Singing in My Soul

Singing in My Soul

Black Gospel Music in a Secular Age

JERMA A. JACKSON

The University of North Carolina Press

CHAPEL HILL & LONDON

© 2004 The University of North Carolina Press
All rights reserved
Manufactured in the United States of America
Set in Galliard and Citizen types by Tseng Information Systems
The paper in this book meets the guidelines for permanence and
durability of the Committee on Production Guidelines for Book
Longevity of the Council on Library Resources.

Library of Congress Cataloging-in-Publication Data
Jackson, Jerma A.
Singing in my soul : black gospel music in a secular age / Jerma A. Jackson.
    p. cm.
Includes bibliographical references (p.) and index.
ISBN 0-8078-2860-2 (cloth : alk. paper) — ISBN 0-8078-5530-8 (pbk. : alk. paper)
1. Gospel music—History and criticism. 2. African Americans—Music—History
and criticism. 3. Popular music—United States—Social aspects. I. Title.
ML3187.J23   2004
782.25'4—dc22   2003024973

cloth   08 07 06 05 04   5 4 3 2 1
paper   08 07 06 05 04   5 4 3 2 1

For my father, Reginald N. Jackson, *1916–1988*

Contents

A section of illustrations can be found following p. 68.

Acknowledgments

Researching and writing about gospel music has been an enriching and transformative experience for me, both intellectually and emotionally. I have not taken this journey alone but have been accompanied by a multitude of strangers, friends, and colleagues whose wisdom, stories, knowledge, and support have nurtured and shaped this project.

The thought of writing a dissertation about music seemed daunting when I began this project as a graduate student at Rutgers University. My knowledge of the subject was virtually nonexistent, and few historians at the time engaged the topic. Yet a community of friends and scholars more than compensated for these apprehensions. Conversations about religion with Sharla Fett, Katherine Bassard, and Pamela Walker raised provocative questions and provided me with a vibrant source of intellectual engagement. Members of my dissertation committee—Donald Gibson, Allen Howard, Deborah Gray White, and Virginia Yans—taught me how to give structure and life to an idea. T. J. Jackson Lears, my advisor, taught me to see value and possibility in ambiguity, insisting that vital cultural changes, never clearly identifiable, are diffuse and murky.

A dissertation fellowship from the Smithsonian Institution's National Museum of American History planted the seeds for the pillars of this project: commerce and music. Charles McGovern schooled me about the workings of the music industry. Charlie, who regarded my naïveté about popular music as a virtue, engaged and encouraged my questions. Bernice Johnson Reagon introduced me to the world of early gospel recordings. More important, she put a tape recorder in my hand and insisted that this project hinged on oral history. My residence at Florida International University provided a supportive and intellectually enriching environment for writing, with the history department providing generous feedback. Conversations with Joseph Patrouch and Felisse Lipsitz on religion in early modern and medieval Europe supplied me with depth and perspective on religion in the twentieth century. Dan Cohen offered much-needed practical advice, reminding me that the best dissertation was a done dissertation.

My colleagues in the history department at the University of North Carolina at Chapel Hill have offered intellectual engagement. Jacquelyn Hall and Donald Mathews, who read early drafts of the manuscript, provided invaluable insights. Peter Filene, Genna Rae McNeil, Lou Pérez, and Yasmin Saikia have been a consistent source of personal, professional, and intellectual support. The classroom has enriched this project in more subtle ways. Students at Eugene Lang College and at Chapel Hill have supplied a vital training ground for translating abstract concepts into meaningful ideas. They have posed questions that have increased the depth and scope of concepts I thought I completely understood. The challenge of engaging and reaching students has inspired me to try to create that same engagement in writing.

Many resources have facilitated my research and writing. A McKnight Doctoral Fellowship at Florida International University provided critical support for writing. Years later a Carolina Minority Postdoctoral Research Fellowship gave me time away from teaching and enabled me to do additional research. A semester at the Institute for the Arts and Humanities at Chapel Hill provided a scintillating environment for writing. The burden of last-minute research and production expenses was lightened by a Spray-Randleigh Fellowship from Chapel Hill. Librarians and archivists helped me locate critical pieces of evidence. Wayne Shirley at the Music Division of the Library of Congress was particularly helpful in aiding my understanding of the copyright process. Generous individuals shared materials they had collected over the years. Some, like Ray Funk, were professional collectors of gospel music; others, like Mamie Thompson, simply kept church programs over the years. Sherry DuPree and her family offered hospitality and kindly shared their very extensive collection of materials on the Church of God in Christ. Michael Kramer and especially David Sartorius managed to track down indispensable material with only threads of information.

I am deeply grateful to the men and women who made the time and opened their homes to share their stories and experiences with me. Over the years Curtis Lyles has become a treasured friend. His support and unbridled enthusiasm have meant a great deal. Curtis raised thoughtful questions about some of my guiding assumptions and perspectives. Minister Marie Knight supplied me vital lessons about working with oral history. She counseled me on the patience and time this project required, explaining that I would have to stitch together the stories she and others were sharing in interviews. Such insight and wisdom would comfort me when I began revising the dissertation. Our conversations and my experiences at Gates of Prayer have given me vital insights into gospel and much, much more. The strong fellowship forged inside the walls of the church transformed a tiny church into a beacon of light. I owe considerable thanks to M. Jacqui Alexander, who accompanied me on the interviews with Knight. Less concerned about gospel music than the spiritual trajectory of Knight, Jacqui helped enrich and deepen our conversations. Discussions about gospel inevitably offered insights about life.

My writing group has been an indispensable part of my revising process. William Dargan, Pamela Grundy, and Jill Snider read numerous drafts of chapters, raising incisive questions about overarching themes and specific details as well as narrative structure. While grueling, these sessions provided a wellspring of support and a tremendous amount of clarity and direction. I owe a special thanks to Pamela for the amazing assistance she provided in the final stages of preparing the manuscript. Through the University of North Carolina Press, two readers offered criticism and suggestions that helped me transform the manuscript into the book it has become. Thanks to Stephanie Wenzel and especially to my editor David Perry for his steadfast enthusiasm and his willingness to guide me through the maze of publishing.

My community of friends has enriched this project in countless ways. In my travels to Charlotte the Ehrman-Dupre family supplied me with overnight accommodations and lighthearted reprieve from the intellectual rigor of my writing group. Beth Kivel, Melissa Exum, Kim Diggs Freeman, Karen Glynn, Thomas Burton, and Joseph Thompson have provided wonderful sources of support, at home and from afar. Elsa Barkley Brown, Tera Hunter, and Carmen Whalen have been with this project from the beginning. Each has offered encouragement at crucial times and instructive criticism at others. In the early stages, when I had second thoughts of doing a project on music, Tera encouraged me to embrace the work as an adventure. Elsa provided enthusiasm and feedback at pivotal moments. Carmen gave me perspective and a helping hand when I could not find my way. In the process each of them has deepened the meaning of friendship.

I owe a special debt of gratitude to my family, which has had to endure the burdens of this work. My partner, Consuella Brown, came into my life just when labor on this project intensified. Her gentle prodding and support helped push me in new directions at a critical time. The extraordinary patience and support my brother and especially my mother have rendered provide me with important lessons about unconditional love. My deepest thanks, however, go to my father, who died just before I began this project. He loved to sing and taught both my family and childhood friends a litany of songs. Long-distance car trips and social visits with friends and family were never complete without dad taking time out to lead us all in song. "Okay, let's hit that chord," he would say. His spirit and the love of music he inspired have sustained and nurtured me.

Singing in My Soul

Introduction

At the dawn of the twentieth century when W. E. B. Du Bois sat down to consider the future of African Americans in the United States, the music of his enslaved ancestors was ringing in his ears. Published in 1903, *The Souls of Black Folk* has become a legendary text for understanding the ensuing century. Much of this stature stems from Du Bois's success at foreshadowing many of the challenges that the new century would pose. For Du Bois the greatest of these was race. "The problem of the twentieth century," he predicted, "is the problem of the color line." Du Bois invoked spirituals at the beginning of each chapter by creating epigraphs using musical notation taken from the songs. He then devoted the last chapter to a discussion of the songs, which African Americans had forged as slaves. A native of New England born in 1868, Du Bois himself never experienced slavery. Nevertheless, the songs provided a language that captured the emotional dimensions not only of slavery, but also of the racism that would plague the post-emancipation world. Du Bois, who regarded the songs as the "rhythmic cry of the slave," described the wellspring of emotion the songs stirred in him. "They came out of the South unknown to me, one by one," he wrote, "and yet at once I knew them as of me and mine." [1]

Spirituals so moved Du Bois because he saw them not only as heartfelt expressions of human emotion, but also as a reminder of the resilience of the human spirit under hostile circumstances. Slavery, a dehumanizing institution, reduced individuals to chattel, subjected them to harsh working conditions, and separated families at will. Enslaved African Americans used spirituals to transcend the physical world, forging a spiritual universe distinct from the material world. In the process they used music to lend meaning to their circumstances. As slaves, African Americans were regarded as abject inferiors. Yet in the songs they cast themselves as God's chosen people. [2]

In the twentieth century, music would continue to serve as an arena where African Americans forged their hopes and dreams, even as they contended with the racial oppression that remained an integral part of American society. A vital part of the fabric of daily life, music helped solidify community in rural districts as well as the urban enclaves to which so many African Americans migrated in the decades following emancipation. Music percolated virtually everywhere African Americans congregated: in community institutions such as barbershops, schools, and churches; at private parties and barbecues; in spaces of commercial amusement; and on city streets.[3]

Over the course of the twentieth century, as African Americans worked to build new communities and as they moved about the country seeking economic and educational opportunities, they produced a rich variety of musical styles that reflected the range of experiences they encountered. In jazz compositions, blues songs, classically arranged spirituals, gospel anthems, and many other forms of musical expression, musicians gave voice to community aspirations and invoked the extremes of feeling and experience that were part of modern black life. Blues singers articulated the despair of daily life, but the community context in which they plied their craft helped create the possibilities for conquering that pain. Gospel singers laced their songs with upbeat rhythms, but the wails and cries used to punctuate the melodies made the pain of daily living an integral component of the good news supplied by religious faith.

Even as music comprised an important part of black community culture, it was also drawn into an expanding commercial economy by individual entrepreneurs and corporate entities eager to mass-produce forms of local musical culture and distribute them across the nation. As a growing entertainment industry came to wield increasing influence in American life, the popular appeal of African American music elevated a small corps of black singers and musicians to national stardom, making them some of the most recognized figures in black America. Studies of twentieth-century black experiences frequently point out that African Americans remained on the margins of industrial development until the advent of World War II. But the gospel music industry opens a window into a corner of the industrial economy where African Americans played a significant role, as well as into the ways that the expansion of material values and the development of technologies of mass production and communication influenced African American life. Considering gospel musicians, the communities of which they were a part, and the audiences who embraced them makes it possible to examine some of the ways in which African Americans contended with a society marked not simply by racial discrimination, but by the growing influence commerce wielded over daily affairs.[4]

Most studies of twentieth-century black music have focused on secular music, particularly blues and jazz. Asserting that secular values comprise a cornerstone of modern life, scholars often argue that the worldly outlook of these styles together with the cultural authority they exerted rendered blues and jazz quintessential symbols of the modern age—an era marked by expanding industrialization, the growing power wielded by large, impersonal corporate entities, and the spread of consumer and material values. As scholars rightly point out, these styles became arenas where men and women celebrated pleasure, fame, fortune, and the material aspects of living. This emphasis on pleasure and materialism would in fact come to comprise an important component of the expanding consumer values that became a cornerstone of twentieth-century commerce. As the twentieth century advanced, the pressures of material concerns would make increasing inroads into every corner of black American life.[5]

An exclusive focus on secular values, however, overlooks the enormous significance religion continued to hold for African Americans. Over the course of the twentieth century, black men and women forged a rich array of religious institutions that became an integral part of daily affairs, a powerful source of individual and community identity, and an important component of social and political struggles. The forms of sacred music that took shape within these religious arenas provide an especially rich lens for witnessing the ways African Americans made sense of modern life.

Solo gospel, a style of sacred singing marked by an upbeat tempo and by intense rhythms generated through percussive instrumental accompaniment, holds particular resonance for this endeavor. In the first half of the twentieth century this music emerged from a group of small churches on the margins of black religious life to became the most popular form of sacred music in the country as well as a huge commercial success. With these developments came new burdens and new possibilities. As a black religious music that enjoyed great commercial acclaim, gospel came to inhabit multiple worlds, serving as a meeting point for sacred and secular concerns and for local black communities and mainstream popular culture. As a result gospel became a critical arena in which African Americans contended with questions about the nature of faith, as well as the shape and meaning of racial identity.

Solo gospel also illuminates some of the many roles African American women took on in black religious life. While men dominated most forms of African American music, including the evolving tradition of the gospel quartet, women became important innovators in solo gospel. The female-dominated arena of the church made it a supportive training ground where women could secure critical music skills. Barred from the pulpit, women used musical forms that became the rudiments of gospel to testify to their religious convictions, sustain fellowship, and pursue missionary work. In the process they helped shape the contours of gospel's solo tradition. Their influence was not confined to the church. The proscriptions against female preaching that initially inspired women to pursue gospel also gave them an incentive to push the music beyond church doors, as they ventured first onto city streets and then into the commercial arena. Historians studying black churchwomen have tended to focus on the social reform efforts pursued by the middle class. The musical evangelism of sanctified women offers an important counterpoint to these portraits.[6]

——— Not until the 1920s did African Americans actually begin to apply the term "gospel" to a body of sacred music. Yet the impetus for the solo gospel tradition came in the 1890s with the emergence of a small religious movement that would eventually coalesce into a set of independent black congregations and denominations known as the sanctified church. In contrast to many mainline churches where leaders privileged restraint over emotional expression, sanctified churches regarded exuberant worship as an expression of the Holy Spirit's presence in believers' souls and bodies—a moment of religious communion that formed the central doctrine of sanctified belief. The belief that music flowed out of a holy encounter, and the emphasis placed on personal testimonies to the power of the Spirit within individuals, fostered a mode of worship that nurtured solo expression and instrumental accompaniment that ranged from washtubs to trumpets to guitars. Chapter 1 traces the development of the religious convictions that helped shape this musical expression, and sets it in counterpoint to the emphasis on education and restraint encouraged in many mainline churches—an emphasis that took musical form in the classical arrangements of slave spirituals that became staples at mainline services and in black colleges.

In the 1910s and 1920s the sanctified movement flourished across the country as African Americans migrated to urban centers. Women, who made up the bulk of church members, assumed particularly prominent roles in building churches, spreading the faith, and further shaping their distinctive musical style. As female missionaries embarked on city streets to reach the unregenerate, they took their music with them, transforming it from a mode of worship into an evangelical tool that they shaped to catch and hold the attention of passersby. When mass communication technology became available in the form of sound recordings, some of these women entered the recording studio, seeking to turn the new technology to their evangelical ends. In the process they took a first step in moving gospel beyond the realm of the church and into the commercial arena. Chapter 2 follows these women on their journeys, examining the religious zeal that nurtured a range of female talents and considering the musical and evangelical paths with which they pursued their missionary ends.

The 1930s saw the exuberant religious movement expand from the margins of black religious communities toward the center of black religious life. This shift began with the efforts of Thomas Andrew Dorsey, a blues musician who turned his skills to writing upbeat, blues-influenced religious songs, which he called gospel music. Facing the opposition of mainline ministers who remained committed to ideals of restrained worship, Dorsey and his associates, most notably former sanctified singer Sallie Martin, launched a range of efforts to build support for the music through other channels. As well as organizing a series of independent gospel choirs and distributing Dorsey's songs through the sale of sheet music, gospel's advocates cast upbeat rhythms as a key component of black heritage. With these efforts, they helped build a popular groundswell of enthusiasm for gospel that eventually won the music a place within mainline churches as well as in popular African American culture. In Chapter 3 I examine these efforts, looking at the songs Dorsey wrote, the faith he developed in black capitalism as a means for distributing his music, and the degree to which gospel's growing popular diffusion created an arena for religious conviction that lay outside the church.

By the 1940s, even as gospel gained new acclaim in African American circles, it also secured a foothold in mainstream popular culture, thanks to the popularity of Sister Rosetta Tharpe, who had emerged onto the national scene in the 1930s. Tharpe, a remarkable artist who had been nurtured in the tradition of sanctified evangelicalism, caught the eye of musical promoters eager to capitalize on the interest in black music generated by the popularity of swing. Tharpe's decision to perform gospel music in nightclubs and theaters outraged many believers, but the power of her artistry secured a large following among both blacks and whites. Chapter 4 looks at the many challenges Tharpe faced as a religious singer in a commercial, profit-centered world and the changes her experiences worked on her music and her faith.

Gospel entered what many consider its "golden era" in the years after World War II, when it became immensely popular among African Americans and the leading form of sacred music in mass commercial culture. An array of gospel groups and singers became national stars, acquiring the conventional trappings of fame and fortune. Such successes, however, caused consternation among many African Americans, who worried that the profit-centered entertainment industry robbed gospel of its sacred significance, desecrating not only a form of sacred expression but also a music that had gained wide acceptance as a cornerstone of black cultural heritage. Chapter 5 begins by considering the process by which musicians and promoters helped build gospel into a national commercial phenomenon. It then looks at commercial gospel's critics, laying out both their critique and the strategies they fashioned to keep gospel within the protective embrace of the church. In the process it illuminates a range of African American perceptions on commercialism, racial identity, and the nature of religious faith.

——— As Du Bois clearly recognized, the twentieth century would bring its own set of unique challenges. With the rise of legal segregation, the color line he insisted would define the century became a wall separating blacks from mainstream American political and economic life. Race, however, would play out differently in the realm of commerce, culture, and religion. In the case of gospel, the boundaries of the color line would blur as men and women wrestled with not only a variety of racial issues, but also the meaning of religion, the seductions and elusiveness of fame and fortune, and the degree of control individuals and local communities could exert over cultural traditions. The communities and institutions that took shape around gospel, along with the joys and sorrows the music so vividly expressed, would be influenced by race but never wholly defined by it.

CHAPTER 1 **Exuberance or Restraint**

Music and Religion after Reconstruction

In 1909 the renowned Fisk Jubilee Singers gathered in front of a recording company microphone to render the well-known spiritual "There Is a Balm in Gilead." The singers had gained worldwide acclaim with their performances of classically arranged versions of slave spirituals, and power in their performance rang clear from the first note. A lone male voice began the song by singing out the first line, enunciating each word, "There is a balm in Gilead." Immediately, the remaining members of the group joined in the singing to complete the first line, "to make the wounded whole." Almost instantly a single voice became a mosaic of rich harmonies. The a cappella singing gave added emphasis to the lyrical quality of these trained voices. Each voice was so carefully modulated that even as the group delivered the chorus in unison, no single voice dominated. They paid tribute to enslaved African Americans with an orchestrated precision that matched the highest standards of Western classical tradition and melded each voice into a seamless whole.[1]

Almost two decades later, in 1927, sanctified singer Bessie Johnson gave voice to her spiritual convictions in a far different fashion. While Johnson recorded her songs with an ensemble, her voice dominated each record. In "He's Got Better Things for You," Johnson called attention to the depth of her religious beliefs by bringing an intense passion to her singing. "My friends I want to tell you because I love your soul," she sang almost plaintively into the microphone, "I have no doubt you've been converted, but the other half ain't never been told." As she began to inform her listeners about the divine gifts that would make their lives whole, the volume of her singing increased and her vocals assumed a rough, gravel-like quality. The slow tempo in which she began the song gained momentum once her singing group joined in the performance. The quickening tempo and the uneven singing that sometimes elapsed into shouting made for an impassioned recording.[2]

Throughout the late nineteenth and early twentieth centuries the arranged spirituals of the Fisk Jubilee Singers gained recognition as the quintessential African American sacred music. The early date of their recording, at a time when few African Americans had the opportunity to participate in the fledgling recording industry, was testimony to their broad-based reputation. The renown of Bessie Johnson, whose music appealed primarily to a small group of faithful at the margins of black religious life, paled in comparison. But despite her relative obscurity, Johnson's recording foreshadowed a far different future. The solo singing, upbeat accompaniment, and impassioned delivery captured on the discs she made formed the bedrock of gospel, the form of religious music that would soon rival the spirituals in popularity both among African Americans and in mainstream American culture. The religious communities that nurtured this music thus had meaning beyond their number.

The recordings made by Johnson and by the Fisk Jubilee Singers captured much more than two divergent styles of sacred music. They embodied the competing meanings that African Americans gave to religion in the decades following emancipation as they faced the challenges of freedom, of industrialization, and of the racial prejudice that saturated American life. As African Americans turned to religion to make sense of the changing world around them, they inevitably modified the worship practices and outlooks that enslaved African Americans had found meaningful. The precise renditions and disciplined harmonies of arranged spirituals grew out of a worship tradition grounded in restraint and middle-class respectability. The emotional dynamism displayed by Bessie Johnson and other, similar singers sprang from an alternate tradition governed by emotional expression. As African Americans wrestled with the many dilemmas of the twentieth century, these competing traditions, along with the music they generated, would help define the terms of their struggle.

——— The gradual development of gospel music cannot be separated from the racial politics that erupted during the late nineteenth century, politics that would both nurture the music and keep it at the margins of black religious life. As African Americans worked to secure a place for themselves as equal citizens in the aftermath of slavery, the journey from slavery to freedom became a struggle for fundamental human rights, namely political and economic freedom. Part of the struggle that ensued stemmed from the enormous social and economic change that unfolded during the post-Reconstruction era. With the end of the Civil War came a new industrial order giving rise to new social and economic structures that significantly transformed social relations. Economic production grew on a scale once thought unimaginable, as machines increasingly replaced handcraft production. These economies of scale generated unprecedented wealth for some Americans and gave rise to a new class of elites. The rise of machine production also contributed to a growing class of unskilled laborers, as more and more capital was directed to machinery and away from labor. The many labor strikes that erupted during the 1890s bear testimony to the intense class tension that engulfed Americans during this period.[3]

Mechanized production transformed daily life for all Americans as more and more people moved to cities, where they found work in the growing number of factories that developed there. Increases in the scale of production fostered enormous demand for labor filled by immigrants from southern and eastern Europe. Immigrants and native born, men and women, and rich and poor all tried to secure a footing in the new social and economic order.

In this period of enormous change, race gained newfound significance as it emerged as a vehicle for explaining the social divisions industrialization produced. The growing significance of race can be found in the rise of Social Darwinism and its concept of civilization. In Social Darwinism race emerged as a critical measure of human development. According to this theory, the Anglo-Saxon race stood at the apex of civilized development, as evidenced by the material and cultural accomplishments of Anglo-Saxon societies. African Americans were cast as members of a separate, far less developed race and thus were set outside the bounds of "civilized" society.[4]

With the advent of Social Darwinism, the anxieties and social tensions of industrialization were frequently projected onto the bodies of black men and women, often with horrendous results. The pervasive discrimination, lynchings, and riots that emerged during the 1890s have led historian Rayford Logan to dub the period the nadir of race relations. Racial discrimination kept African Americans locked out of factories and industrial employment so that the vast majority of laboring black men and women were forced to domestic service jobs. Whites turned to physical violence and brutality as they made African Americans the target of their discontent. The period also witnessed the emergence of vicious racial stereotypes in mass circulation magazines, which also reinforced notions of black inferiority. In the South these developments culminated with the emergence of the social and legal caste system known as Jim Crow.[5]

The pervasiveness of racist ideologies led African Americans to build an impressive array of institutions to address their own social, economic, and political needs. These institutions included not only churches and religious institutions but also schools, businesses, and mutual benefit societies. While these institutions failed to dismantle racism, they fostered a sense of community to combat prejudice for African Americans. With the advent of Social Darwinism, the vast majority of non-black Americans looked down on African Americans. As African Americans worked to build new lives and communities, they adopted a range of strategies for confronting these notions of black inferiority, both within individuals and in the world at large.[6]

In the late nineteenth century the most prominent of these strategies was pursued by a growing black middle class eager to convert race from a mark of derision into a source of pride. These men and women, who articulated their racial pride by designating themselves as "race" men and women, poured their energies into schools, clubs, and churches seeking to improve the conditions in which all African Americans lived.[7] They placed particular emphasis on education, a concept that encompassed much more than learning to read and write. Within the growing number of black educational institutions, education became a vehicle not only for the acquisition of knowledge but also for the proliferation of values such as thrift, refinement, and industriousness.[8]

These new values formed the bedrock of a distinctive middle-class outlook geared toward upward mobility. The professionals and experts who swelled the ranks of the middle class counseled upward mobility as a way to cope with the changes that accompanied industrialization. In a society increasingly governed by intense competition, social strife, and class divisions, self-discipline, hard work, and refined behavior seemed to offer the best possibility for individual advancement. For African American educators eager to advance the race, middle-class values took on added meaning. In their minds these values would facilitate racial progress and help eradicate prejudice and discrimination.[9]

The educational institutions and culture that advanced middle-class visions of education would make serious inroads in the way African Americans practiced religion. Such changes were especially evident in the convention movement that emerged inside the black Baptist church. The movement, which took shape during the final decades of the nineteenth century, culminated in the National Baptist Convention, a denomination of black Baptist churches separate and distinct from white Baptist organizations. Led by individuals trained in southern black schools and colleges, the convention movement identified education with progress and upward mobility. As a result education emerged as both a remedy for prevailing social ills and a vital source of collective empowerment. True to their belief in individual and church autonomy, Baptist churches would always embody a range of outlooks and worship styles. But uplift-minded leaders would wield enormous influence over church practices.[10]

The particular version of education advanced by the convention movement led leaders of some Baptist congregations to curb spontaneous forms of worship that had prevailed during slavery. For enslaved African Americans who actively engaged their gods, worship had been a participatory experience that included ecstatic shrieks, moans, and groans as well as energetic hand clapping and foot stomping. In the aftermath of slavery, Baptist leaders increasingly associated such physical and emotional involvement with superstition and ignorance. One minister made the connection explicit by asserting that the conventions involved "the amassing of a force of intelligence that will sweep from our worship the last vestige of superstition and ranting which has characterized it for so many years." For this minister and many in the convention movement the notion that "emotional religion" amounted to nothing more than ignorance compelled them to direct their attention to the wholesale repression of religious emotion.[11]

In place of emotion and spontaneity, Baptist leaders stressed education and restraint. The widespread adoption of hymnbooks and the institution of church choirs were two marks of this approach. During slavery most hymns were "lined out." A leader spoke or sang each line of a song, and congregation members, most of whom could not read, sang the line back, often elaborating on the melody and augmenting the words with the shouts and moans of religious ecstasy. Hymnbooks and choirs removed spontaneous singing from religious fellowship, emphasizing the importance of education and bringing greater structure and restraint to worship. This strategy was aimed at outside observers as well as the faithful themselves. It stemmed from the assumption that supposed evidence of black inferiority resulted from impoverished social conditions rather than any qualities inherent in race, and that evidence of black accomplishments would help alleviate prevailing discrimination and prejudice. Armed with this agenda, these leaders waged an aggressive campaign to advance and uplift the race that included mandating educational requirements for the ministry as well as toning down ecstatic worship.[12]

Strategies of racial pride and uplift assumed their most potent musical form in the arranged spirituals pioneered by singing groups that sprang up at African American colleges in the late nineteenth century. In the 1870s, newly opened Fisk University achieved worldwide renown with the Fisk Jubilee Singers, a group of well-trained performers who toured the Northeast and Great Britain. Their concerts featured temperance songs, operatic arias, and parlor tunes as well as a group of slavery-era spirituals that had been rearranged according to the principles of Western classical music. The concerts proved an enormous success, raising much-needed funds for the struggling university. Music critics and sympathetic clergy expressed particular enthusiasm for the arranged spirituals. The success the group enjoyed stirred a jubilee movement, leading black colleges such as Hampton, Morehouse, Livingstone, and Tuskegee Institute to sponsor similar ensembles. Black newspapers included many references to college jubilee groups between 1870 and 1910.[13]

Arranged spirituals offered a felicitous convergence of African American heritage with the politics of uplift. Performers and arrangers replaced full-throated singing and frequent melodic turns with the smooth singing, precise tones, and even melodies that demonstrated African American mastery of Western classical forms. But the arrangements used a call-and-response structure that embraced the lining-out tradition, and the spirituals' origins in slavery highlighted the accomplishments of a distinctly black culture.[14] The enthusiasm the Fisk Jubilee Singers generated, for example, led composer Antonín Dvořák to point specifically to the spirituals as the bedrock for a distinctive American music: "These beautiful and varied themes are the product of the soil. They are American. They are the folksongs of America, and your composers must turn to them. In the Negro melodies of America I discover all that is needed for a great and noble school of music." [15]

The attention the songs garnered on the concert stage provided African Americans with a useful vehicle for refuting prevailing notions of black inferiority. During the 1910s and 1920s, black scholars such as John and Frederick Work, James Weldon Johnson, and Nathaniel Dett collected spirituals and arranged the songs in a Western classical format. Some African Americans pointed to the revised spirituals to assert that "music comprised the Negro's contribution to American civilization." [16] Another described the songs as "the finest contribution [America] has to offer the world." [17]

Leaders of the National Baptist Convention took particular pride in the classical renditions of the spirituals. Choirs taking shape in black Baptist churches featured the songs, and during the 1920s many congregations sponsored musicales devoted to spirituals. In 1921 the publishing arm of the convention issued its first hymnbook, *Gospel Pearls*.[18] The publication contained a range of sacred songs, including anthems, hymns, and spirituals. The editors of the collection articulated their pride in the spirituals through their arrangement of the contents of the hymnbook. Spirituals appeared in a special section at the end, and the editors pointed to the songs as "the rarest and prime favorites—the result of long hours of research and hard work, collecting and making popular throughout the land." [19] In 1927 the National Baptist Convention published *Spirituals Triumphant*, devoted exclusively to spirituals.[20]

——— The shift toward hymnbooks, trained choirs, and arranged spirituals had far-reaching implications and sparked considerable controversy. Daniel Webster Davis, who began teaching in public schools in Richmond, Virginia, during the 1880s, conveyed how the meanings imputed to education led leaders in his religious community to adopt printed hymnbooks for use during worship services. The decision transformed how services were conducted. Adoption of the printed books displaced the lining-out tradition, which had encouraged the congregation to actively participate in singing. In addition the decision shuttled the unlettered, often the elders of the community, to the sidelines of church polity. Davis described these changes in "De Linin' Ub De Hymns," a poem he published in 1897:

De young folks say 'tain't stylish to lin' 'um out no mo';
Dat dey's got edikashun, an' dey wants us all to know
Dey likes to hab dar singin'-books a-holin' fore dar eyes,
An' sing de hymns right straight along "to manshuns in de skies."

Dat it am awful fogy to give 'um out by lin',
An' ef de ol' folks will kumplain 'cause dey is ol' an' blin',
An' slabry's chain don' kep' dem back frum larnin' how to read—
Dat dey mus' take a corner seat, an' let de young folks lead.
. . . .
Well, p'raps dey's right, I kin not say; my lims is growin' ol',
But I likes to sing de dear ol' hymns, 'tiz music to my soul;
An' 'pears to me 'twont do much harm to gin 'um out by line,
Dat we ol' folks dat kin not read may foller 'long behin'.

But few ub us am lef' here now dat bore de slabry chain,
We don't edikate our boys an' gals, an' would do de same again;
An Zion's all dat's lef' us now to cheer us wid its song—
Dey mought 'low us to sing wid dem, it kin not be fur long.

De sarmon's highfalutin', an' de chuch am mighty fin';
We trus' dat God still understan's ez in de days ub min',
When we, 'do' ignunt, po' an' mean, still wushuped wid de soul,
Whil' oft across our peaceful breas' de wabes ub trouble roll.

De ol'-time groans an' shouts an' moans am passin' out ub sight—
Edikashun changed all dat, an' we belebe it right,
We should serb God wid 'telligence; fur dis one thing I plead:
Jes' lebe a leetle place in church fur dem ez kin not read.[21]

Davis conveyed how the emphasis on education helped alter worship practices. Without education blacks had "wushuped wid de soul," but as he pointed out, education "changed all dat," and now blacks worked to "serb God wid 'telligence." As a schoolteacher Davis recognized the importance of education. Yet he displayed decided ambivalence when assessing its impact, pointing to the changing stature of the unlettered elders of the church to highlight how the use of hymnbooks altered social dynamics.

While Davis merely called for tempering the push for educated worship, other African Americans rejected the strategy outright. One result of this rejection was the Church of God in Christ, a new denomination that would nurture many of the singers that helped create and popularize gospel. Rather than dismissing the ecstatic worship that had prevailed amongst slaves, these men and women infused it with new meaning by linking ecstatic outpourings to the beliefs of the first-century Christians. Over time the religious practices they forged drew on the slavery era's vernacular music while also paving the way for a new mode of music to take shape.[22]

The Church of God in Christ, which emphasized close study of the Bible, also drew on the push for education that marked the aftermath of slavery. But church leaders turned their learning in a far different direction. During the late nineteenth century Charles H. Mason, a traveling minister from Arkansas, and Charles P. Jones, a minister of a small Baptist congregation in Mississippi, embarked on a new tradition, which they referred to as "bible religion." At some point in the 1890s Jones organized a small study group to bring his church members together for serious religious reflection. As they read the Bible closely, Jones made a radical discovery: the ecstatic worship that had been a mainstay of religion among African Americans during slavery had also been a vital component of early Christianity. The discovery that the more sedate religion he practiced carried "none of the signs spoken of in the Scriptures" convinced Jones that they "were not toting fair with Jesus." "I began then," Jones wrote, "to seek Him with all my heart for that power that would make my life wholly His, so that I might realize the blessedness and usefulness of real Bible Religion."[23]

Jones found a kindred spirit in Charles Mason, and together they published *The Work of the Holy Spirit in the Churches*, described as a "treatise on the 12th chapter of First Corinthians." The two men pointed to 1 Corinthians to put forth what they felt constituted true religion, namely the manifestation of divine presence. The chapter described how the divine bestowed individuals with an array of gifts that included wisdom and prophecy, the ability to heal and work miracles, ecstatic speech known as speaking in tongues, and the capacity to interpret that speech.[24]

In their search for authentic religion, Mason and Jones found a congenial spirit in the white-dominated Holiness movement, which had developed a detailed doctrine of sanctification—the dwelling of the Holy Spirit within a believer. This movement, which took shape inside the Methodist fold during the mid-nineteenth century, flourished in the wake of the Civil War.[25] John Wesley, instrumental in spreading Methodism in America during the 1840s, had introduced the doctrine as a way to liberate the body from sin and secure grace and salvation in this world. Yet over the course of the nineteenth century, sanctification lost its footing in Methodism as more and more congregations came to embrace religion as ritual and custom rather than out of deep-seated conviction. Participants in the Holiness movement grew dissatisfied with these developments, pointing to them as proof that the Methodist church had begun to compromise with the world. Intent on rescuing true faith, those who embraced sanctification set themselves the task of making the divine an integral part of their lives. These men and women believed that salvation made it possible for the Holy Ghost to dwell inside the soul of an individual. While such presence offered the possibility for Christian perfectionism, participants recognized that it was never a condition one attained but was part of a continual process that had to be actively engaged. Armed with this recognition, members of the movement stressed holiness, the daily work of keeping the world at bay and making the divine an integral part of their lives. As they worked to elaborate on their understanding of true religion, Jones and Mason would embrace many aspects of the Holiness movement.[26]

Unlike the Baptists, who drew on slave songs to promote a sense of racial pride and distinctiveness, black members of the Holiness movement rarely spoke about the significance of race. This was evident in both their embrace of the early Christians and the interracial nature of some aspects of the movement. At a moment when black Baptists were separating themselves from denominations controlled by whites, black members of the Holiness movement reached beyond racial boundaries. This was most clearly evident in the Azusa revival. Between 1904 and 1907, African American minister William J. Seymour led an extended revival at the Azusa street mission in Los Angeles. This revival was notable both for its emphasis on speaking in tongues —which marked the advent of Pentecostalism—and for interracialism. Seymour, who believed that religion provided the only real tool for transforming social mores and manners, saw the outpouring of religious enthusiasm as a vehicle for creating an inclusive church that transcended the color line. Religious scholar Douglas J. Nelson points out that the minister articulated his vision by installing an unorthodox seating arrangement at the mission. The minister placed the pulpit at the center of the room rather than at the front. This arrangement prevented Seymour from assuming an elevated position. At the same time the pews, which formed a circle surrounding the pulpit, placed all who assembled on the same level.[27]

News of the revival sparked considerable interest among blacks and whites in the Holiness movement. Scores of men and women, including Charles Mason, descended on Azusa eager to learn more about what many considered an extraordinary turn of events. Since the seating arrangement Seymour designed made no special provision for race, blacks and whites openly engaged in religious fellowship. One white participant from the South described the impact of the experience: "I, being southern born, thought it a miracle that I could sit in a service by a colored saint of God and worship, or eat at a great camp table and forget I was eating beside a colored saint, but in spirit and truth God was worshiped in love and harmony."[28] For many like this man, the racial openness intensified the sacred significance of the experience.

The Church of God in Christ, previously an all-black congregation, acquired a number of white members in the wake of the enthusiasm generated by Azusa. Ultimately, however, such interracialism was unable to withstand the pressures of the white supremacy that had come to permeate American life. By 1914 the church's white members had left to form the all-white Assemblies of God. As a result, the musical innovations nurtured by the Church of God in Christ took shape within a distinctly African American context. But for church members, who centered their identity on religion rather than race, the racial dimensions of their worship style seem to have sparked little discussion.[29]

The Church of God in Christ became an official denomination in 1907, one of a number of new Holiness and Pentecostal denominations that found appeal primarily among the ranks of the working class. Throughout the 1910s and 1920s, these men and women forged a variety of independent congregations and denominations: the United House of Prayer in Charlotte, North Carolina; the Church of the Living God in Chicago; and the Church of Christ, Apostolic Faith, in New York City. While membership in many churches was quite small, the proliferation of congregations designating themselves as Holiness or Pentecostal proved so great that the term "sanctified church" emerged in black communities to refer to these collective congregations and denominations. By the 1930s and 1940s some denominations had become so well established that memberships in black Holiness and Pentecostal churches began to rival their mainstream counterparts, and by the 1950s the Church of God in Christ was one of the fastest-growing African American denominations.[30]

──── The music that took shape within the Church of God in Christ as well as other sanctified churches was inseparable from the way members comprehended religion and the significance they gave to corporeal experience. Sanctification precipitated a moment of profound ecstasy as an individual felt the presence of the Holy Spirit. The experience, however, hinged on the willingness of individuals to commit themselves to God in pursuit of holy living. More than an abstraction, such commitment or holiness compelled individuals to consecrate all aspects of their lives to God and required considerable discipline in the consumer-oriented society in which they lived. The emphasis placed on physical experience made the denomination extremely strict in some arenas of life and worship and highly innovative in others.[31]

Holiness imposed strict regulations on conduct and appearance. To experience God fully sanctified individuals devoted their lives and consecrated their bodies to the divine. For the sanctified, religion encompassed much more than a Sunday ritual. Services often took place every night of the week. One man described how services would last for hours at a time: "Arriving early Sunday morning for Sunday School, families came prepared to stay all day. Homemade lunches were brought because many families stayed through the evening services, which sometimes lasted until midnight."[32]

In the sanctified church, belonging to the community of faithful entailed considerable work and required a serious personal commitment. At a time when the secular values of pleasure and indulgence were gaining growing influence in American public culture, living a holy life entailed making one's body a holy temple. Such work demanded enormous physical discipline and sacrifice. The sanctified understood that the body was a critical intermediary between the world and the Holy Spirit. The body could be flesh, in which case it engaged with the world. That same body could be a temple for the Spirit, in which case it separated itself from the world. In this context fasting and prayer emerged as sacred acts that the sanctified embraced to consecrate their bodies to God and to keep the world at bay.

Consecration also influenced physical appearance. Disdaining any trends of fashion, the sanctified individuals wore plain, modest dress — a choice that would become especially noticeable when flashier styles emerged in the 1920s. Women did not use makeup or wear dresses with bold and vibrant colors. Instead they donned dark, colorless attire and rejected the fashionable pumps of the day for unadorned oxford shoes. Men did not wear neckties and chose modest suits. More than a means of distinction, these modes of dress held deep religious significance as the sanctified used their attire to consecrate their bodies to God. In this regard physical appearance served as a daily reminder that they were children of God.[33]

——— Even as the concept of consecration required physical discipline, however, the very idea that the divine abided with an individual made God tangible and dynamic, allowing for a wide range of worship practices. Jones related the importance of experience. "Do not be satisfied with the attitude merely that holiness is right. Get the experience, get saved, get a knowledge of it."[34] Frank Bartleman, a journalist who was part of the Holiness movement, vividly described his experience of speaking in tongues:

> After a time of testimony and praise, with everything quiet, I was softly walking the floor praising God in my spirit. All at once I seemed to hear in my soul (not with my natural ears), a rich voice speaking in a language I did not know. . . . It seemed to ravish and fully satisfy the pent up praises in my being. In a few moments I found myself, seemingly without volition on my part, enunciating the same sounds with my own vocal organs. It was an exact continuation of the same expressions that I had heard in my soul a few moments before. It seemed a perfect language. I was almost like an outside listener. I was fully yielded to God, and simply carried by His will, as on a divine stream. I could have hindered the expression but would not have done so for the worlds. . . . The experience was most sacred, the Holy Spirit playing on my vocal chords, as on an Aeolian harp.[35]

In experiences such as this, the Holy Spirit not only occupied a believer's soul but also seized control of his or her entire body.

Members of the Church of God in Christ regarded music as an extension of worship. Horace Boyer, who grew up in the Church of God in Christ, came of age almost a half-century after the revival at Azusa. Yet his words made clear that the emphasis on spiritual gifts, including music, persisted over generations. "The Lord gives each person some kind of gift," Boyer remembered being told. "He gives some the gift of smiling, some the gift of talking soothingly to people, some the gift of praying, some the gift of preaching . . . some the gift of singing."[36]

The close relationship between music and worship reflected how members of the Church of God in Christ regarded religion as a corporeal experience in which the physical and emotional reinforced each other. As parishioners spoke in tongues, considered the most sacred divine gift, they made external an experience that was private and internal and in the process helped generate a community. Maudelle Oliver, who experienced conversion in 1922 at age fourteen, related how the corporeal experience of the Holy Ghost moved believers to dance:

> MO: The Spirit would come on you and you would do things. And we just enjoyed what the Lord did. And we'd dance you know what I mean. Do you know what the holy dance is?
> JJ: I've heard of it. I was wondering if you could tell me what it is.
> MO: Oh Lord have mercy. You just rejoice instead of wrestling may I say. You know some churches the folks be happy, and the folks hold them. But we never held nobody, just keep them from hurting anybody else if they would probably to fall down. You know in those days we would see the Lord knock people out and purge them. Well we just enjoyed seeing the Lord work.[37]

As believers consecrated their bodies to God and celebrated God's presence, they also moved away from the a cappella singing that characterized vernacular music during slavery. Music served as both a vehicle for religious fellowship and an arena for individual expression. Describing a religious experience he had in 1907, Mason conveyed how collective and individual singing could reinforce each other. "More light came," he wrote, "and my heart rejoiced! . . . Some said, 'Let us sing,' [and] I arose and the first song that came to me was 'He Brought Me Out of the Miry Clay; He Sat My Feet on the

Rock to Stay.'" Moved by the presence of the Holy Spirit, Mason looked past the suggestion that the congregation begin singing and arose from his seat to deliver the song that came to him. The sight of someone so moved by the Spirit seems to have inspired those assembled to catch the song and join him in the music.[38]

Over time, testimonies like the one Mason gave in 1907 became a formal part of worship. The critical role such testimonies assumed can be discerned from fieldwork conducted by anthropologist Hortense Powdermaker during the 1930s. Living among members of a Church of God in Christ community in the Mississippi Delta, Powdermaker provided a rich description of the services she witnessed. She recalled that members began worship with chanting, which they followed up with a scripture lesson. "Then comes the testifying," Powdermaker explained, and she recalled the interaction between spoken word and song: "Each witness stands up and starts a song, in which the others join. When they stop singing, the testimony is given. . . . Some are very shy and speak so low that they can hardly be heard. Others shout at the top of their voices that they are living and sanctified. One looks particularly exalted as she sways back and forth, crying out that Jesus is in her and keeps her sanctified; otherwise, she could not escape the sins of the world."[39]

As congregations devoted an entire segment of worship to testifying, they also modified the lining-out tradition that had dominated vernacular music during slavery. As with arranged spirituals, testifying did not eliminate the call-and-response that ensued between leader and congregation. Rather, it made the call-and-response structure more fluid and spontaneous. Instead of a designated individual leading the congregation, any member who was moved to testify might start a song. Testifying encouraged individuals to display the divine gifts they possessed, a process that would nurture the solo singing tradition that lay at the heart of solo gospel.[40]

In their search to resurrect intense religious experiences such as speaking in tongues and testifying, members of the Church of God in Christ laid the groundwork for distinctive elements of solo gospel: intensely emotional singing and upbeat instrumental accompaniment. Even as church members eschewed changes in fashion, they embraced the flood of new, affordable musical instruments created by industrial production. Members of the Church of

God in Christ used a wide spectrum of instruments to accompany singing, including washtubs, drums, trombones, and trumpets, as well as tambourines and guitars.[41] One man captured the interactive dynamic between instruments and religion when he described how Pentecostals of the 1920s and 1930s transformed music and dancing into mediums for praising God. "Our music," he said, "was tambourines and sometimes a guitar. The Holy Ghost would come and we would dance for hours and hours. . . . We praise God in the dance and plays music."[42]

The recordings made by Bessie Johnson in 1927 dramatically illustrate the rise of solo singing as well as the music's roots in the vernacular sounds of slavery. Nowhere is this pattern more evident than in the textured vocals that account for some of the music's emotional intensity. Much of the singing dominating sanctified churches featured guttural sounds and shrieks, both hallmarks of vernacular spirituals. The richest source for textured vocals comes from recordings the sanctified made during the 1920s. When Bessie Johnson made her solo recordings, she delivered each song with a full-throated vocal style that lent a textured, worn quality to the music. The style was so pervasive in sanctified circles that the faithful may have used it to convey that music making was fundamentally a religious experience that involved reaching inside one's soul and giving voice to the gift of song bestowed by the divine.[43]

Men and women in sanctified communities forged more modern, vernacular sounds with the instrumentation they used to accompany singing. More than a few observers commented on how the emphatic rhythms that laced the music had more in common with blues than with sacred music. Blues guitarist T-Bone Walker noted that he first heard boogie-woogie piano playing in the sanctified church in his Texas hometown. The suggestion that gospel resembled blues must have struck the sanctified as preposterous, especially given that blues musicians voiced little interest in divine subjects. Yet both sets of musicians were rooted in rural communities and working-class urban enclaves, and both celebrated the power of emotion over worldly circumstances. As blues musicians used their instruments and voices to reflect on the pain and misery of life, the power they elicited through personal expression created the possibility for transcending that pain and misery. While the sanctified used music to engage a religious rather than a secular experience, they offered their own path to transcendence. As individuals made manifest the presence of the divine, they transcended the self.[44]

Many black Christians shunned any association with blues music. The prevalence of the guitar in blues, for example, tainted the instrument's reputation in mainstream denominations. In his autobiography blues composer W. C. Handy offered a dramatic illustration of the results. Sometime in the 1880s a young Handy selected a guitar as his first musical purchase. He described the outrage and disbelief his parents felt when they learned of his choice: "'A box,' he gasped, while my mother stood frozen. 'A guitar! One of the devil's playthings. Take it away. Take it away, I tell you. Get it out of your hands. Whatever possessed you to bring a sinful thing like that into our Christian home? Take it back where it came from.'" The Handy family belonged to the African Methodist Episcopal Church, an African American denomination whose leaders, like those in the National Baptist Convention, worked to bring greater restraint to religious worship. For the Handy family the organ was synonymous with religious music. Handy related how his father would meet with his teacher to "hear how I was progressing in sacred music." Conversely, he explained that his father "was brought up to regard guitars and other stringed instruments as devices of Satan." The objections raised by his parents involved more than matters of sin and holiness, as Handy intimated how notions of middle-class ambition were also at stake. Charles Handy demanded that his son exchange the guitar for a dictionary. The elder Handy maintained that the guitar was a mere "plaything," while the dictionary was "something that'll do you some good."[45]

The possibility for transcendence gave sanctified musicians far greater musical latitude. Stressing the importance of holiness, they imputed a sacred meaning to instruments and rhythms typically associated with secular music. For members of mainstream denominations, who felt a decided anxiety about style and expression, the form of sacred music and the instruments used to generate the music assumed extraordinary importance. Such anxiety did not pervade the sanctified church, because it engaged music as a vehicle for experiencing the divine. As a result, the particular form music assumed or the instrument one played seemed almost incidental.

———— While arranged spirituals gained worldwide renown, the sacred singing that inspired gospel remained sequestered in local religious communities throughout the 1910s and early 1920s. Only with hindsight can we discern the development of critical components that would later serve as the foundation for a distinctive form of sacred music. Sanctified communities never envisioned themselves as pioneers of gospel music between 1890 and 1930. Although they surely realized that their music differed from the hymns, anthems, and arranged spirituals that prevailed in educational institutions and mainline denominations, Mason and his contemporaries had little inclination to regard the music as a distinctive sound or style, since they saw music and dancing as synonymous with worship. Histories produced by the Church of God in Christ call attention to this outlook. These sources, which focus on the development of the denomination, give only scant attention to music. References to music are usually dispersed throughout the histories and can most often be found in testimonies describing religious experiences.[46]

In their search for authentic religion, the sanctified embarked on a new religious movement. Grounding respectability in holiness, they worked to make religion meaningful in a world where secular values wielded ever-greater sway. The increased emphasis accorded education by mainstream religious leaders symbolized this transformation. Education encompassed a constellation of values that offered possibilities for advancing the race, and in a world where racism and prejudice prevailed, these possibilities mattered. Yet they revolved around material, not spiritual, concerns. The sanctified sought a different path.[47]

The new styles of worship that emerged from Bible religion would work another change: bringing women to the forefront of worship. Women dominated lay membership in churches across the denominational spectrum. The emphasis sanctified churches placed on spontaneity and individual testimony, however, gave women a more powerful voice in sanctified services. Tellingly, when Hortense Powdermaker described the combination of song and expression that marked the testimony segment of a Church of God in Christ service, she noted that "only women testify." As they raised themselves before the congregation to sing and share their personal experiences of the Holy Spirit, sanctified women developed critical musical and leadership abilities. Bessie Johnson must have summoned those skills in 1927 when she stood in the recording studio poised to deliver her song into a microphone. Sanctified women would assume a vital role in spreading gospel music during the 1920s and 1930s. It is to these women that we now turn to explore the role they played in the development of gospel music.

CHAPTER 2 **I Just Do What the Lord Say**

Gospel as Women's Missionary Work

Sister Rosetta Tharpe, one of gospel music's pioneering stars, did not set foot inside a theater until she was in her early twenties. Tharpe had been raised in the Church of God in Christ, and she spent much of her youth as an itinerant missionary, singing in churches and on city streets in search of lost souls. Her mother, Katie Bell Nubin, stuck strictly to the denomination's proscriptions against worldly living. As the women moved from place to place, Nubin carefully sheltered her daughter from the growing range of commercial amusements that occupied increasing amounts of Americans' free time. As a result, when Tharpe first saw moving images on a big screen, she became so frightened that she jumped up and ran out of the theater.[1]

Less than a decade later, however, Tharpe herself would grace the stages of theaters. Gone would be the oxford shoes, dull colors, and long, decorous sleeves that set sanctified women apart from their more worldly counterparts. Dressed in an elegant evening gown, Tharpe faced audiences with confidence, her fingers moving across the strings of her guitar to accompany her singing. By the late 1930s Sister Rosetta Tharpe was one of the biggest names in the growing field of commercial sacred music, playing a major role in pushing the music beyond the church and into the realm of commerce. She would tell the story of her first encounter with moving pictures again and again, underscoring the cultural distance her musical talent had carried her.[2]

In some ways Tharpe's popular stardom marked a sharp departure from her days as the sheltered daughter of a zealous missionary. But it could also be seen as a logical outgrowth of her upbringing. In the early decades of the twentieth century, sanctified women such as Nubin and Tharpe drew on their religious fervor to fashion a powerful female culture that nurtured musical talent and sought to turn worldly institutions to spiritual ends. As growing numbers of African Americans migrated to cities, many among the faithful recognized that public arenas such as parks or street corners could be converted into sacred spaces. Not surprisingly, they also seized on the new technologies of mass communication that infused commercial culture, recognizing that these technologies might be harnessed to spread religion to vast numbers of people.

Music played a major role in these women's efforts. Like most formally organized African American denominations, the Church of God in Christ barred women from the pulpit. Music, however, was another matter. The belief that musical ability represented the power of God working through an individual gave women great latitude in developing and deploying their musical skills. When record companies set out to reach black consumers in the 1920s, sanctified women ventured to recording studios where they re-created religious fellowship typically found in churches and revivals. These efforts helped drive the tremendous growth that the Church of God in Christ enjoyed in the 1920s. They also played a pivotal role in making inroads for sacred emotion in the commercial arena, laying the groundwork for the more aggressive efforts Tharpe would pursue in the 1930s.

——— Tharpe's life was built on the expanding terrain sanctified women traversed as they pursued their evangelical callings. She used gospel to lead revivals—critical missionary work that consumed her early life and developed her music skills. The activities Tharpe pursued comprised part of a woman-centered world that emerged in black churches across the denominational spectrum. In Baptist churches dedicated to racial uplift, women translated their religious ideals into social reform efforts. In the sanctified church, women directed their religious zeal toward missionary work. Approaching this work with steadfast commitment, they seized the public realm to reach the unregenerate. Such initiative proved instrumental in building and expanding the Church of God in Christ and eventually would inspire Tharpe and other women to push their distinctive sacred sound beyond church doors.[3]

Tharpe maintained that the missionary work she embarked on as a child helped make possible her widespread recognition, stressing to audiences that her career began long before she entered the national spotlight. One sheet music collection emphasized her roots in the church: "At the age of six," the description ran, "my work began. The first program was at a church on Fiftieth and State Street, Chicago, Illinois. We had over 900 people in attendance, and here is where my career began."[4]

Tharpe's life was consumed by church work from the start. Born in 1915, she grew up in Cotton Plant, Arkansas. During the late 1910s and 1920s, as the name makes clear, cotton farming dominated this rural district. Census schedules from the 1920s show that most African Americans in Cotton Plant resided on plantations. Yet spiritual work rather than farming seems to have driven the rhythms of Tharpe's early life. Her mother, Katie Bell Nubin, served as a missionary in the Church of God in Christ, then based in Memphis. In the early decades of the twentieth century the stronghold of the denomination encompassed the tristate region that included Mississippi, Arkansas, and Tennessee. The era was one of fervent evangelical activity, and Tharpe accompanied her mother as Nubin traveled about the local area conducting revivals.[5]

Tharpe seems to have displayed extraordinary musical talent as a child. One playbill pointed to the program that launched her career as a moment of reckoning: "Rosetta had her first musical triumph at the age of six with the guitar which one of her gospel singing relatives taught her how to play."[6] This "gospel singing" relative may well have been her mother. Nubin, described as very protective of Tharpe, probably played an active role in teaching Tharpe basic chords and techniques.[7] Nubin played the mandolin, a fretted instrument very similar to the guitar. But by the early twentieth century, guitars had become far more accessible, a shift that likely influenced Tharpe's choice of instrument.[8]

Since musical talent was perceived as a divine gift in the Church of God in Christ, the community encouraged and nurtured such talent. Whereas other young black children attended school or worked on the farm, Tharpe was able to focus on spiritual work. Tharpe and her mother seem to have traveled extensively. Richard Cohen remembered that the two worked their way through the South doing religious programs and revivals when Tharpe was a teenager. "She played the guitar," Cohen recalled, "and the mother played the mandolin."[9] The mother-daughter team also spent time in Chicago during the 1930s. Sometimes they played in church—"I remember her being with

Elder P. R. Favor's church quite a bit," Musette Hubbard recalled.[10] But they also struck out on their own. Agnes Campbell recalled Tharpe and her mother "having church on the street."[11]

Trekking across the South and Midwest, Tharpe moved back and forth between rural districts where the vast majority of African Americans resided and urban centers to which large numbers of African Americans were migrating. The travel must have given Nubin added incentive to keep a tight rein on her daughter and make all spaces of amusement off-limits. Isolated from the ways of the world, Tharpe was ensconced in religious circles dominated by women. In a concert she gave in 1956, Tharpe described the close ties that resulted: "I remember we used to live in the country, and the womens you know, they wouldn't think about anything. They would go to one another's house and they would hate to leave one another. That's when the sweetness was in the land then. . . . We used to stay at one another's house and when our friend get ready to leave, we wouldn't want them to go."[12]

Migration served as a critical engine for ushering African Americans into the urban-industrial world taking shape around them. African American migrants brought their rural sensibilities to bear in the neighborhoods where they resided. The demands of urban life also inspired new outlets and avenues of expression. As growing numbers of African Americans migrated to urban areas during the 1920s, churches became a stronghold for women—a development that would have significant consequences for gospel music. In 1933 religious scholar Benjamin Mays, who studied black churches in twelve cities, reported that women outnumbered men at a two-to-one ratio. "It is the opinion of pastors," he wrote, "that there are more women members than men, and that women do more of the church work."[13]

This female dominance had limited effects on formal church authority. Susie Blakeny joined the Church of God in Christ in the late 1930s when she and her family migrated from Louisiana to Kansas City, Kansas. In a 1993 interview she described the major roles women played in her denomination, even as she made clear that formal leadership remained the province of men:

SB: In my opinion it was the women who actually kept the church going.
JJ: How did they do that?
SB: It was so many of them, the members. They were the ones who cooked

the meals and sold them and raised the money to keep the bills paid. . . . If there was a congregation of 20 people, about 16 or 17 of them were women and a few men—the preacher, the preacher's son maybe. And it's still that way not just in the Church of God in Christ only. Almost all churches including Catholic churches.[14]

Horace Boyer, who also grew up in the Church of God in Christ, described the contrast between female and male roles in starker terms: "With the exception of administration, the black church is a female church I don't care what anybody says. You know it runs like fifty women to one man. And now the men when they come in of course want to be the administrators. . . . So that you'll have a church full of women, and a head deacon and a pastor and a chair of the trustee board, and they're all men. I don't know how women let men do that, but that's the way it is."[15]

Some women challenged strictures on female preaching, arguing that the religion encompassed much more than the church. In their thinking, the relationship between an individual and God, which remained the most essential relationship, transcended any authority a minister wielded. During the 1920s and 1930s some women began to serve as ministers of independent congregations. One social scientist, who completed a street-by-street survey of black churches in Chicago, recalled how a former member of Quinn Chapel, the oldest black religious institution in the city, pointed to the divine call that led her to establish a new church: "Mrs C. prays much during the day, even being in an attitude of prayer while engaged with house work. The knowledge that she was to found a church came to her at such a time. She had been troubled for a long while about 'the worldly practices' that had crept into Quinn Chapel."[16] Many of the churches led by women consisted of small congregations that were part of the sanctified church. One exception was All Nations in Chicago, founded in 1928 by Lucy Smith. This small congregation soon gained a large following, and Smith took pride in the church building she and her congregation built.[17]

Despite these successes, the persisting strength of gender proscriptions can be seen in the criticism these pioneering women encountered. In fact, some African Americans pointed to female preachers to ostracize the sanctified church generally. The presumption seems to have been so widespread that it became a source of childhood banter. Richard Cohen, who came of age during the 1930s, recalled that "there was a kind of strained relationship between Pentecostalism and what they'd call mainline religions. And you know we were harassed in school." Female authority became a subject of such harassment. "I can remember," Cohen continued, "that one of the things kids use to tease us about was that they assumed that all Pentecostal churches had women preachers." Cohen denounced the perception as absurdity, proudly pointing to the strictures against female preaching that prevailed in the Church of God in Christ. Female preaching, he stated, was "just taboo and still is."[18]

The vital role women like Tharpe played in sacred music, however, should caution against making the pulpit the sole barometer for ascertaining how gender operated in the religious realm. To understand how a shift in gender relations became part of an emerging social order, we must move beyond issues of formal authority. The growing cultural emphasis on secular values presented the faithful with a critical question: how might they use their faith to lend meaning to both spiritual values and the society in which they lived? The 1920s and 1930s marked a period of tremendous religious plurality as Americans, black and white, engaged this issue. Moving beyond the pulpit, women were instrumental in engaging the public arena to make religion meaningful. In the process they marshaled spiritual and material resources at their disposal to carve out space for themselves as dedicated reformers and missionaries.[19]

In middle-class institutions, women often focused on social reform. Black Baptist women, for example, established separate women's societies at the state and local levels and later at the national level. These societies, known as the Women's Convention, were an autonomous wing of the National Baptist Convention. In the wake of urban migration these women joined forces with secular institutions seeking preventive remedies for social ills. As historian Evelyn Brooks Higginbotham explains, foremost among such efforts was the formation of the National Training Institute for Women, through which black Baptist women set out to professionalize the domestic work that was available to many African American women. The programs of formal training they created sought to reduce the drudgery and monotony of domestic work and to make it more respectable.[20]

Women in the Church of God in Christ, on the other hand, focused on missionary work. They viewed political activism as an impediment to religion, since it focused more on social matters than on individual salvation. Their Women's Department encouraged women to use the public arena to reach the unregenerate. Histories of the denomination consistently point to the spiritual work women pursued. One history described the vital role women played in expanding the denomination: "Just as God has said to our Father Adam, 'It is not good for man to be alone,' so it is in the church along with our men Great Women helped pioneer the Church and suffered persecution bravely for Christ."[21] Although he denounced female preaching, Richard Cohen embraced the separate administrative structure where women exercised considerable authority. "The Church of God in Christ," he recalled, "had a female counterpart to any position that a man had in the church."[22] Lizzie Roberson, who spearheaded the Women's Department between 1911 and 1940, laid particular stress on missionary work.[23]

Women brought steadfast commitment to their missionary endeavors. Roberson's own life and work exemplified the aggressive evangelizing women pursued in the Church of God in Christ. Initially she traveled with her husband, with whom she helped establish a church in Omaha, Nebraska. The couple settled there, and her husband became the church's pastor. Roberson, however, did not abandon her missionary work to assume the duties of a minister's wife. While her husband focused on the congregation in Omaha, Roberson continued her missionary work, traveling now with other women in the denomination.[24]

Marriage took Tharpe's work in a different direction. During her travels in Chicago she met Thomas J. Thorpe, a minister in the Church of God in Christ. The couple married in 1934, and Rosetta, then nineteen, assumed the name Thorpe, which she later changed to Tharpe. Rather than continuing to travel with her mother, she now began doing revivals with her husband. He preached the word, and she continued to evangelize with her music. Richard Cohen recalled that the two later relocated to Miami when his father enlisted Tharpe for a weekly radio broadcast. According to Cohen, the couple would crisscross the South during the week and return to Miami in time for Tharpe to do the radio broadcast on Sundays.[25]

Extensive travel rendered missionary work a formidable force in Tharpe's early development. Marie Knight recalled how it prevented Tharpe from securing much formal education.[26] Richard Cohen believed her itinerant lifestyle motivated Tharpe to maintain strong connections to people. He described the affection Tharpe showed toward his family: "She always said my mother and father took her in like one of their children, so she always called us sister and brother." Although Tharpe would emerge as a national celebrity during the 1940s and 1950s, she did not lose contact with Cohen and his family. "You know some people as they move along," Cohen explained, "they forget. Rosa kept up with folks she knew from childhood up until she died." He remembered the enthusiastic reception she gave him and his sister when they went to her dressing room after a performance she gave in 1960. The conversation that ensued was as warm and sincere as if they were all back in Miami.[27]

The collective efforts of Tharpe, Roberson, Nubin, and others help account for the phenomenal growth that the Church of God in Christ enjoyed during the 1920s and 1930s. In one ten-year period, for example, the denomination grew from nine congregations across the state of Illinois to twenty-four congregations in the city of Chicago alone.[28] George Hancock recalled that during that era, which members refer to as the "pioneer period," "the women started this thing."[29] Although women were barred from the pulpit, Hancock explained that "the only way that a church got built was a woman missionary went out and built it." The establishment of the first church in Chicago provides an example of how women acted as the advance guard of church building. In 1915 there was no Church of God in Christ in Chicago. However, Anna Davis and Lillian Coffey arrived in the city that year, and on their arrival the two women began to bring together local residents for prayer and Bible study. Davis used her home to accommodate the faithful. The prayer band grew over the next two years, and ultimately William Roberts moved to Chicago to serve as pastor of the community. As this story suggests, the prayer and Bible bands women established supplied the critical seeds from which communities of faithful grew.[30]

As they moved from place to place teaching about the Bible and testifying to the power of God that dwelled inside themselves, female missionaries like Davis and Coffey acted as unofficial preachers. In so doing many looked past the restrictions on preaching and simply followed the dictates they received from the Holy Spirit. Agnes Campbell, born in 1915, did not begin evangelizing until the late 1950s. Yet she grew up in the church and began singing at an early age. She described the range of activities female spiritual workers carried out and alluded to the murky boundaries between preaching and teaching:

> You teach the Bible. You make altar call for people to be saved. Or you might pray for the sick, whatever is needed in this particular church. Maybe someone come that want to be saved. Maybe another person is sick and you pray for them. Maybe somebody else say, "I have a special unspoken request." You pray for them. And then you teach or preach. Sometimes when I was very young they used to say, "The women don't preach, the men preach." But now they say, "The women teach and preach so don't worry about it." I tell them, "I just do what the Lord say, y'all can call it what you want to."[31]

As the denomination expanded into cities and more churches took shape, women also expanded the scope of their evangelism. Daily life in the city moved at a faster pace than in rural areas, and spaces of amusement helped turn play into routine activity. Like all institutions, churches had to contend with the new environment. Some churches set up vocational training classes. Others sponsored recreational activities.[32] The Church of God in Christ adapted to city life by holding more frequent revivals. Susie Blakeny, who grew up in a small Louisiana town, described the annual revivals she remembered as a child: "In the South they would have a revival at least once a year—an annual thing. And that was the big event of the year. And everybody who don't belong to the church, you are asked and begged you know . . . you should seek religion as they called it." In contrast, when Blakeny moved to Chicago and joined the Church of God in Christ, the denomination "had revivals all the time."[33] The Church of God in Christ sponsored annual statewide and national convocations, but revivals seem to have been more spontaneous affairs. Rather than following the calendar, Alva Roberts recalled, revivals occurred at the church her father-in-law pastored "just when Papa felt led to." The frequent revivals provided women with a wellspring of opportunities to spread the word of God. Katie Bell Nubin, for example, directed much of her missionary work to conducting revivals.[34]

Women fulfilled their missionary duties with great zeal. In 1922 Maudelle Oliver ventured to Crawfordsville, Arkansas, from Memphis with a group of other women. She recalled how the enthusiasm around holiness and sanctification compelled women to take initiative. "Well see as I said we were just inclined to do. We weren't sent by nobody. But when the people found out what we had, then they wanted to use us."[35] Women like Lizzie Roberson devoted themselves to full-time missionary work, sometimes logging so many miles that they became virtual itinerants. During the 1910s and 1920s Lillian Daniels traveled throughout the Midwest reaching out to the unregenerate in private homes, churches, and missions and tents across Kansas, Missouri, Oklahoma, Iowa, South Dakota, and Illinois.[36] Life as an itinerant could be demanding and difficult and seems to have offered little, if any, financial remuneration. Travel imposed particular hardships on married women, since it took them away from family responsibilities. Yet the commitment female missionaries displayed toward their spiritual work suggests that religious obligations comprised a part of their identity that they took as seriously as they did their commitment to family and loved ones.[37]

Women endured the hardships of travel because they imagined themselves as carrying out the Lord's work. In fact, missionary work offered a degree of satisfaction and pride that significantly differed from the drudgery that characterized wage labor. Historian Sharon Harley explains that the low-status work available to black women gave them little incentive to ground their self-perception in their work.[38] Instead, female missionaries perceived themselves as doing the Lord's work and grounded their self-perception in working for God. During the 1920s Nancy Gamble conducted meetings across Illinois and Indiana and also worked in New Jersey, where she helped build a church. Gamble took great pride in her work: "I did all I could to the glory of God," she explained.[39]

This zealous pursuit of lost souls often led female missionaries to city streets, which held an especially important place in black urban neighborhoods. Every urban enclave had a commercial street where men and women gathered for work and play. There an array of vendors peddled their wares. Some were engaged in a formal market economy; others turned their attention to the informal, underground economy. Thus all manner of businessmen and -women shared the street, including the tailor, the bootblack, and the barber as well as the streetwalker, the pimp, and the bootlegger. The street became especially active at night as men and women congregated in theaters, dives, saloons, and other spaces of amusement lining the commercial strip. With so much activity, the street also became a social gathering place. Men assembled on street corners and shared gossip. Many of the women who gathered came to shop, though shopping supplied its own outlet for gossip and storytelling. The commercial strip rendered the street a vital thoroughfare that blacks used to move about the city. As both center and thoroughfare, the street inevitably lured musicians, most of whom were men, seeking to attract community patronage.[40]

While most street activities were profoundly secular, missionaries learned that the street could be transformed into an ephemeral sacred space through music and preaching. Lillian Daniels ventured onto city streets across the Midwest to teach about the word of God. Ann Bailey evangelized on the street as she traveled throughout the Northeast helping to establish missions in New Jersey, Connecticut, New York, and Massachusetts. "Mother Bailey," according to one source, "worked untiringly in the ministry, in the missions and on the streets playing her guitar and singing to win souls."[41] Agnes Campbell remembered accompanying her father, William Goodwin, on Chicago's Taylor Street, where he led street meetings: "We would go out on Taylor Street on the west side. I sang all the time. I would be singing and then he would preach."[42]

Tharpe also turned to the street to conduct missionary work in urban areas. As a child, gospel singer Marion Williams remembered hearing Tharpe singing on the streets of Miami. Agnes Campbell recalled seeing Tharpe and her mother ministering on the streets of Chicago in the summers. Tharpe "would play her instrument and sing," Campbell related, "and then her mother would teach."[43] The street seems to have occupied such an important place in Tharpe's work during the 1930s that when she later emerged as a national celebrity and trekked across the country doing concerts, she paid homage to the street. Frequently, according to Abner Jay, her manager, Tharpe returned to the street in the 1950s to give money away:

AJ: And money, money, money, money, money, money she gave away more than anybody.

JJ: Who did she give it to?

AJ: Street corners, stop on the street corners. Start throwing it out the window, "It's Sister Tharpe." Stop in front of the schools and children be turning out. Stop on the street corner, "Come here mama, you need a new dress. Here's fifty dollars. Sister Rosetta Tharpe give it to you." And she—like we stayed in them homes, they's the places where we stayed. Like Spartanburg, South Carolina, for instance. Told this woman say, "Mama, you need a new stove and refrigerator. Come on let's go downtown." Bought that woman a new stove and refrigerator.[44]

The story points to Tharpe's empathy with other women. It also recalls her earlier experiences as a street missionary. Tharpe seems to have returned to the street as though she were returning home.

———— Music assumed a particularly important place in female missionary activity. Because members of the Church of God in Christ placed music within the rubric of sanctification, they regarded musical talent as the manifestation of a divine gift. Agnes Campbell related the deeper significance behind this concept. For Campbell, who began singing in the church at a young age, music was the physical manifestation of a profound spiritual experience. "I used to just stand up," she recalled, "and the spirit of the Lord would take me over and I would start singing 'He's Coming Back Again,' I think it was." In that moment Campbell's body, which no longer belonged to her, became a vessel for God to act.[45]

The experience Campbell described accorded her little agency, so that she became a passive instrument. Yet since the experience was sacred and came at the hands of God, the sanctified recognized its power. Marie Knight, who grew up in the Church of God in Christ, conveyed that power in a 1997 interview. Knight described how outside requests for songs intervened in the spiritual experience that singing encompassed: "Now songs to me is a story, and that story most of the time has something to do with me, that's why I can't sing requests. Because see they might come up and say, 'I want you to sing such and such a song.' Maybe that's not what's dwelling on my mind or the stage that I'm in. And I can't deliver it. I can't. I have to be original, how it comes to me. The song drives a message to me." Since music emanated from an internal, spiritual experience, Knight explained that the decision of what particular song to sing had to come from inside.[46]

The concept of music as an act of communion with God rather than of individual volition meant that women's musical abilities were nurtured and celebrated, even as the pulpit remained a male domain. As a result women enthusiastically engaged music in their missionary work. No single pattern dominated women's use of their abilities. Some combined music and teaching, whereas others devoted themselves exclusively to music. Maudelle Oliver, for example, integrated music into the services she led and assisted. Speaking of the church work she did during the 1920s, Oliver related how missionaries like herself "would call the people to the altar, sing and pray with them and tarry."[47] One history of the Church of God in Christ stressed Ida Baker's use of music in her missionary work. Baker, the daughter of Lizzie Roberson, seems to have drawn regularly on one particular song in her efforts to reach the unconverted. As one history put it, "Ida used to sing to cheer them, 'I'm climbing the hills of Light, I'm singing along my way, My faith is bright as day, I'm seeking a better home.'"[48]

Women's music also took on a range of forms. Some women, like Baker, directed their energies to singing. Others, like Arizona Dranes, played piano. Remembered for the distinctive "black bonnet trimmed in white" that she wore, Nancy Gamble sang and played the guitar as she worked to build communities of faithful.[49] The extensive travel some women undertook in their spiritual work made the guitar a particularly practical instrument to pursue because it was so portable. Sister Rosetta Tharpe and Ann Bailey, who both traveled extensively, used the guitar in their missionary work.[50]

The spiritual dimensions of sacred music accorded women a level of musical authority for which women in secular fields often had to struggle. The guitar dramatizes this disparity. The instrument assumed an important place both in sanctified communities, where religious singing prevailed, and in the clubs and juke joints of southern rural communities, where blues dominated. Memphis Minnie, a blues guitarist who recorded during the 1930s, developed her music skills on the streets of Memphis and in traveling shows. Establishing herself in these settings, Minnie had to demonstrate to her male peers that she was tough, could take care of herself, and could play a guitar as well as any man. Blues guitarist Johnny Shines described how Memphis Minnie had to protect herself: "Any men fool with her, she'd go for them right away. She didn't take no foolishness off them. Guitar, pocket-knife, pistol, anything she'd get her hand on, she'd use it."[51] In contrast to Minnie, sanctified female musicians did not seem to have to demonstrate their toughness. As Bailey, Tharpe, Gamble, and other women used their guitars to demonstrate the power of the divine working in their lives, their skills were celebrated rather than challenged.

Women used this leeway to push their music in new directions, shaping it to fit their circumstances. The experience of street evangelism seems to have been a particular source of innovation. When women took sacred music to the street, they put it to a new use. Within churches, music was part of a mode of worship that testified to the power of the Holy Spirit and nurtured the gathered faithful. Effective street evangelism depended on the power of a singer or musician to attract and hold an audience amid competition and distractions.

Rosetta Tharpe's guitar playing offers a cogent example of the way women adapted to the street. Observers recalled her ability to pick the instrument. One woman, who grew up in Chicago, related how Tharpe "could pick that box, baby. Oh, she could pick that box."[52] Another recalled how Tharpe "would just make that guitar talk."[53] These memories of Tharpe, all from the early 1930s, suggest that she adopted a technique used by blues musicians, who plied their craft on the same streets where she evangelized. Making a guitar "talk" involved playing single notes rather than chords, turning the instrument into an extension of the vocal line and creating a second voice that made for a more dynamic performance. In addition to playing single notes, blues musicians slid devices such as pocketknives and bottlenecks along the guitar strings to reproduce shadings of the human voice.[54]

The innovations in Tharpe's guitar playing demonstrate the autonomy that sanctified women exerted in the public realm, as they forged a culture that fostered a commitment to aggressive spiritual work. The public missionary activities these women pursued would prove auspicious for the emerging field of gospel music. When companies began making records that appealed to black consumers, women embraced recording technology as another vehicle for spreading religion. As they displayed the considerable skills they had developed, they helped push the precursors of gospel music into commercial culture.

———— The advent of recording technology at the turn of the twentieth century radically transformed the selling of music, creating new markets and helping initiate local cultures into the entertainment industry. Sheet music publishers, who had dominated the business in the nineteenth century, had used live performances to disseminate their songs. Recording technology distilled music from its performance context, giving the sound and feel of music a material quality it had not possessed before. The technology also offered a new medium for distributing music, namely records.[55] Americans eagerly responded to this development. In 1922 American consumers purchased nearly 100 million phonograph records.[56]

In the early years of record making, African American participation was limited to a handful of particularly prominent artists and groups, such as the Fisk Jubilee Singers. That would change in 1920. The decisive moment came when Okeh Records, a division of the General Recording Company, issued a recording by blues singer Mamie Smith. The *Chicago Defender* called attention to the record as an important symbol—a recognition by the recording company that "we are here for their service."[57] But it was more than that. The Smith recording sold 75,000 copies within the first month of its release and launched a new recording market known as race records. Increasingly, record companies began to employ black singers and musicians to make recordings geared specifically to black consumers. Companies developed special catalogs and used certain inventory numbers to designate a separate race series. Over time, race records included a range of music encompassing sacred as well as secular realms.[58]

Blues dominated the earliest race recordings to such an extent that many in the trade press regarded the two as synonymous. Noting how race recordings were transforming the music business, one publication described the attention blues garnered in company inventories: "One of the phonograph companies made over four million dollars on the Blues. Now every phonograph company has a colored girl recording Blues." Given the obscurity of blues in company catalogs prior to 1920, the trade magazine described what must have seemed like a meteoric rise of the music. In addition, it conveyed how thoroughly women dominated early race records.[59]

Many of the blueswomen who cut early recordings were veterans of show business and had gained tremendous name recognition among African American audiences while working on the vaudeville circuit. Ma Rainey, for example, already enjoyed immense appeal among African Americans in the South when Paramount Records began recording her in 1924. Eager to capitalize on her popularity, the company invoked her live performances in the advertisements they placed in black newspapers. In one ad the company promoted Rainey's recording by tapping into the memories of her admirers. The advertisement described the blues singer as "the wonderful gold neck woman who starred for five years in three theaters in Pensacola, Atlanta and Jacksonville" and then alluded to the reputation Rainey enjoyed: "'Ma' Rainey is the only Blues singer in the world elevated to the heights of 'Madame.' Now she sings exclusively for Paramount."[60]

Like women throughout commercial culture, blueswomen exerted authority through sexuality. In theaters and other places of amusement Rainey and other blueswomen used music to highlight the sexual power they possessed. Intent on seducing their audiences, these women appeared onstage wearing glistening, glittering gowns and jewels that sparkled.[61] The reputation she earned as the "gold neck woman" suggests how the elaborate costumes Rainey wore onstage became her trademark. Celebrating the body as a source of pleasure, blueswomen adorned themselves in the most extravagant attire. Clyde Bernhardt, who remembered seeing Rainey during the 1910s, described her seductive powers. "Yes," he pointed out, "she was ugly. But . . . she had such a lovely disposition, you know, and personality you forget about it." He went on in a tone of near-disbelief, "She'd commence to lookin' good to you."[62]

As the popularity of race records continued to soar, record companies moved beyond the vaudeville circuit and broadened the spectrum of music they recorded. They soon hired their own personnel and enlisted independent talent scouts to comb black neighborhoods in search of men and women to record.[63] These scouts and record men employed a range of devices for finding talent. Independent talent scout H. C. Speir, who operated a record store in Jackson, Mississippi, combed the area around Jackson and New Orleans looking for talent.[64] Frank Walker, who worked at Columbia Records, made periodic trips to the South, where he set up temporary recording units and invited local people to record. He recalled that he would advertise in the newspaper and people would come from miles around eager to perform. It seems as if there was significant word of mouth about the recording companies. Walker recalled that most of the people were less interested in making money than in the novelty of hearing themselves on a recording: "And these people would show up from eight or nine hundred miles away. How they got there I'll never know, and how they got back I'll never know. They never asked you for money. They didn't question anything at all. They were just happy to sing and play, and we were happy to have them."[65]

Sacred music featured prominently in this new phase of recording. Ministers from the sanctified church and the National Baptist Convention recorded sermons. University ensembles like the Fisk Jubilee Singers recorded arranged spirituals. Quartets sponsored by local secondary schools and by companies recorded sacred music, as did street evangelists. These recordings provide an aural portrait of the variety of sacred styles that prevailed in black communities during the 1920s. They also offer a repository of the early manifestations of gospel.[66]

Sanctified women formed a key component of this conglomeration. Given the recording companies' initial fascination with the glamorized sexuality of blueswomen, recording studios might seem unlikely ground for sanctified women. But these women could draw on a long history of turning secular spaces to sacred ends. On the street they had distinguished themselves from the prostitutes and pleasure-seekers with whom they mingled through their severe styles of dress and their sacred message. Lizzie Roberson, who was so instrumental in forging female work, gained a reputation among members of the denomination for the strict dress codes she put in place. According to one account, "Women had to wear shoes with their toes inside; dresses were well below the knees; women could not wear jewelry and women did not wear feathers."[67] In recording studios, women like Roberson could simply let their music speak for them.

When they stepped before the recording companies' microphones, women drew on their experiences as public missionaries to make an unfamiliar technology serve their purposes. The sterile atmosphere of the studio removed singing from the realm of human interaction to which these women were accustomed. But just as they had done on the street, women turned the recording studio into an ephemeral sacred space. Even when a woman dominated a recording, rarely did she sing alone. Most often women either had vocal accompaniment or comprised part of a group. As they sang into the microphone, the individuals assembled engaged in religious fellowship. When Sister Clara Hudmon sang out "Now is the needy time," the men and women in the studio responded with "Sing it, sing it," "Oh now you're telling," and "If there ever was." Later, when Hudmon began to hum the melody, the other singers reiterated the verses she had sung. Another source of spontaneity can be found in the uneven tempo of the recordings women made. In 1930 when Bessie Johnson and Her Sanctified Singers recorded "Key to the Kingdom," they began with a slow tempo that gathered momentum as members of the group experienced the song. Johnson's booming contralto dominated the recording, suggesting that members directed much more attention to feeling the Spirit than to generating a precise, even sound.[68]

The ways that women met the challenges of the studio were especially apparent in the recordings of Arizona Dranes, a blind pianist from Texas who emerged as one of the most acclaimed sacred songsters of the 1920s. Dranes recorded sixteen sides during the late 1920s. In her first sessions Dranes appeared to be rushing through her songs rather than letting the music move through her. No doubt her urge to rush through the music was triggered by the unfamiliar environment of the recording studio, where she was a lone individual singing into a microphone rather than part of a dynamic human interaction. By the next session, however, Dranes had remedied the situation by enlisting members of her religious community to join her in the studio and provide vocal accompaniment.[69]

Dranes's recordings vividly captured the fervor dominating music in sanctified churches. In every recording she prominently featured a percussive piano style in which her left hand generated a driving rhythm as her right hand wove in and out of that rhythm to provide the melody. This style was a staple of blues piano playing commonly known as barrelhouse. Dranes, however, deftly turned it to sacred purposes. In her recording of "I'm Going Home on the Morning Train," for example, she pushed the piano to the background so that the instrument served largely as a source of rhythm. In so doing she used her vocals to call attention to the importance of divine deliverance. "All my sins," Dranes sang out to begin the song, using her sharp, clear vocals to convey the depth of her convictions. The sanctified minister Rev. F. W. McGee in unison with his Jubilee Singers sang back the line. "Been taken away," Dranes continued, and the Jubilee Singers responded once again. With the sentiment now delivered, Dranes, McGee, and the Jubilee Singers abandoned the call-and-response structure to sing the complete line. "All my sins been taken away," they cried out together, with Dranes's vocal fervor directing the pace and course of the song. After moving through several verses, Dranes then pushed the piano to the foreground to deliver a solo, using the instrument to elaborate on the melody line. Once singing resumed, Dranes returned her piano to the background but deepened the instrument's syncopation. As the singers moved through each successive verse, the song slowly acquired a life of its own.[70]

Dranes's piano and vocal styles serve as further examples of the degree of musical latitude sanctified women enjoyed. As Dranes highlighted the percussive dimensions of the piano, she invoked a technique that prevailed in the saloons, rent parties, and dance halls where blues flourished. Outside vaudeville circles, the world of blues was dominated by male musicians. Thomas Andrew Dorsey, who pursued a career as a bluesman before turning his attention to gospel, conveyed how men dominated these arenas:

> Blues would sound better late at night when the lights were low, so low you couldn't recognize a person ten feet away, when the smoke was so thick you could put a hand full of it into your pocket. The joint might smell like tired sweat, bootleg booze[,] Piedmont cigarettes and Hoyettes Cologne. . . . The piano player is bending so low over the eighty-eight keys, you would look for him in time to swallow the whole instrument. He is king of the night and the ivories speak a language that everyone can understand.[71]

Blues clubs offered few opportunities for a blind woman such as Dranes to develop musical skills. Similarly, barrelhouse piano would not have been welcomed in many Baptist churches. In sanctified communities, however, concerns about holiness, not style or gender, governed how music evolved. Several members of the Church of God in Christ in Chicago pointed to the rapid-fire tempo of Dranes's piano playing as evidence of the divine at work. In a recent interview they recalled the programs Dranes put on when she traveled to Chicago to record. Alva Roberts, who had migrated from Iowa to Chicago in 1925, vividly recalled Dranes. "She was blind," Roberts said, "but she was gifted." Elizabeth Spearmon, who arrived in Chicago in 1923, recalled the dramatic techniques Dranes deployed, noting that "she could stand up and sing and play the piano." Given the fast tempo of the songs Dranes recorded, standing up and singing must have been a feat for a blind musician, emphasizing the power of divinely inspired skill. "The Lord had given her that gift," Roberts explained, "and she could play a piano."[72]

Dranes's clear, fiery vocals serve as a striking example of how women continued to stretch gospel in new directions as they embarked on recordings. This style distinguished Dranes from other sanctified missionaries, male and female, who featured grittier, more textured vocals. While gritty vocals embodied a more impassioned delivery in settings of religious fellowship, they often resulted in murky lyrics on recordings. Dranes may well have recognized that clear vocals could both convey religious passion and reach out to distant, amorphous audiences. Her style seems to have influenced others. A number of women who later recorded adopted it. Most notably, when Rosetta Tharpe began recording in the late 1930s, she would use the clear vocals Dranes deployed to frame her songs.[73]

Race records brought Dranes a level of visibility she could hardly have imagined. As soon as the first recordings were pressed and began selling, Okeh, the company that recorded Dranes, arranged another session. Moreover, the company promptly marshaled its resources to promote Dranes. Her records were plugged on the radio. Large posters of her appeared in record stores in many cities. Dranes had enjoyed a reputation within her home religious community of Fort Worth, Texas, but that recognition paled in comparison to the renown brought by commercial promotion. Dranes channeled the attention into her missionary work, using the recordings as advertisements to secure engagements at churches across the Southwest, including Texas and Arkansas.[74]

Religious singers would face daunting challenges in a profit-driven music business. For Dranes, spreading her evangelical message and reaching consumers seemed virtually indistinguishable. Yet as the music business expanded, religious singers encountered increasing difficulty fusing missionary work and commercial interests. To broaden the range of audiences they reached, recording companies encouraged sacred songsters to entertain as well as evangelize. Such pressures, as Sister Rosetta Tharpe would discover, could potentially mute the evangelical message.

Company executives also found sacred records a challenge. When companies recorded blueswomen, they could build on connections these women had to the entertainment industry. With sacred music, however, they often had to improvise. Correspondence between Dranes and Okeh highlights the initiative the company took to school Dranes in the importance of selling her records. As one manager counseled, "You must remember that the sale of records is what counts in the popularity of the artist." Okeh also clearly saw Dranes as a potential conduit to broader religious markets. One manager, for example, asked Dranes to retrieve the names of churches in the Texas area that might be interested in her recordings:

> I am writing to ask if you will learn through Rev. Samuel Crouch if it would be possible for us to obtain the names of different churches throughout your section of the country, whose congregations might be interested in these records. We can write to each pastor and ask him to advise the congregation that these records are now for sale and endeavor to get them started in this manner. At Dallas, Texas, Miss Dranes, the jobber there handling Okeh records is James K. Polk Co., and I would suggest your getting in touch with them, advising that you live right there where they are and would be willing to do anything possible to assist them in exploiting the sale of your records.[75]

Dranes, too, was interested in selling records. In evangelical terms more records would mean more souls touched. In addition, Dranes had her own interest in the profits record sales could generate. In a religious world where most salaried positions—those of preachers—were reserved for men, female missionaries were forced to rely on the day-to-day generosity of the people whose hearts they moved. As a blind woman unable to do other work, Dranes was particularly dependent on this community patronage. She clearly looked to recording royalties as a valuable supplement to her income.

Dranes approached her financial interactions with Okeh with the same assertiveness that women in the sanctified church deployed to conduct their missionary work. She made sure that the company reimbursed her for every aspect of the travel that recording required. While traveling at company expense between Dallas and Chicago, she often arranged stopovers to play at churches along the way. She also seems to have closely monitored the distribution of her records and often corresponded with the company regarding its strategy for issuing the recordings. Despite such efforts, however, her recordings never produced the kind of income she hoped for. In 1928 Dranes expressed frustration about not receiving her royalties:

> I failed to get any letters from you and our contract will soon be at an end and you promised to send me some more Royalty from my Records I've only received one 50 dollars from you and that was Jan 28 1927 of coarse I dident know anything about record making or prices on them and I dident even consult our White friends down here I took what you said about everything and was confidence that you would treat me fair now I'm asking that you consider me as I am disable to work now and have to be confined to my room for awhile.[76]

This letter captures the predicament that many musicians encountered. Dranes had given Okeh exclusive rights to all her compositions in exchange for 25 percent of the gross royalty paid on any of those compositions. But while this agreement entitled her to a generous share of profits, monitoring the sale of records was difficult for musicians removed from the marketing and distribution process. As a result, despite her efforts, Dranes had difficulty ascertaining just how much money she was entitled to.

Although Dranes's recordings sold well, her recording career was short, highlighting the limitations of commercial success. Faced with mounting personal problems and financial difficulties, Dranes soon became a liability to Okeh. These troubles began soon after Dranes started recording. When influenza broke out in Memphis in 1926, Dranes became ill and never fully recovered. The illness hampered her ability to travel, a critical component of her missionary work, and Dranes approached the company for loans. After initial hesitation, company personnel began to supply some of the requested funds, drawing against future royalties. But her constant travel made her difficult to locate, illness affected her ability to fulfill recording obligations, and she began to quarrel with some of the men and women who accompanied her on her recordings. She made her last recordings in 1928 and slipped back into the sanctified world from which she had emerged.[77]

Despite these troubles, Dranes's recordings were spiritual and artistic triumphs that generated enormous enthusiasm, particularly in sanctified circles. Collectors remark that the copies of her recordings they find have been played so much that they are unusable, and in the 1990s many members of the Church of God in Christ in Chicago still vividly recalled her music. In addition to testifying to Dranes's formidable abilities, this enthusiasm points to the important role women played in the development of gospel. Dranes managed to translate the fervor of her faith onto her recordings precisely because she drew on the wealth of spiritual resources and strategies sanctified women cultivated in their own communities. These rich resources reveal another side of the restrictions Katie Nubin placed on Sister Rosetta Tharpe. In barring her daughter from movie theaters and other secular amusements, Nubin ensured that the female culture prevailing in sanctified circles would mold Tharpe's sensibilities. As a result, when Tharpe ventured into the very theaters from which she had once been restricted, she went armed with the confidence and the spiritual resources that would enable her to negotiate the challenges posed by the commercial world.[78]

With their recordings Dranes and other sanctified women secured a commercial foothold for the sounds and rhythms that would soon acquire the name gospel. The inroads they made for the music created the possibility for gospel to move beyond the sanctified fold, posing a challenge for Baptist and Methodist ministers who sought to tamp down the teeming rhythms and emotional fervor dominating music in sanctified churches. In the 1930s another group of believers would take on that challenge directly, launching a grassroots movement for gospel inside black Baptist churches and moving the music to the center of black religious life.

The Grassroots Campaign for Gospel

In the mid-1930s, sanctified singer Sallie Martin traveled from Chicago to Cincinnati on a spiritual mission. It was a trip that sanctified women had made many times before as they traversed the country, intent on building churches and saving souls. Martin's journey, however, had a different goal. Rather than taking to the streets in search of lost souls, Martin was recruiting members from mainline black churches to build a network of "gospel choruses" designed to introduce the sounds and rhythms that marked sanctified music to a broad range of African American believers. The upbeat tempo and emphatic rhythms that characterized the emerging field of black "gospel" music did not sit well with some ministers, who continued to prize the decorum, restraint, and refinement their predecessors had championed in the decades following emancipation. Many churchgoers, however, felt differently. The gospel choir that Sallie Martin organized in Cincinnati became part of a broad-based swell of grassroots African American enthusiasm for upbeat religious music, a shift that would transform the sound of black religious life and carry gospel well beyond the church.[1]

Sallie Martin, who would be one of the central figures in gospel music's spread, had deep roots in the sanctified church. She first entered the fold as a teenager in Georgia. After migrating to Chicago, she directed her energies to a small congregation on the city's South Side. In 1932, however, Chicago's musical landscape began to shift, and Martin set her sights on a broader field. Sometime that year an ambitious young composer named Thomas Dorsey had formed a gospel chorus at Pilgrim Baptist Church, one of Chicago's most prominent Baptist institutions. In contrast to the restrained music that had dominated mainline Baptist services, Dorsey's chorus swayed to upbeat rhythms with an exuberance that echoed the emotions of sanctified worship. Black Chicagoans were flocking to Pilgrim to hear the new sound, and sheet music bearing at least one of Dorsey's compositions was making its way around the city. Black religious music was on the verge of a major transformation, and Sallie Martin was determined to be part of the movement. She auditioned for Dorsey, and when he turned her down, she tried again. When he finally hired her, she became a tireless promoter of the new gospel music, helping to organize dozens of gospel choruses around the country and playing a major role in the development of the gospel sheet music industry.[2]

The appeal of Dorsey's compositions, combined with innovative strategies of organization, would soon give gospel a following great enough to rival that of secular music. "Here, indeed is church music that can hold its own against anything on the hit parade," cultural critic Arna Bontemps observed in 1942, noting that even Chicago's taxicab drivers tuned their radios to gospel broadcasts.[3] As gospel's popularity grew, the efforts of Dorsey, Martin, and others to win institutional legitimacy for the music would also help elevate sounds and rhythms that had once been confined to the margins of black religious life to a place alongside the cherished spirituals as an icon of African American culture.[4]

The music that caused such a stir resembled in many ways the music that had developed in sanctified churches. Both styles had been nurtured on the streets and in the gathering places of working-class black neighborhoods, and both used the power of rhythm and emotion to touch listeners' souls. Recordings vividly captured these similarities. Dorsey made two sacred recordings in 1934, playing the piano in a style that shared important similarities with that of Arizona Dranes. Both Dranes and Dorsey embellished the melody of their songs by deploying improvisational runs at selected intervals. Dorsey used his runs to punctuate certain elements of his songs. Dranes displayed her runs with piano solos in which she elaborated on and extrapolated from the melody line.[5]

There were, however, important differences. Rather than emerging from sanctified music circles, Dorsey had developed in parallel with them. He had gotten his musical start as a bluesman, plying his trade amid the clubs, theaters, and storefront churches of Atlanta's Decatur Street. He had then honed his skills on the vaudeville circuit and in the burgeoning race record industry, where he worked as a performer, composer, and arranger. The religious songs he composed bore the mark of these experiences. His gospel lyrics focused on the individual joys and sorrows that so infused blues music, and they were rendered with a polished professionalism that eliminated the rough edges so common among blues and sanctified singers. In fact, Dorsey initially turned down Sallie Martin because of the roughness in her sanctified sound.[6]

Like the evangelical singers who had seized on race records to broadcast their message, Dorsey saw the realm of commerce as fertile ground for reaching beyond conventional church institutions to spread his religious and musical message to a broad public. Unlike his sanctified predecessors, however, Dorsey carefully steered clear of the corporations that were coming to dominate the popular music industry. His experiences as a blues musician at the heart of the vaudeville and race record industries had shown him all too clearly that profit, not the good of individuals or communities, drove corporate enterprise. With the help of Sallie Martin, he turned instead to a different form of commerce—entrepreneurial black capitalism—which he saw as offering the advantages of modest profits and commercial distribution while remaining tied to the values and goals of the communities it served.[7]

As with so many cultural endeavors, the gospel campaign would have multifarious effects. Gospel's supporters would put in place a set of institutions, most notably an independent gospel publishing industry and the National Convention of Gospel Choirs and Choruses (NCGCC), that nurtured a long line of church-based gospel singers and drew African Americans together across denominational boundaries. The role Dorsey played in these developments, along with the popularity his compositions garnered, won him the title "Father of Gospel Music." At the same time, however, the popularity that gospel's supporters generated for the music helped move it further into the treacherous currents of popular culture. There it became the focus for a range of uses and interpretations that at times dovetailed with supporters' religious goals and, at others, seemed to run directly counter to them.[8]

——— Born in 1899, Thomas Andrew Dorsey was the son of an itinerant Baptist minister. His musical sensibilities, however, were shaped on Atlanta's Decatur Street, in the city's black commercial district. While the carefully sheltered Sister Rosetta Tharpe found her first encounter with commercial entertainment frightening, for a youthful Dorsey the experience was intoxicating. "Like all youngsters," he explained, "I wanted to get out where the 'lights' were brightest, where times were gayer, and the field was more lucrative."[9] As a youngster Dorsey moved with his family from rural Georgia to Atlanta, seeking economic reprieve from the harsh conditions of sharecropping. Dorsey became enamored with the vaudeville theaters that lined the city's commercial district, where the secular values of a commerce-driven society were on extravagant display. Recounting his experiences at one theater, the Eighty-One, Dorsey pointed to the litany of celebrities who appeared there: "The late Eddie Heywood—not the one who wrote about Canadian Sunset, but his father—was one of the top artists who came there regularly. It was at this theater that I first met the legendary Ma Rainey. . . . I met Bessie Smith there too. . . . Butterbeans and Susie used to come to the theater too. They were wonderful singers and terribly funny on stage when they wanted to be. There was a large procession of big stars."[10]

Dorsey initially saw music as a way out of the poverty his family had been unable to escape. He began this quest by securing a job at the Eighty-One "selling five cent quick drinks." He then used the opportunity to foster relations with piano players like Ed Butler, who accompanied the moving picture shows. Dorsey recalled arriving at the theater early so that Butler might show him "how to play the song that so and so sings." So strong was his commitment that Dorsey would go home at night to practice those songs on an organ his family owned.[11]

His ambitions eventually led him from Atlanta to Chicago, where he relocated in 1916. "In my late teens," he explained, "I began thinking that there must be something better out there in the world. . . . I wanted better musical experiences, better chances to advance. I came North to live."[12] Pursuing his goals in true middle-class fashion, Dorsey began taking courses at the Chicago College of Composition and Arranging. He flirted with sacred music in the early 1920s but soon turned his attention to the opportunities created by the advent of race records, which brought blues and jazz to new heights of popularity. Dorsey, who found these possibilities enticing, recalled how the potential fame and fortune looming on the horizon compelled him to return to blues: "The time rolled on. Then stage bands, and blues singers were becoming very popular. I felt that I wanted to make some quick and real money.

So a band was looking for a piano player at $40.00 a week. This excited me. I quit the church and went with the band and began to drift further and further away from the church."[13]

Dorsey readily availed himself of the new opportunities in blues. He composed blues songs and sold his compositions to music publishing companies eager to capitalize on the enthusiasm surrounding music. He made a number of recordings, both sacred and secular. Perhaps the most successful included the series of recordings he called "hokum blues," in which he teamed up with guitarist Tampa Red. Dorsey also toured with blues singer Ma Rainey as the leader of her backup band. Finally, he worked behind the scenes of a race recording company scoring songs of prospective recording artists.

By 1932, however, Dorsey had left blues to devote himself exclusively to sacred music. The critical moment came in the late 1920s when he became seriously ill during his tenure with Ma Rainey. The predicament unleashed a profound spiritual crisis that fundamentally changed his life and convinced him to turn to sacred work. The illness so incapacitated Dorsey that he was unable to work for eighteen months. Physicians and health specialists were unable to alleviate his condition. Dorsey and his wife, Nettie, lived on their savings for a while, but as the illness lingered, they found themselves "with no income and no one to look [to] for help."[14]

The illness persisted until a minister urged Dorsey to seek divine guidance. The advice, which proved a critical turning point in his recovery, helped Dorsey recognize the ephemerality of the fame and fortune he had so assiduously pursued. Reflecting on the experience in his autobiography, Dorsey described his suffering as a vehicle God had devised to teach him about the importance of faith. "God had to call me in, put me down where I could take time to reason and think," he wrote. "I wasn't as sick physically as I thought. . . . It was my soul and mental thinking that was sick."[15]

After he recovered, Dorsey was determined to consecrate his life to God and devote his attention to sacred music. For many African American singers and musicians, religious conversion prompted a wholesale renunciation of secular music. Dorsey, however, did not take that path. Rather, he sought to put the skills he had learned as a bluesman to sacred ends. Some years earlier, he had been deeply moved by a musical performance in which a Baptist minister riveted his audience by embellishing a hymn with the twists and turns that bore a striking resemblance to the enhancements Dorsey used to give his blues songs emotional force. As Dorsey began to compose religious songs, he sought to create the same effects.[16]

Fired with a new religious zeal, Dorsey made a decision that would have broad consequences for gospel music. The most obvious place for a man in his position to turn would have been the ministry. But Dorsey had little interest in preaching. Neither did he turn to evangelizing, where sanctified musicians whose style so closely resembled his own had enjoyed such great success. Rather, he sought to make a place for blues-inspired sacred music in established black churches.[17]

Convincing mainline denominations of the value of his work would prove an uphill battle. But Dorsey had a formidable range of resources to deploy. He also began his work at an auspicious time, when some mainline churches were rethinking their approach to worship. By the 1920s, proponents of restrained worship dominated most of the major black congregations in Chicago, where Dorsey was based. The issue of worship style, however, had never been completely laid to rest, as many rank-and-file church members had never been fully convinced of the virtues of restraint.

Pilgrim Baptist Church, where Dorsey would organize his first gospel chorus, exemplified this ongoing dilemma. The church began in 1915 as a small prayer meeting club made up of men and women who had recently migrated to the city. One year later when the band of worshipers decided to organize a church, they took the name Pilgrim Baptist to honor their origin as a prayer group that pursued sacred goals in a new environment. During the 1910s and 1920s the church grew rapidly. To accommodate its increasing numbers, the congregation occupied a range of different structures on the south side of the city. In 1916 they worshiped in a storefront facility. Over the next four years they occupied three different church structures, each larger than its predecessor. In 1921 the congregation finally found a permanent home in a former synagogue. The new home reflected not only the congregation's expanding size but its growing social status. The elaborate display of ornamentation found in the vaulted, wood-paneled ceiling that adorned the worship hall, the concentric arrangement of pews, and the gallery that curved around the sides and back of the hall stood in sharp contrast to the humble, makeshift storefront facility of 1916.[18]

The increased ostentation of its church building was not the only change that Pilgrim Baptist underwent. Emotional expression comprised an important element of worship when the congregation was small and the environs more humble. Yet as the congregation became more affluent, finding a consensus about worship practice proved more difficult. In the 1920s the church moved toward restraint. When minister Junius C. Austin came to Pilgrim in 1925, for example, he altered Sunday morning worship by removing the prayer service from the main sanctuary to the basement of the church. The prayer meeting, a ritual of spontaneous singing, had traditionally preceded the more restrained Sunday morning services. Austin also hired Edward Boatner, who enjoyed an esteemed reputation in the classical field as both composer and singer. Boatner was widely regarded for the work he did to champion spirituals, and he had arranged hundreds of the songs. A fitting symbol of the mission Austin had undertaken, Boatner served as chorister for the National Baptist Convention, which had championed the virtues of restraint over emotion since the late nineteenth century.[19]

With the onset of the Great Depression, however, Austin clearly saw the need to strike a new balance between restraint and emotion. Skyrocketing unemployment, expanding breadlines, and deepening destitution required that parishioners contend with new strains on their already inadequate financial resources, and black communities were left with few material resources for dealing with the crisis. It hardly seems surprising that Austin would look for additional sources of spiritual nourishment to comfort his parishioners through the difficult times. In 1932 Austin asked Thomas Dorsey, who had belonged to Pilgrim for more than a decade, to organize a gospel chorus. Since the choir Boatner directed appealed to members who regarded restraint as the measure of religion, Austin likely saw a gospel chorus as a way to appeal to those members for whom emotion comprised a more meaningful articulation of religious experience.

The decision proved immediately popular. While the church's established choir featured stately "anthems, hymns and spirituals," member Joan Isbelle recalled, the music of the gospel chorus was "foot tapping music and, you know, spirit-filled."[20] The chorus enlivened participation among existing parishioners and even attracted new members to Pilgrim. Austin's son recalled how "folk crowded out that church" to hear the music and preaching.[21] The gospel chorus seems to have inspired lapsed members like Isbelle to deepen their church commitment. Isbelle also described the impact the music had on her mother, Fannie Reinhart, who joined the chorus. According to Isbelle, before joining the chorus, Reinhart "just went to church." The rehearsals and travel required of chorus members encouraged Reinhart to become much more active.[22]

The popularity of the Pilgrim chorus did not dispel the controversy that had surrounded religious emotion since the late nineteenth century. For people like Edward Boatner, the driving rhythms served as ample evidence that the songs were not sufficiently religious. Boatner recalled his first impression of the music Dorsey was creating and endorsing: "At that time I never knew what a gospel choir was. But I know that when I heard him play the piano, I knew what was happening. He was sitting in the church one day and he was playing a gospel hymn or song for some lady who was sitting there. And it was nothing but jazz, the rhythm of jazz. You can look at any of them today, any of the gospel songs. They have that same jazz type of form."[23]

As Boatner's comments suggested, Dorsey's initial endeavors met a combination of indifference and resistance. Leaders of the National Baptist Convention did not necessarily see the songs as helping to advance their religious interests or their efforts to promote racial progress. In later years Dorsey described the rebukes he encountered from ministers:

I recall one experience which happened right here in Chicago. I asked a certain pastor for a chance to say something about my gospel songs. I figured that I could meet the folks as they left the church and sell them my sheet music. This way, I wouldn't interfere with the service or the collection. This preacher—I won't call his name; he's dead now—he said to me: "Oh sure, Brother Dorsey, I'll be glad to give you a chance." I sat up there in the front pew of his church as the services began. The choir marched in. Announcements were read. Scriptures were recited. The choir sang a few songs. The preacher gave his sermon. The doors to the church were opened for people to come join. The offering was taken. Doxology was said, and the minister dismissed the congregation. There I was sitting in the front pew. And that minister looked me straight in the eye and said: "Oh Mr. Dorsey! I forgot all about you."[24]

Dorsey insisted that the apology offered by the minister was nothing more than deliberate deception. He recounted a similar story in other interviews, suggesting that this insidious dismissal had come to symbolize the degree of opposition he encountered.[25]

The chorus did, however, create an opening for a more sustained public discussion about the meaning of religion. Dorsey, who availed himself of all the opportunities his position at Pilgrim could provide, seized the moment to mount an aggressive campaign for gospel in black Baptist churches. Drawing on his experience with the sheet music dimension of the popular music industry, Dorsey began publishing his songs as sheet music. He initiated a letter-writing campaign to interest ministers and made direct contact with church leaders in and around the Chicago area in an effort to garner their support. In addition Dorsey organized gospel singing groups to demonstrate his songs on street corners, over the radio, and at the annual meetings of the National Baptist Convention.[26]

The Pilgrim chorus became a particularly effective vehicle for gospel promotion. Joan Isbelle noted that as Dorsey carefully schooled chorus members in his songs and their performance, he launched a broader campaign for gospel music itself: "He told them what to sing because you see they didn't know his music. See he hadn't printed a book, and he just had his music in sheet music. And it wasn't in all the churches. . . . So he had the music, and he would give them the sheet music and he would play."[27] The Sunday morning services at which the chorus performed at regular intervals gave Dorsey a ready-made audience for his efforts.

The opportunity at Pilgrim, however, was just a beginning. Dorsey only had to look at the small number of gospel choruses in Chicago—three in 1932—to realize the extent of the resistance that he faced. This situation gave Dorsey incentive to use his position at Pilgrim to mount a community-wide campaign for gospel. He and the two other gospel chorus directors—Theodore Frye at Ebenezer and Magnolia Lewis Butts at Metropolitan Community Church—organized a citywide chorus. Over time the popularity of this chorus prompted other churches to organize gospel choirs. Ultimately the citywide chorus turned into a union of Chicago-based gospel choirs and choruses, which provided a forum to generate broader support for gospel choruses and gospel music.[28]

The success of the Chicago union convinced Dorsey that a national coalition of choirs and choruses could help boost gospel further. The idea sparked the formation of the NCGCC, a coalition of individual gospel choruses with no formal church ties. The organization, which met annually in different cities across the country for a week of singing and fellowship, transcended denominational and congregational boundaries without abandoning the church. The first meeting took place in 1933. Dorsey was elected president and would serve in that capacity for more than thirty years.[29]

The expansion of gospel choirs nurtured a groundswell of support that turned into a movement for expressive worship with gospel at its core. And as in sanctified churches, where the significance music gained in worship practice gave women a prominent role in sanctified services, gospel's growing acclaim created openings for women to exercise greater influence within mainline black religious life. From the beginning, gospel choirs were dominated by women. Additionally, it would be the drive and ingenuity of Sallie Martin that transformed Dorsey's dreams for gospel music into realities. When Martin joined Dorsey, his sheet music operation was a struggling venture and had published only four gospel songs. Martin soon criticized his business operation and remembered saying, "Really you have something here but you don't know what to do with it."[30] According to Martin, Dorsey challenged her to do better and paid her four dollars a week.

Over the years, Dorsey's inventory increased as Martin found a way to connect the NCGCC to the publishing concern. As she explained, "I told him to let me go travel, then carry the music and sell it when I finished singing." Dorsey's publishing company became a self-sustaining enterprise, as Martin traveled across the country organizing gospel choruses. In the process she helped generate support for gospel across regional and denominational lines by organizing existing choirs and choruses into unions.[31]

The work of organizing choirs differed from the missionary work sanctified women conducted during the 1920s. Whereas her predecessors had focused on sanctified communities and the broad public arena, Martin was moving across denominational boundaries. The outlooks and values Martin imbibed in the sanctified church made her a formidable organizer who recognized that her work was divinely inspired. As a result, she was not shaken when she encountered indifference or resistance. Instead she drew on her religious convictions and encouraged the women she met to move beyond the church altogether. Her experiences in Cincinnati were emblematic. When "I could not interest the pastor," she explained, "I organized what we call a community gospel chorus." When an angry local pastor "called me in a conference," she later recalled, "the Lord guided my tongue."[32]

These independent ventures and the developing gospel publishing industry transformed the production, dissemination, and distribution of black sacred music. Until the Depression the church had exerted tremendous control over the dissemination of sacred music, which was principally distributed through the hymnals that specific denominations published. Dorsey and Martin's decision to venture beyond the auspices of the church to sell and promote gospel music also created new opportunities for African Americans, particularly women, in the commercial arena. The corporate dominance of the popular music industry meant that most economic opportunities for African Americans in blues rested in performance, not in the business side of the music. Similarly, religious recording artists such as Arizona Dranes found themselves with little influence over the corporations for which they worked. Gospel, however, during the 1930s and 1940s was dominated by small-scale entrepreneurs such as Dorsey. Consequently the field offered opportunities for African Americans in publishing, composing, and retail as well as performance. Many of the gospel music publishing studios that took shape in the 1940s were either led by or partnered by women, including Roberta Martin, Sallie Martin, and Lillian Bowles. Reflecting on his career in an interview for a blues publication in the mid-1970s, Dorsey commented on such capitalism as a source of black pride: "But hear me and hear me well: gospel singing; gospel songs; gospel song books and gospel stores where they sell gospel songs; has been lucrative and has brought in more money to many more people than the blues."[33]

Dorsey's own sheet music business captured his emphasis on spreading gospel rather than maximizing profits. Sheet music may have seemed a bit outmoded, relative to recording technology.[34] But Dorsey turned sheet music into an innovative and economic way of disseminating gospel among a mass black public. During the early 1930s he was among the few independent gospel publishers in the nation. In fact, during the 1930s gospel sheet music became so synonymous with Dorsey that people referred to it as "Dorseys."[35]

Dorsey's reliance on his own compositions pointed to another of his priorities: he was more interested in maintaining control of his music than in building an expansive enterprise. With the exception of a small number of spirituals that he arranged, Dorsey limited his operation to songs that he composed himself. This practice distinguished Dorsey from the corporate publishers of popular music who inspired him. These enterprises either devoted small attention to composing or abandoned it altogether. Depending on the size of their operation, many purchased copyrights from other songwriters, bought the catalogs of companies going out of business, or hired individuals to write exclusively for the company. Limiting his catalog to his original compositions, Dorsey received only modest economic rewards. "He got a little money," according to one person who knew Dorsey, "and he was satisfied."[36]

The lack of interest Dorsey showed in expanding his commercial horizons reflected his religious sensibilities. He certainly recognized the potential of commerce for accumulating wealth. During his tenure with Ma Rainey he had made a good deal of money. In 1930 he secured an additional windfall when "It's Tight Like That," a blues song he wrote and recorded, became a hit record. Yet in both instances money proved to be ephemeral. These experiences convinced Dorsey that divine assistance was a much more reliable resource than wealth. He conveyed this perspective while reflecting on the economic difficulties he faced in the 1930s. "I opened my own publishing company," Dorsey recalled and then quickly added, "or the Lord opened it for me 'cause I didn't have a cent."[37]

Dorsey and his supporters demonstrated the degree to which carefully configured commercial involvement had the potential to bypass gospel's opponents and to further meaningful religious work. For Dorsey, commerce was not an incubator of material values that undermined religious faith. Rather, commerce comprised a vital middle ground between the sacred world of religion and the profane world of popular culture. While Dorsey clearly recognized the limits of wealth, he did not consider such limitations intrinsic to commerce.

In Dorsey's view commerce provided a viable arena for bringing African Americans a more responsive worship practice. He conveyed this perspective in the way he scored his sheet music. Dorsey recognized that since much of the music in African American communities sprang from oral performance, music notation had little import. Consequently he regarded his sheet music as a sketch to guide consumers. His scores included lyrics, and he presented basic melody and harmonic patterns. This approach resulted in straightforward, simple notation, a significant departure from the variety of melodic ornamentations and rhythmic syncopation that were part of performance. Marion Peeples, who joined the gospel chorus at Pilgrim Baptist during the 1940s, conveyed how Dorsey made the distinction between notation and performance in rehearsal. She described how Dorsey used his sheet music as a teaching tool that he abandoned in performance:

> MP: Right we always had music. We always used music to rehearse. But when we get up, [Mr. Dorsey would say,] "Put that book down."
>
> JJ: So you had music to rehearse . . .
>
> MP: Now see like senior choirs, they would put their portfolio—their folders with the music—and they sang from the music. We did not. We sang from the music in rehearsals.
>
> JJ: But not when you [performed]?
>
> MP: No, no!
>
> JJ: And did he have any music when he was directing?
>
> MP: No, no, no.[38]

Dorsey used his sheet music as a mechanism for training and disciplining members of the chorus rather than as a script for performance. The precision he demanded makes unlikely the possibility that chorus members spontaneously departed from the music notation during performance. Instead, the point of departure probably occurred in rehearsal. The distinction Peeples made between the senior choir and the gospel chorus underscores the innovations Dorsey brought to his sheet music.[39]

Even as he employed commerce to reach a black mass public, Dorsey made a concerted effort to remove the stigma that had shrouded emphatic rhythms and emotional expression. To do that, he turned his sheet music into a platform for celebrating the virtues of gospel. He made a case for the music with the advertising slogans he used to promote his songs. Dorsey referred to his music as "songs with a message" and called attention to the lyrics. In addition to echoing sanctified approaches to music, the focus on lyrics captured Dorsey's own personal journey from blues to gospel. He related how he geared the blues songs he wrote to the market—what might sell—but he approached his gospel songs differently. His gospel compositions reflected his personal experiences. The slogan also served as a subtle rejoinder to critics like Boatner who pointed to the rhythms of Dorsey's songs as evidence that the music had more in common with jazz than with religion. Highlighting his lyrics, Dorsey reminded consumers that while his songs might bear some resemblance to secular music, the words laid bare the distance between his songs and secular concerns.[40]

In addition to stressing the sacred content of gospel lyrics, members of the NCGCC sought to cast the rhythm that so infused the songs, and also served as a source of their appeal, as a virtue rather than a vice. For this they turned to history. In books, essays, pamphlets, speeches, and newspaper columns Dorsey and his supporters insisted that rhythm not only had religious significance, but it formed a key component of black heritage. To make these arguments, they challenged conventional wisdom about the origins of upbeat religious music. Most observers placed gospel's origins in the late nineteenth century, when Dwight Moody and Ira Sankey conducted a number of fervent urban revivals that gave birth to a series of hymnbooks bearing the title *Gospel Hymns*. Ruth Smith, who belonged to the NCGCC, rejected this conventional wisdom. In her 1935 work *The Life and Works of Thomas Andrew Dorsey*, Smith asserted that Sankey and Moody's innovations were rooted in black spirituals. Rhythm became her prime evidence: "I claim the Gospel Hymn to be a derivative of the Negro Spiritual in that they carry the same lively trend so given to our nature; songs that exhilarate and captivate. I feel that had our forefathers been educated and familiar with the rudiments of music it would be readily seen to whom this type of hymn would be accredited."[41]

Using the term "lively trend" to refer to rhythm, Smith sought both to link gospel to African American roots and to reclaim the songs from classically minded arrangers such as Boatner. For her the rhythmic dimensions of gospel were not only a source of pride but also comprised a critical part of African American heritage. Similar sentiments appeared in an essay that the Illinois Writers' Project devoted to gospel. The essay, "Spirituals of Today," referred to gospel songs as modern-day spirituals. Like Smith, the essay highlighted the rhythmic dimensions of the music and cast rhythm as intrinsic to African American life. "The music is usually in spirited rhythm and touches answering chords in the make-up of a people in whom a love for rhythm was born."[42]

In addition to making rhythm a critical component of African American heritage, Dorsey and his colleagues gave his syncopated rhythms religious significance. Citing biblical authority, Dorsey maintained that the term "gospel" had relevance as good news, and the shape and form that news assumed was irrelevant. "Gospel's good news," he asserted, "as far as the Bible's concerned."[43]

The notion of "gospel" as good news marked a significant departure from the meaning that the National Baptist Convention assigned to the term in 1921 when the organization titled its first songbook *Gospel Pearls*. At that time leaders of the National Baptist Convention adopted the term as it had been coined in the 1910s by Ira Sankey, who used it to distinguish contemporary sacred songs from more traditional numbers. A decade later Dorsey invoked an older definition that gave the word "gospel" biblical importance. The gospels consisted of the four initial books of the New Testament that told the story of Jesus Christ's birth, baptism, ministry, healing, death, and resurrection. Derived from the word "God-spell," the term "gospel" referred to the "good tidings" conveyed by these divine acts. Referring to gospel music as "good news," Dorsey made the rhythmic dimension of the music synonymous with this older definition of "gospel" and its religious significance.[44]

As Dorsey and members of the NCGCC called attention to the virtues of rhythm, they helped turn their campaign for the music into a movement for expressive religion. As many pointed out, the rhythms that made gospel so distinctive elicited an emotional and physical response. Describing the influence of Dorsey's songs, one observer referred to "a Dorsey beat" that "caused people to run and shout, to clap their hands and tap their feet, to sway and move about."[45] For Joan Isbelle the music's ability to generate such emotional and physical responses held a decidedly religious significance, which she invoked when she spoke of Dorsey's songs as being "spirit filled."[46]

The link Dorsey and his colleagues drew between rhythm and black heritage played a key role in this endeavor, engaging both the interest black leaders had developed in identifying distinctive features of African American traditions and the growing national interest in exploring the mores and manners of a range of American cultures. In yet another effort to call attention to the contributions of African Americans to the American past, black leaders eagerly seized on this national interest in black folkways to refute lingering notions of black inferiority. Placing gospel in this context proved highly appealing. For Dorsey and members of the NCGCC the cultural politics of the Depression era provided the added opportunity of responding to the criticisms Baptist church leaders had long waged against Dorsey's songs. As gospel grew more popular during the 1930s, the music emerged as a symbol for expressive worship, paving the way for expressive worship practices to gain acceptance in mainline black churches. Once considered by many Baptist church leaders as a sign of primitive, backward behavior, expressive worship gradually came to be seen as a vital component of black culture and history.[47]

———— The movement for expressive worship, which Arna Bontemps described in 1942 as a "new religious ecstasy," provides important insights about the changing place of religion in twentieth-century black America. Discussions about expressive worship cannot be separated from larger concerns about the broader meanings African Americans gave to their faith. Just what place should emotion assume in religious worship? Should worship be governed by restraint or give way to emotion? These questions, which hovered over the struggle Dorsey and others waged for gospel, recalled the efforts of Charles H. Mason and Charles P. Jones to use the first-century Christians as evidence that ecstatic worship comprised a component of early Christianity and therefore constituted "authentic religion."

Significant differences, however, separate the Depression era movement from its late nineteenth-century counterpart. In the late nineteenth century the movement was grounded in churches. By using the doctrine of sanctification to shape worship rituals, Mason and Jones helped forge a new religious movement that culminated in the sanctified church. In contrast, the spread of gospel was not confined to churches. Rather, Dorsey's efforts to bypass disapproving church hierarchies helped establish gospel as a space for religious expression connected to and yet separate from religious institutions. The success of this new arena provides particularly telling evidence of how the place of religion in African American society changed over time. In contrast to a doctrine such as sanctification, music was decidedly ambiguous. Consequently it could appeal to people with very different religious outlooks. Thomas Dorsey and Sallie Martin, both central figures in the gospel campaign, came from disparate religious backgrounds. Dorsey grew up in the Baptist church and joined Pilgrim Baptist Church in 1921 at a time when many Baptist leaders frowned on expressive worship. Martin was part of the sanctified church. She had joined a sanctified congregation as a young woman, and Dorsey recalled that when the two met in 1932, Martin was "aspiring to the ministry" in a "small holiness church on Federal Street."[48]

The ambiguity and fluidity of music could easily camouflage differences in religious outlook. The subjects of Dorsey's songs were also particularly conducive to bridging boundaries. Gospel's supporters often pointed to the Bible as the foundation of gospel and the source of its distinctiveness. As George Lewis asserted in an Illinois Writers' Project essay, "All gospel songs are written around some verse or saying taken from the Bible and the words are so couched that they reach the heart of their hearers."[49] Yet the Bible did not always figure prominently in gospel, particularly the songs Dorsey composed. Religion for Dorsey had more relevance as personal experience than as biblical text, a perspective that no doubt accounts for the absence of biblical scriptures in his otherwise deeply religious autobiography. Seeking to convey "the realness of God," Dorsey produced songs that revolved around the application of broad Christian principles in everyday life.[50]

For Dorsey, faith revolved around action and behavior, namely, the willingness to seize faith and hold onto it during moments of difficulty. In his songs Dorsey often reflected on his personal relationship to the divine. His most famous composition, "Take My Hand, Precious Lord," provides a concrete example of how Dorsey used his songs to make God alive and vibrant:

> Precious Lord, take my hand,
> Lead me on, let me stand,
> I am tired, I am weak, I am worn;
> Through the storm, through the night.
> Lead me on to the light:
> Take my hand, precious Lord,
> Lead me home.[51]

Dorsey wrote the song in 1932 when the death of his wife and unborn son catapulted him into the depths of despair. Awash in misery, Dorsey sought divine guidance. In the resulting song, Dorsey conveyed the realness of God by asking the divine to give him direction at a difficult time. "Precious Lord," he entreated, "take my hand." With this simple request, he conveyed to audiences both his own vulnerability and the power of the divine to protect and deliver him from the pain and misery he felt. The song had little to do with religious doctrine. Instead, Dorsey called attention to religion as a deeply personal experience. In this song and others he wrote, Dorsey carried readers inside his personal relationship with the divine. In the process God emerged as immediate and intimate.[52]

The focus of these songs significantly differed from that of those recorded by the sanctified during the late 1920s and early 1930s. Whereas Dorsey wrote songs grounded in personal experience, the sanctified recorded songs that either featured biblical themes and characters or reflected on the power of God. A typical example was Arizona Dranes's rendition of "Lamb's Blood Has Washed Me Clean":

Lord Lord (Lord Lord) Ain't gonna live in this world no longer
Lord Lord (Lord Lord) Lamb's blood has washed me clean
Jesus knew what I needed most
(Lamb's blood has washed me clean)
Filled my soul with the Holy Ghost
(Lamb's blood has washed me clean)
Lord Lord (Lord Lord) Ain't gonna live in this world no longer
Lord Lord (Lord Lord) Lamb's blood has washed me clean.[53]

The song combined two potent biblical symbols: Jesus as the Lamb of God and the shedding of his blood to underscore the doctrine of sanctification. The Holy Ghost was able to dwell inside their human bodies precisely because Christ's crucifixion had freed them from the burden of sin. Dranes pointed to the blood of Jesus to remind listeners that they had been washed clean and rendered holy and righteous. In other recordings, sanctified singers highlighted the magnitude of divine power. "In Jesus Is My Air-O-Plane," Mother McCollum likened God to an airplane:

Oh Jesus is my air-o-plane,
He holds this world in his hands.
He rides over all,

He don't never fall,
Jesus is my air-o-plane.[54]

An emblem of technological power and might, the airplane was a potent symbol in the 1920s and 1930s. McCollum used that symbol to remind listeners that divine power surpassed any power technology commanded. Unlike ordinary airplanes, which could crash, McCollum emphasized that Jesus would never fall.

Dorsey, in contrast, created a balance between human and divine agency. In many of his songs he devoted serious attention to human vulnerabilities and frailties. In "Take My Hand, Precious Lord," for example, Dorsey accorded his own misery and despair as much attention as the power of God to deliver him from that misery. He captured this dual agency in the first line of the song's refrain: "Take my hand, precious Lord." With these words Dorsey did not plead with God to protect him but gently commanded that God come to his assistance. Deploying this command, Dorsey accorded individuals like himself with a certain degree of human agency. Yet even as he uttered this order, Dorsey carefully pointed out that it was a desperate plea to a powerful and indeed precious divine for help and protection. Creating stories in which the divine shared center stage with mortals, Dorsey made God comprehensible on the scale of everyday life.

The popularity of Dorsey's music and the fluidity of his message helped spread gospel beyond individual churches and across denominational lines. They also carried it out of his reach. In his effort to build grassroots African American support for the music, Dorsey had deliberately remained separate from the corporate-dominated popular music industry. But he could not control how others interpreted his songs or where they would take the music. Even as Dorsey and his supporters were promoting their music within African American circles, jazz-derived swing music became a highly profitable national sensation, sparking great enthusiasm among blacks as well as whites. The same promoters that profited from this development began to turn their eyes to black sacred music, sizing up its potential to appeal across racial lines. In gospel, they found what they were looking for.

Katie Bell Nubin traveled across the country holding revivals and prayer meetings during the 1910s and 1920s. Women like Nubin dominated the sanctified church, where gospel took shape as a mode of worship. Female missionaries eschewed popular fashions of the day for the plain dress Nubin displays in this photograph: oxford shoes, long sleeves, and long skirts. Courtesy Michael Ochs Archives.Com.

Arizona Dranes, a blind sanctified pianist, seized the recording studio to conduct her missionary work and helped push gospel into the commercial arena. In the late 1920s her sacred recordings were extremely popular among African American audiences. Okeh Records distributed this sketch of Dranes to sell her recordings.

Gospel composer Thomas Andrew Dorsey, center, began selling his songs as sheet music in the late 1920s. To demonstrate his songs Dorsey organized singing groups like the female quartet in this photograph. During the 1930s Dorsey along with Sallie Martin, on the far right, ignited a choral movement that help push gospel into mainstream black churches so that it reached a broad spectrum of African Americans. Frank Driggs Collection.

In 1938 Sister Rosetta Tharpe, having traveled across the country singing in sanctified churches and revivals as well as on city streets, moved to the nightclub and theater circuit to pursue her missionary work. In this her earliest publicity photograph, the sanctified singer-guitarist relinquished the oxford shoes and long skirt common among sanctified female missionaries for a silk evening gown. Courtesy Michael Ochs Archives.Com.

Sister Rosetta Tharpe stood singing before the congregation at the Harlem-based Church of God in Christ. In 1939 Life *magazine included this photograph in an essay it devoted to Tharpe bearing the headline "Singer Swings Same Songs in Church and Night Club." Once a gospel industry had taken shape, Tharpe would focus exclusively on the commercial arena. In the late 1930s, however, Tharpe conducted her missionary work both in churches and on the nightclub circuit. Courtesy Time Life Pictures/Getty Images.*

In this 1939 photograph, also part of the Life *magazine essay, Tharpe appeared at New York's Cotton Club singing gospel, promoted then as "swinging spirituals." The appeal she garnered at the nightclub brought gospel national exposure and transported the music from black communities, where it had been sequestered, to mainstream American culture. There gospel began to gain visibility among white middle-class audiences.*
Courtesy Time Life Pictures/Getty Images.

Sister Rosetta Tharpe, seated at the piano, and Marie Knight, standing, enjoyed considerable acclaim during the mid-1940s when they began collaborating. Taken in the 1950s, the photograph gives the guitar a conspicuous presence, signaling that the instrument had become a trademark that set Tharpe apart from other gospel singers. Courtesy Michael Ochs Archives.Com.

The Famous Ward Singers were among the increasing number of soloists and groups who enjoyed tremendous acclaim during the 1950s, the "golden age" of gospel. As gospel gained a foothold in commercial culture, many female gospel singers donned robes, perhaps to distinguish themselves from their counterparts in the secular arena. The Famous Ward Singers brought a distinctive flamboyance to the robes they selected, lining the buttons, cuffs, and necklines with sequins. Left to right at bottom: Gertrude Ward, Kitty Parham, Francis Steadman, Marion Williams, Willa Ward. Center (standing): Clara Ward. Courtesy Michael Ochs Archives.Com.

CHAPTER 4

With Her Spirituals in Swing

Sister Rosetta Tharpe, Gospel, and Popular Culture

On 13 October 1938 Sister Rosetta Tharpe picked up her guitar and delivered a version of "Hide Me in Thy Bosom," one of the many gospel songs Thomas Andrew Dorsey had composed. Tharpe had been evangelizing for so long that it had become a familiar way of life. Yet this night was unlike any other. Rather than standing on city streets surrounded by ragtag onlookers, Tharpe was singing on the stage of the Cotton Club, a renowned New York nightclub where African American singers and musicians performed. The enthusiasm Tharpe generated quickly prompted offers from an array of nightspots around the city and across the country. It also encouraged Tharpe to expand her missionary work beyond the church and even the street. During the 1930s and 1940s Tharpe increasingly turned to nightclubs and theaters to save souls.[1]

Tharpe's decision to sing at the Cotton Club gained her a national reputation. Almost overnight her professional and personal activities received coverage in black newspapers and music trade publications across the country. Even *Life* magazine, which rarely turned its attention to African American personalities, devoted a photo essay to Tharpe.[2] Such fanfare would become almost routine for gospel music stars in the years after World War II, when a spate of record companies took interest in the genre and turned gospel into big business. In those postwar "golden years," gospel songs would make the record charts, and gospel programs, once held almost exclusively in churches, would give way to extravagant concerts held in civic auditoriums and theaters. But when Tharpe walked through the Cotton Club stage door and into the public eye, she was stepping onto uncharted ground. With that step and her subsequent achievements, Tharpe secured a prominent place for gospel within the massive music industry that would soon dominate American popular culture.[3]

For many observers Tharpe's movement beyond the sheltered religious circles in which she had grown up seemed a sharp departure from her roots. The move would spark harsh criticism from members of her community, who questioned whether the religious convictions she possessed had ever been sincere. But viewed another way, Tharpe was following in the footsteps of women such as Arizona Dranes, who had proclaimed the word of God through any means she could.

Tharpe's greatest break with her past lay not in her performance but in her audience. The Cotton Club was known not only for its array of African American stars but for its well-heeled white audience. Since the collapse of interracialism in the Holiness movement, gospel had remained largely sequestered in African American communities. Sanctified evangelists focused their efforts on black streets and black neighborhoods. Race records were marketed in black communities and purchased mainly by black consumers. Thomas Dorsey and his supporters had worked largely through and around black churches. Sister Rosetta Tharpe's rise to stardom, on the other hand, introduced the music to middle-class white audiences. The enthusiasm she generated caught the eye of key figures in the rapidly consolidating American music business—men who had turned white enthusiasm for blues and jazz into a national craze and a highly profitable industry. Tharpe's appeal suggested that black sacred music might prove a similarly lucrative field, and she had no shortage of opportunities.[4]

During the next three decades Tharpe negotiated an ever-shifting line between religion and commerce. As she contended with the demands of performance and promotion as well as the material rewards that came with national stardom, Tharpe reshaped both her music and her religious views. In addition to demonstrating the critical role that the commercial arena played in the development and evolution of gospel, her story offers rich insights into the development of a twentieth-century religious outlook.

———— According to legend, Tharpe's rise to stardom began when renowned bandleader Cab Calloway heard her singing on the streets of Miami. Calloway's interest eventually resulted in an invitation to appear in the Cotton

Club's fall revue. Each year the club featured two musical productions, and the array of celebrities in the 1938 revue was especially distinguished. "Audiences," the *Chicago Defender* announced, "are to witness one of the most brilliant star-studded revues in theatrical history when the fifth Cotton Club Parade will have its premiere on Thursday night." Stars included Cab Calloway and his band and the dance team of Fayard and Harold Nicholas. Both Calloway and the Nicholas Brothers had been featured in major motion pictures and were expected to draw large numbers of people. Legendary blues composer W. C. Handy also made an appearance, as did the Dandridge Sisters, a singing group of rising stars. Tharpe was cast in a supporting role along with promising new figures in black entertainment such as the Lindy Hoppers, a dance troupe consisting of young men and women from the celebrated Savoy Ballroom in Harlem.[5]

Many of the men and women who graced the Cotton Club stage had honed their craft in smaller clubs that catered to black audiences. Tharpe, who had never before sung in a commercial venue, was an exception. Still, she brought a fresh sound to the stage that more than made up for her commercial inexperience. One newspaper referred to Tharpe as "Broadway's latest sensation" and noted how audiences were electrified by her music. "Everyone from waiters to patrons," the paper reported, "was caught in the mood of her husky voice, accompanied by her guitar." Given that the Cotton Club catered to white audiences, the warm reception Tharpe received enabled her to expand gospel beyond the black community.[6]

The sensation Tharpe generated at the Cotton Club brought her opportunities to perform before white and black audiences. Not long after her debut, she was engaged to appear in a number of theaters where African Americans congregated. The *Washington Afro-American* reported that Tharpe "was able to bring down audiences at the Paramount Theater in New York for one week."[7] She also appeared at the Apollo Theater in New York, the Royal Theater in Baltimore, and the Circle Theater in Indianapolis. Many more black men and women also soon gained access to Tharpe's music through the records she made. Around the time she appeared on the stage at the Cotton Club, Tharpe signed a recording contract.[8]

The decision in 1938 marked a critical watershed in Tharpe's understanding of the missionary work she had been pursuing, a shift that would prove auspicious for the commercial development of gospel music. After devoting much of her life to singing at revivals and impromptu street meetings, Tharpe turned increasing amounts of her attention to commercial venues such as nightclubs and theaters. *Life* magazine chronicled the transformation of her missionary work in a 1939 feature. "Singer Swings Same Songs in Church and Night Club," read the headline of the essay that included two especially telling photographs. One showed Tharpe on the stage of the Cotton Club with a caption noting that "Sister Tharpe's revival songs are swing hits." A second showed her singing to a sanctified congregation. Together the images vividly captured how the missionary work that she began as a young child remained connected to churches but also expanded beyond them.[9]

From 1938 through 1945 Tharpe devoted more time to commercial venues than she did to churches, securing a place for herself, and thus gospel music, on the nightclub and theater circuit. On the heels of her Cotton Club triumph, Tharpe appeared in the Carnegie Hall "From Spirituals to Swing" concerts, conceived by independent producer John Hammond to introduce white audiences to a broad spectrum of African American music. When the Cotton Club opened its spring show in 1939, Tharpe was again among the performers featured. The enthusiasm she generated in the "From Spirituals to Swing" concert gave her an honored place at the Café Society, a nightclub that catered to New York leftist intellectuals.[10]

The emergence of gospel as part of popular culture grew out of a long series of developments that encompassed not only performance but the changing shape of the popular culture industry. As the experiences of Thomas Dorsey and Arizona Dranes make clear, the advent of race recordings allowed a small corps of singers and musicians to become self-supporting professionals and in the process move away from the economic margin of society and venture toward the center. The same recordings that provided opportunities for singers and musicians, as well as hours of joy for the many black consumers who purchased them, dramatically altered the production and dissemination of music in black communities and, indeed, local communities across the country. Such changes proved so fundamental that they transformed the place of music in American society. Music was no longer solely a space of cultural expression; it also became a space of commerce.[11]

Once records transformed music into commodities that could be bought and sold, music increasingly emerged as part and parcel of commerce. Over the course of the twentieth century a music industry took shape that ultimately became part of a more encompassing entertainment industry. For African Americans music that had once been under the exclusive auspices of their own communities gradually emerged as a product whose control was increasingly shared with a group of profit-minded outsiders, most of whom were white men.[12]

Thomas Dorsey had envisioned commerce as an arena between the sacred and the profane, sufficiently malleable to foster race pride. This view of commerce was possible as long as it remained dominated by small entrepreneurs like himself who had a stake in the community as well as their own financial well-being. But as an industrialized economy spread across the nation during the twentieth century, commerce increasingly became the province of large corporations with fewer direct ties to their customers. Music would prove no exception.[13]

During the early decades of the twentieth century, the music industry was a relatively diffuse operation. Its two major components—commercial entertainment venues and sheet music companies—were separate and distinct entities. During those early years few theater circuits even existed. Instead, the entertainment field was dominated by a rather motley collection of individual entrepreneurs. Some organized and supervised theatrical troupes. Others managed theaters and recruited troupes to perform. Still others turned their attention to sheet music. Some music publishers operated large, corporate enterprises and worked with retailers and musicians to promote their music in stores and on the stage. Publishers like Dorsey, who were poised on the periphery of the industry, maintained significantly smaller operations.[14]

Over time, however, operations that once comprised separate domains grew less isolated as managers in these different sectors built networks with one another. An endless array of stylistic and technological developments meant that entertainment never became a vertically integrated industry in which a single individual managed or controlled all aspects of production and distribution. In the 1910s, for example, the advent of recording technology posed a significant threat to music publishers. During the 1930s the sale of recordings was devastated by the emergence of radio. Still, as the industry became more consolidated, it was increasingly dominated by a small corps of managers able to forge connections among various entities that helped produce and distribute entertainment, including theaters, publishing houses, record companies, and radio networks.[15]

The move toward consolidation had decided consequences for the role played by race in American popular culture. During the 1920s, when the industry was much more diffuse, few major companies directed their attention to black consumers, convinced that such a strategy would yield little profit. Not until a small company marketed a recording to black consumers did record companies realize that black men and women could be avid record purchasers. The discovery prompted companies to begin recording significant numbers of African American musicians. The greatest change occurred, however, when it became clear that black music could be marketed to a far larger and more lucrative pool of white consumers. The popularity of jazz-inspired swing, which became the dominant form of popular music during the 1930s and 1940s, signaled an important watershed: the ascendancy of black music in mainstream American culture.[16]

The career of music publisher Irving Mills, a pioneer in the mass production and distribution of black music, illuminates the process by which swing became a major product of a dynamic but quickly consolidating industry. When records posed an increasing challenge to sheet music during the 1920s, Mills began managing swing bands to diversify his publishing operation. The concept of managing artists enjoyed little currency during the late 1920s. Most bands at the time were cooperatives and dealt with booking agencies and record producers on their own. But as Arizona Dranes's experience made clear, navigating the increasingly complex channels of production and promotion could be a daunting task. Mills demonstrated the value of outside managers. To secure lucrative contracts for the bands he managed, Mills negotiated with radio networks, record companies, concert halls, and nightclubs.[17]

Mills used the Cotton Club as leverage for securing contracts for his clients. It was hardly coincidental that the house bands for the club during the 1920s and 1930s included those led by Duke Ellington and, later, Cab Calloway, both clients of Mills. As Mills worked to introduce black talent to white middle-class audiences, he transformed the Cotton Club from a little-known cabaret into a preeminent institution for showcasing African American talent to mass audiences. Although the club catered to a fairly narrow band of elite whites, an appearance there conferred a level of importance far beyond these circles. Mass circulation newspapers from both the trade and the black press routinely reported on the shows featured there. A weekly radio show was broadcast live from the club, giving African American audiences access to performances they were unable to see in the segregated nightclubs. Tharpe's successes on the Cotton Club stage would set this machinery in motion on gospel's behalf. Eager to capitalize on the music's commercial possibilities, a group of powerful men inadvertently forged a place for gospel in mainstream popular culture.[18]

Tharpe's Cotton Club triumph ushered her into a swirl of booking agents, publishers, promoters, record men, and independent producers who recognized her moneymaking potential. The men Tharpe worked with between 1938 and 1945 comprise a veritable who's who in the music industry. Mills published a collection of her songs as sheet music. She recorded with Decca, one of the leading record labels of the day. In 1941 Moe Gale, the top booking agent for black singers and musicians, scheduled her concerts. Her overnight success was often portrayed as miraculous, with one reporter referring to her as "Cinderella."[19] But her sudden popularity was, in fact, precisely the kind of product that industry consolidation had been designed to produce. The significance of these connections was clear to her long-term singing partner, Marie Knight, who recalled that when the two teamed up in 1943, "Rosetta was already with the musical center—with the Jews, with the Italians that have the money." As a religious singer at the heart of a well-established popular culture industry, Tharpe would encounter both advantages and challenges.[20]

The industry's promotional machinery smoothed her path to stardom. A decade earlier, when recordings made Arizona Dranes a religious celebrity, Okeh record executives had been uncertain about how best to promote her music. As a result, they called on her to arrange her own performances and much of her own publicity. Tharpe, on the other hand, benefited from an elaborate array of promotional strategists who arranged her bookings and carefully shaped her public image. The deployment of such strategies shows in the efforts to link her music to two of the most prominent forms of African American music: spirituals and swing. The enormous popularity of swing had piqued promoters' interest in black sacred music. They also recognized the cultural weight that spirituals carried among whites as well as blacks.

Thomas Dorsey and his followers had sought legitimacy for their efforts by casting gospel music as a direct outgrowth of the spirituals. Mills followed the same path. When he published a collection of Tharpe's songs in 1938, he titled it *Eighteen Original Negro Spirituals*. In the preface he cast spirituals, including Tharpe's work, as the foundation of swing: "Countless numbers of people both in this country and in Europe have become interested in American music and negro spirituals—so much so that they have created a market for a type of standard rhythmic music which might be said to have been wholly inspired by the negro spiritual."[21] A few years later, managers at Decca Records would make even more explicit connections. Rather than calling Tharpe's music "gospel"—a description still largely confined to African American communities—they promoted it as "spirituals in swing."[22]

Still, even as this promotional strategy helped make Tharpe into a major star, it pointed to the gap between the priorities of the music industry and those of a sanctified evangelist. Promotional materials focused on the power of her artistry and the authenticity of her sound rather than on the meaning of her message. Growing up in the sanctified church, Tharpe and others had used their individual talents to testify to the power of the divine in their lives and to convey that power to others. Such spiritual concerns had little place within the music industry, where music was seen primarily as raw material from which a multitude of different commodities could be produced.

Marie Knight vividly described the corporate culture that pervaded the industry, providing a look behind the glitter and glamour of popular culture. "There's more to recording than just walking in the studio," she explained. "Every minute is counted. All the minutes you burn up." For a musical group, she continued, "all the time that's wasted comes out of the leader's check."[23] Similarly, the success or failure of any singer or musician did not rest solely on skill but also hinged on the willingness of managers to invest in the music. "It's not what you know," Knight reiterated on several occasions, stressing the importance of what she called "financial background." "It's who you know. If you expect to go anyplace, you got to have a background."[24] In the 1930s Thomas Dorsey had turned to the commercial arena to make gospel accessible to the masses of black people, freeing it from church leaders who worked to contain and suppress it. But his vision of commerce rested on small-scale, entrepreneurial capitalism, in which entrepreneurs such as himself retained connections to the communities they served. Corporate capitalism was a different matter.[25]

As well as negotiating the gap between religious conviction and mass appeal, Tharpe had to contend with the racial and gender conventions of American popular culture, which departed sharply from those that prevailed in the female-centered world of black sanctified religion. Black singers and musicians were expected to grin and smile for white audiences, conventions that hearkened back to nineteenth-century minstrelsy. Women were judged by physical appearance and sex appeal as much as for their musical ability. One reviewer, for example, felt compelled to comment on Tharpe's appearance before even considering her talent, describing her as a "comely femme, who, to self-guitar accompaniment, gives the gospel hymns a killer-diller inflection."[26]

The emphasis on sex appeal over musicianship was especially evident during the 1940s for the women who worked as vocalists with male bands. The sentiments of Lionel Hampton, a member of the Benny Goodman band, illustrate how male bands often had more respect for female members as cheerleaders than as singers capable of making a distinct musical contribution to the group. In a weekly column he wrote for the *Washington Afro-American*, Hampton announced that the band was looking for "a GOOD girl singer" and invited all who were interested to contact him by mail. Hampton went on to stipulate that anyone interested "MUST convince me via mail that you are worth an audition!"[27] The double standard he was employing became clearer several weeks later when interested applicants failed to comply with his instructions. Hampton, outraged, complained that "out of all the avalanche of letters I've received . . . only a very few have followed my instructions!" He went on to reiterate that interested women "must enclose a photo and a return self-addressed envelope."[28]

For Tharpe, then, the decision to strike out into commercial culture involved adjusting to the music business and the corporate milieu it generated as well as familiarizing herself with the expectations and conventions that prevailed in mainstream popular culture. Cab Calloway related how the terrain Tharpe had to negotiate required that she receive special tutelage prior to her debut. On discovering Tharpe, the bandleader, according to one newspaper, "made arrangements for her to come to New York, whereupon he built her up and groomed her in the theatrical world."[29] This building up and grooming was an integral part of the popular culture industry. Thomas Dorsey related how he facilitated the grooming process when he worked at Paramount Records, a recording company that specialized in race records during the late 1920s and 1930s:

> I taught most of the singers who sang for Paramount Records. I was the man that had to hear them. I could make any embellishments that I wanted to in the song. I'd do that and then teach it to the artist that was going to perform. Some of them needed a lot of changes too; some of them come in there was terrible. . . . [The songs] had no expression. The writer didn't know what to say at some places for the punch. I would take them [the songs], feel the words out and then feel the music out and accent them in a way that it will grasp the public.[30]

The transformation of Tharpe's surname provides other clues about the grooming process. When Rosetta married Thomas J. Thorpe, she assumed his last name. Yet she appeared at the Cotton Club in 1938 as Rosetta Tharpe. The practice of assuming stage names was widespread in show business. During the 1920s stage names often contained geographical references. Dorsey, for example, assumed the stage name "Georgia Tom." In the 1930s many black singers and musicians assumed stage names that conveyed a sense of royalty, as when Edward Kennedy Ellington took the name "Duke" Ellington. But while the kinds of stage names might change over time, the impetus behind the practice remained consistent. Just as Dorsey counseled singers and musicians on how to phrase their songs in order to grasp the attention of the public, managers used stage names to achieve the same purpose. The surname "Thorpe" sounded ordinary. "Tharpe" conveyed more pizzazz.[31]

An examination of Tharpe's years in the limelight reveals the strategies she used to bridge the gaps between the worlds of commerce and religion. Despite the claims of some of her critics, Tharpe never abandoned her faith. Music perhaps provides the best evidence of the role religion continued to play in her life. Describing their creative process, Marie Knight related how the divine remained an integral part of Tharpe's life:

> It was a gift. Sound. If she could hear it, she could play it. Sometimes she would be up, like 2 or 3 in the morning. She'd be downstairs at the piano.

And she would say, "You gotta come down, cause we got a song—I got a song that's coming through. . . ." She would get the guitar and I would play the piano, and she'd sit there and we'd word it out. She'd word it out. And that's how we did our recordings. She would hear the songs as they came through. And she would sit there and pick them out on the guitar. The keys and what not. And that's the way she did it. It had to come to her by sound.[32]

Still, the demands of the music industry and the conventions of popular entertainment stood at odds with many tenets of religious faith. As a result, throughout her career Tharpe played with ambiguity. She both engaged and held herself apart from show business conventions. She used her formidable music skills to reveal some parts of herself in some venues and other parts in others. In the process her concept of faith, and of her work, underwent its own changes.

A particularly striking example of Tharpe's use of ambiguity involved the skits that were part of many of her performances—skits that satirized both race and religion. The conventions of nineteenth-century minstrelsy, in which comic black characters were paraded onstage for the amusement of white audiences, still weighed heavily on American popular culture in the 1920s and 1930s. Black preachers were staple characters in minstrel shows, and Tharpe was cast in several versions of these skits. A photograph in *Life* shows her standing in front of a replica of a storefront church with a sign draped across the front window that reads, "Pentecostal Mission." Perhaps the most explicit description comes from a 1939 engagement at the Apollo Theater:

Opener is based on the appearance of Sister Tharpe. Scene is a holy-roller meeting, with gals dressed in bright-colored old-fashioned dresses on folding chairs around the back of the stage. Around a mike in rear center are the Four Alphabets, quartet of male warblers, also dressed in reds and greens. They provide intermittent harmony, while John Mason, Sandy Burns and George Wiltshire, house comics do the preacher stuff from a rickety rostrum and with a telephone book for a bible. Burlesque of holy-roller antics give live opportunity for work.

Sister Tharpe comes in for the finale of the scene. Strums a guitar and sings to the harmony backing of the Alphabets.[33]

Tharpe occupied an ambiguous position in the skit—in it but not wholly of it. The actions of the preachers served as the focal point for the audience's humor. The actors were clearly comedians, not real preachers. Tharpe's appearance at the end marked a moment of transition, when comedy gave way to powerful religious expression. As a result, the precise relationship between her singing and the mockery that preceded it was far from clear.

Tharpe's negotiation of other religious issues as well as of sexual conventions was more completely woven into her broader approach to the music she performed. In this task she brought formidable skills to bear. Many children in the sanctified church had grown up singing gospel. Few, however, had spent so much of their youth moving about the country and using the music to reach the hearts and souls of the unregenerate. The skills and sensibilities Tharpe had acquired over the years made her an ideal person for undertaking the challenge she assumed: making gospel compelling, indeed meaningful, in arenas that occupied a world apart from the religious community that was so familiar. The mores and manners that pervaded the nightclub must have seemed alien to a young woman who grew up in a religious community that sought to separate itself from the world and who was raised by a protective mother who would not even let her daughter go to a movie theater. With its emphasis on making money rather than saving souls, the music business must have been equally alienating. Yet her recordings and live performances give the appearance that Tharpe managed to broker the musical aspects of these challenges with some ease.

Tharpe enjoyed considerable leeway in shaping the musical components of her career. While the managers with whom she worked were all seasoned in the industry, with Tharpe they were encountering uncharted terrain. Sammy Price, a house musician at Decca Records, recalled that in the mid-1940s producers at the company were befuddled about how to record Tharpe. The situation afforded Tharpe some degree of liberty in how she made gospel meaningful. During her tenure at Decca Records she worked with Milt Gabler, who in 1992 explained that Tharpe had complete authority over what she sang, complete control. Gabler recalled how Tharpe would bring her little song book to the recording sessions, where she would choose the songs to record.[34]

Tharpe's choices of songs to record suggest that she deliberately sought to reach as broad an audience as possible. As with Thomas Dorsey's compositions, only a few of her recordings featured the biblically centered themes likely to dominate church and revival settings. Some of her recordings, such as "Nobody's Fault but Mine" and "Moonshine," paid tribute to the religious groups, soloists, and guitar evangelists who recorded during the 1920s. Others, including several of Dorsey's songs, were recent compositions. Almost all of them featured either personal spiritual reflections or deliberations about the general state of religion in the broader society.[35]

Even as Tharpe embraced her predecessors, she created a distinctive sound and helped widen the contours of gospel. With the exception of Arizona Dranes's work, the recordings of the 1920s featured throaty, textured vocals. The pattern was so pervasive that textured vocals emerged as a common idiom among gospel singers and groups. Like Dranes, Tharpe forged a smoother sound by using open vocals to deliver her songs. She did not, however, abandon textured vocals. Instead she deployed texture at calculated junctures within a song and in the process retained the idiom while using it for punctuation and effect.[36]

Tharpe's innovations become particularly evident in comparison with the work of Arizona Dranes. Anyone familiar with the recordings of both women can immediately hear the influence that Dranes's bright vocals and infectious rhythms had on Tharpe. Still, significant differences separated the two. Dranes's rapid-fire, boogie-woogie piano playing so dominated her recordings that her singing often appeared secondary and almost formulaic. Tharpe moved away from formulaic vocals by infusing each song with a variety of vocal techniques that conveyed different shades of meaning. As a result, even as Tharpe repeated verses, her changing inflections built each song to dramatic climax.[37]

The new feel and meaning that Tharpe's innovations gave to gospel were especially evident in her signature song, "That's All." Washington Phillips, a street evangelist, had originally recorded the song in 1927 as "Denomination Blues"; Tharpe recorded it on three separate occasions between 1938 and 1944. Like his contemporaries, Phillips had featured textured, grainy vocals to deliver a forceful lament on religious infighting. "You're fighting each other, think you're doing well," he sang, "and the sinners on the outside going to hell."[38] Tharpe turned Phillips's lament on the state of religion into a lighthearted, sassy song in which she stressed the importance of getting religion. To give the song such a lighthearted feel, she employed several different strategies. Tharpe used her guitar to punctuate the song and give it an upbeat tempo. Rather than pushing the instrument into the background to supply the rhythm or letting it dominate the song, Tharpe turned her guitar into a second voice, which she used to create a dialogue with her vocals. In addition, she carefully phrased the lyrics to combine singing and speaking. This combination helped give the song a playful yet serious air. To emphasize the importance of getting religion, Tharpe then stretched out the line "You got to have religion now."[39]

The innovations Tharpe brought to gospel music signaled concurrent changes in her missionary work between 1938 and 1945. In churches and even on the street, missionaries such as Tharpe had used music to testify to the divine power that dwelled inside them. Slowly Tharpe began using gospel to appeal to and entertain audiences. "That's All" embodied some of the subtle ways this transformation unfolded. After Tharpe reworked the song to give it a light, playful feel, "Denomination Blues" no longer seemed an appropriate title. Rather than a meditation on the infighting that plagued religious communities, the song, in Tharpe's hands, became a fanciful tribute to matters of faith.[40]

This transformation was hardly absolute. Tharpe continued to use gospel to commune with God. In "Savior Don't Pass Me By," recorded in 1939, Tharpe made an earnest plea for divine deliverance. She phrased the song so that it was both a public prayer and a personal conversation with God. To do that, Tharpe made a sharp distinction between the chorus, where she spoke to God directly, and each stanza. She used a combination of singing and talking as she moved through each stanza but reserved the chorus to engage her singing more fully and also feature a guitar solo. The chorus contained a single line that she repeated three times. "Savior, Savior," Tharpe sang, "Savior, don't you pass me by." With each repetition she not only phrased the line differently but moved up an octave. Tharpe used repetition to testify to the place of the divine in her life, making her request for deliverance into a deeply personal plea for divine protection.[41]

During the 1930s and 1940s Tharpe featured lighter songs such as "That's All" in her live performances while reserving her more serious religious songs for her recording repertoire. In these recordings Tharpe engaged the divine with sincerity and purposefulness. It is possible that this strategy reflected a calculated effort to reach a variety of audiences.[42]

During the war years Tharpe broadened her range even further. With the outbreak of World War II, she joined the Lucky Millinder band as the group's official soloist. She had previously pursued informal affiliations with swing bands on the nightclub circuit, appearing with the Count Basie band in a one-week stint at the Paramount, performing with a band led by Al Cooper at the Apollo Theater, and singing with the Benny Goodman band for a radio broadcast. Joining the Lucky Millinder band compelled Tharpe to make significant changes to her repertoire. While gospel had dominated her prewar work, secular songs were featured in her live performances during her tenure with the Millinder band.[43]

Even as she performed and recorded secular songs with the Millinder ensemble, however, Tharpe continued to record religious songs. Applying her trusted strategy, Tharpe directed her solo efforts to her religious audiences and recorded some of her more spiritually reflective songs. In 1942 she made several solo recordings, including "What He Done for Me." As she moved through the first stanza, Tharpe slowly raised the melody an octave. She used this same technique for each subsequent stanza. In so doing Tharpe set up the chorus as the critical focal point of the song. She fashioned a musical testimony about the place of the divine in her life with a guitar solo that recalled the melody of the song, while she sang "Oh what He done for me." By stretching out the word "Oh" fully and completely, Tharpe captured and conveyed precisely what God had done for her.[44]

Whether she used a song to engage divine subjects seriously or merely to touch on them, Tharpe's singing called attention to her artistry—her skill as a singer and a musician. Curtis Lyles, who grew up listening to Tharpe on the radio in the 1940s and 1950s, described her as a "great artist," pointing to the variety of ways she sang her material. He explained, "I think she is constantly creating, constantly creating. She is not limited, she's exploring. If you look at the songs she records, each one—she brings an added dimension to the music. The color, the phrasing of the voice . . ." The versatility Tharpe exhibited helped him appreciate jazz singers like Sarah Vaughan and classical performers like Leontyne Price, even though their styles had little in common with Tharpe's. "Rosetta Tharpe . . . set a standard for me," he recalled; "I think there is a universal quality that she allowed me to develop and instilled in me."[45]

As Tharpe worked to secure a place for gospel in the entertainment industry, she moved back and forth between very different worlds. Her music and the changes in how she conducted her missionary work reflected that movement. At one extreme she engaged religion, and at the other she downplayed religious subjects entirely. Her live performances, particularly those on the nightclub and theater circuit, illustrate the wide spectrum she spanned.

In some instances Tharpe made the religious sentiments of gospel songs decidedly ambiguous. Perhaps none stands out more than "Rock Me," her version of Dorsey's "Hide Me in Thy Bosom." Tharpe recorded the song in both 1938 and 1941 and featured it in many of her nightclub engagements. Thomas Dorsey had written the song as a prayer for divine protection. Reflecting on the circumstances that led him to write the song, Dorsey explained that just as his gospel songs began to circulate, his friends began to reject him. "Some of my friends," he explained, "became distant. Some became envious of my possessed advantages. Some of my associates resented my acquired success."[46] Unable to understand such behavior, Dorsey recalled, he wrote the song as a prayer seeking protection and guidance through the difficult time. The first stanza described his predicament:

> Jesus hear me praying,
> Hear the words that I'm saying,
> Moist my soul with water from on high.
> A world of sin around me,
> While evil thoughts would bind me,
> My Savior, if you leave me I will die.

He then turned the chorus into a plea for guidance and protection:

> Just hide me in Thy bosom til the storm of life is o'er,
> Rock me in the cradle of Thy love.
> Just feed me til I want no more,
> Then take me to that blessed home above.[47]

Tharpe reinterpreted the song and gave the divine succor Dorsey sought an ambiguous quality by eliminating explicit references to divine subjects. For example, she changed the lyrics of the first verse so that the song lost its meaning as a prayer:

Now don't you hear me swinging,
Hear the words that I'm singing,
Moist my soul with water from on high.
While the world of love is around me,
Evil thoughts do bind me,
Oh if you leave me, I will die.[48]

Whereas Dorsey spoke explicitly to the divine, Tharpe couched her plea with vague references that failed to address the divine by name. In 1938 Tharpe was careful not to eliminate the divine altogether and thereby turn the song into a reflection about a man who had left her. Still, such obfuscation veiled the religious content of "Rock Me," giving the song a double meaning. In her 1941 recording with the Lucky Millinder band, the double meaning became even more explicit. She slowed the tempo and sang in a higher octave, which gave the song an emphatic and distinctly female presence. The interplay between Tharpe and the band contributed to the sexual innuendo. Since Tharpe and the band toured together, this song no doubt became a staple in their live performances.[49]

The new and alien world in which Tharpe found herself in 1938 initially seems a bit rarefied. Only a small corps of singers and musicians were successful enough in show business to enjoy the luxury of supporting themselves with their music. But the predicament of having to make sense of a new world was common to African Americans growing up in the late nineteenth and early twentieth centuries. Each successive generation had to adjust to ways of seeing and moving through the world to which they were unfamiliar. These changes assumed a myriad of different forms: the emergence of new technologies, the transformation of the workplace, the growth of urban enclaves, the emergence of new types of leisure activity, and the growing significance accorded consumption and materialism. The enormity of these changes could feel like utter chaos without the solace of the familiar. The black men and women who migrated from southern cities and towns to northern enclaves like Chicago bear testimony to how the familiar could guide one through the morass of change and transformation. Many of the men and women who migrated to Chicago did not abandon their southern mores and manners but held onto those familiar rituals as they made their way in the city. Religion, which provided one set of rituals and practices, supplied migrants with a source of comfort and familiarity. Yet even as migrants embraced religion, its meaning slowly changed over time.[50]

These experiences give meaning to the changes Tharpe underwent as she took gospel on the nightclub and theater circuit. That her missionary work would change seems hardly surprising given the circumstances in which Tharpe found herself. The fact that she changed seems less significant than the process of change and the logic she used to make sense of her circumstances. As she negotiated the world of show business, Tharpe seized gospel as her guide and solace. As her popularity grew during the 1940s, Tharpe could have easily fashioned herself as a jazz singer. Yet gospel remained deeply meaningful for Tharpe even as she made changes to the music. In a world so alien, gospel music remained familiar and perhaps for that reason may have acquired added significance. The changes she brought to gospel and to her missionary work offer important clues about how Tharpe made her way through an enormous array of new circumstances. These changes supply us with important insights about the evolution of her faith.[51]

———— Tharpe initially described her forays into secular venues in evangelical terms. According to one newspaper, she explained to radio listeners that "she sings in a night club because she feels there are more souls in the nighteries that need saving than there are in the church."[52] Over the next seven years, however, her mission substantially changed. Having grown up using music to win souls, Tharpe began using gospel to entertain audiences. This musical outreach won her a legion of fans that not only turned her into a national celebrity but also brought her material benefits. The new circumstances in which she found herself certainly led Tharpe to alter the direction of her missionary work. Faced with this new situation, Tharpe used her faith to make sense of her environs so that her changing circumstances resonated with her religious upbringing. Understanding how Tharpe used her faith offers us a rare glimpse of the evolution of religious outlook in the course of a single life.

The world Tharpe entered when she moved to the nightclub and theater circuit profoundly transformed her daily life. As one newspaper put it, "It is a long way from the platform of a small out of the way Pentecostal church in Miami, Fla., to the brilliant lights of Broadway." Initially Tharpe denied that her musical success made any difference in her personal life. Shortly after she began her stint at the Cotton Club, the *Washington Afro-American* reported that despite Tharpe's newfound acclaim, "none of this has in any way affected her personality. She is still unsophisticated and sincere. She has the same tastes she had when she first came to New York, lives quietly in a modest apartment and is saving her money." For Tharpe, however, even a simple apartment was a significant change. When she and her husband moved to Miami in the 1930s to participate in the weekly radio show, they could not afford their own residence and had to board at the Cohen household. When she relocated to New York in 1938, Tharpe could pay for an apartment of her own.[53]

Over time Tharpe came to relish her celebrity status and the material comforts it generated. Abner Jay, Tharpe's manager, recalled the extravagant lifestyle she led during the late 1940s through the 1950s. Tharpe had recently purchased a large home in Richmond, Virginia, and regaled her audiences with stories of extravagance, reminding them that they had played a role in making such luxury possible: "And she would tell all this about her piano [being] gold. It really wasn't gold, it was gold finish. And the ceilings were mirrors, which they were. And her walls were gold, which was colored gold something. Wasn't no real gold. And she had wall-to-wall mirrors in her bathroom. She would tell the audience about that. And she said, 'You all bought it.' And some of them would laugh, some of them didn't like it. She was kind of brash, she kind of boasted, but she could back up what she said along those lines." Jay also noted that while in the South, Tharpe devised ways to sidestep local Jim Crow laws that restricted African Americans from shopping at exclusive clothing stores. As he explained, "She wore the best evening gowns money could buy. She could stand outside those rich stores where didn't allow colored to go in. . . . She would stand outside to see somebody that she could trust. Said 'Honey, I want you to go in there and get me a gown, size 9. . . .' And she says, 'Here's the money, here.' She would give them a big roll of money." The story symbolized how significantly her life had changed within the span of a decade. Raised in a religious community that stressed the importance of plain dress, Tharpe now wore the nicest clothes she could find.[54]

The growing emphasis Tharpe placed on the material benefits of her success serves as a compelling reminder of the pervasiveness of consumerism and materialism in America. That these values hovered around Tharpe, who grew up in a community founded on the very principle of stemming the tide of material concerns and preoccupations, indicates just how pervasive these values had become over the course of the twentieth century.[55]

Even as Tharpe relished her celebrity status, however, she did not abandon her faith. Rather, she transformed it. Throughout her career, she carefully pointed out that the success and popularity she enjoyed were a measure of her faith. In 1939 a reporter asked her for the secret of her sudden success. "Religion," Tharpe responded with such absolute certainty that the reporter was moved to comment on the singer's unwavering faith. "She has a firm belief that her faith is the cause of her amazing overnight success," the reporter said of Tharpe, "and believes that nothing else can supplant belief in the Lord." The reporter went on to say that Tharpe sincerely believed in the sentiments she articulated in her songs. "And it is with no tongue in the cheek," the reporter wrote, "that she strums the strings of the music box and croons:

> You can go to any college,
> You can go to any school,
> But if you ain't got religion,
> You're an educated fool."[56]

No matter how much her sentiments moved the newspaper reporter, however, they marked an abrupt departure from the religious culture in which Tharpe grew up. Individuals like Charles Mason and Sallie Martin, who were part of the sanctified church, followed the dictates of the Holy Spirit they believed dwelled inside their souls. In his autobiography Mason made repeated references to biblical scriptures. He used these references to point out to his readers that the Holy Spirit guided his actions. Similarly, Sallie Martin recalled that her decision to move beyond the church in one community and organize a community choir came from directives she received from God. Unlike Mason and Martin, Tharpe apparently made few if any references to tangible divine intervention that compelled her to embark on her new venture. Instead, the sheer popularity she garnered seems to have convinced her that she was following divine will. Her assertions suggest that she considered popularity and material success as the benchmarks of her faith.[57]

Tharpe was not alone in her shift. The popularity she gained among both black and white audiences indicated that her decisions resonated with many others. Support from church members, including her husband, corroborated this. Tharpe seems to have worried about what her husband would think about her move. Tharpe had married Thomas J. Thorpe in 1934, and according to Richard Cohen, she shrouded the Cotton Club engagement in secrecy. Cohen recalled that Tharpe "was very deceptive about it, because she told her husband . . . she was going home to see about her mother."[58] Such fears were allayed when Thomas Thorpe relocated to New York to join her. One newspaper article inadvertently revealed how Rosetta and especially Thomas perceived the engagement at the Cotton Club as a serious missionary endeavor. The paper reported that Thomas reprimanded Rosetta for violating "revival meeting etiquette" by singing onstage without wearing a hat. The photographic essay on Tharpe that appeared in *Life*, which included a photograph of her singing before a Church of God in Christ congregation in Harlem, indicates that other members of the church perceived her activity as a serious spiritual undertaking.[59]

Tharpe's new missionary course and her changing ideas about faith signaled larger changes that were unfolding in the sanctified community. The sanctified church had taken shape in the midst of spiraling consumerism and materialism. To curb these developments, members insisted that holiness had to be made tangible and concrete—a religious outlook that helped to nurture gospel. The music in fact grew out of corporeal religion, the notion that the body was God's holy temple. Corporeal religion occupied a critical dimension of spiritual practice in the sanctified church. Dress codes, which helped distinguish the faithful from other religious communities, attest to the importance of corporeal religion in the sanctified church. As consumerism and materialism grew more pervasive over the course of the century, however, differences arose in sanctified communities over what holiness entailed.

Richard Cohen reflected on how the faithful searched for ways to make holiness meaningful in a rapidly changing world. In a series of interviews in

1992, Cohen related how this struggle for meaning generated tensions and disagreements in his religious community. A question about the way female missionaries dressed prompted Cohen to discuss how the standards for holy living had become much too strict and unrealistic. The subject seems to have been a topic of considerable discussion within the Cohen household. Cohen recalled a story that his mother, Mamie, often recounted when the subject of holiness came up for discussion. "You put this stuff so high," she used to say, "'til you can't even get up there yourself. And when you find out you can't get up there yourself, then you gonna find out that you're gonna have to ease it back down." When open-toed and high-heeled shoes became popular, members had a hard time finding the oxford shoes that they considered appropriate for holy living. Cohen recalled that his mother used the occasion to convey her ideas to members of the congregation. "I guess none of y'all are going to heaven now," he remembered her telling members of the church, "because you got your toe out."[60]

Richard Cohen recalled that some members of his father's church expressed outrage at the things Amaziah Cohen allowed his children to do. Richard explained that although many members considered going to the movies a sin, his father took his brothers and sisters to the movies. Amaziah defended his action on the grounds that children had to be children. "The Bible says you cannot make children adults," Richard recalled his father saying to members of the church. The minister used the occasion to stress that what an individual felt in his heart took precedence over outward appearances. "You know all this stuff we talk about, that's not what it takes."[61]

The pervasiveness of consumer values inspired critical questions about the meaning of holiness for members of the sanctified church. In the late nineteenth century, holy living encompassed a way of life that included both heart and body. The sanctified insisted that attending church and possessing faith were not sufficient for holy living. Individuals had to commit their lives and bodies to God. As society grew more materialistic and commercial, individuals had increasing difficulty maintaining the old standards of holiness. For some the strict dress codes and modes of behavior from the turn of the century felt increasingly outdated. Some individuals had difficulty reconciling the physical with the emotional.

The discussions that took place in the Cohen household occurred in other communities that made up the sanctified church. Lillian Coffey, who as the International Supervisor of Women held the highest female position in the Church of God in Christ, made a concerted effort in the 1940s to display a more modern look than her predecessors. Cohen recalled that Coffey "just dressed up. You know she went downtown and she saw a designer dress, she bought it. She wore it; the sleeves were short, she wore it." Mother Coffey, as she was called, used her position to convey to women in the denomination that plain dress—long skirts, oxford shoes, and long sleeves—was not a prerequisite for holy living. Cohen remembered Coffey telling women, "Y'all walking around here with these long black skirts dragging the ground got more hell under them than some folks out there in a bathing suit."[62] Coffey still believed that women should display modest dress but advocated a modern standard of modesty to replace the plain dress that hearkened back to the early decades of the twentieth century.[63]

The sentiments expressed by Coffey and members of the Cohen family raised questions about the meaning of holiness. Was it grounded primarily in the heart, or did it have more to do with outward appearances? Even as the question hovered over churches and congregations, no real consensus emerged. Instead, members held a range of views on the subject. Some, like the Cohen family, stressed the importance of grounding holiness in the heart and encouraged members to embrace a standard of dress more in keeping with the society in which they lived. Other members were less willing to make such compromises and insisted that strict modes of plain dress and behavior had to be maintained at all costs. Such divergent perspectives generated increasing concern about sincere religious expression.

The corporeal religion that had been an important component of the sanctified church had generated a common measure of what holiness entailed. Without that guide, individuals voiced growing concern about whether a particular expression of faith was sincere or merely a ruse. People could not always agree about what comprised sincere religious expression. Cohen alluded to the problem when asked how members of his religious community perceived emotion. Eager to counter images of his community as overly emotional, Cohen quickly recalled what Amaziah Cohen used to say about religious fervor. "Folk would be dancing in the church," he remembered his father saying, "they're not always under the spirit." Amaziah Cohen insisted that sometimes dancing under the spirit was nothing more than youth exercising their desire to move. Richard recalled his father saying that "because they're young and they got that energy, they want to move." The story illustrates the absence of any consensus about what constituted sincerity in religious expression.[64]

Changing ideas about holiness were especially noticeable in the response of Tharpe's mother, Katie Bell Nubin, to her daughter's commercial endeavors. Nubin did not raise her daughter with the kind of permissiveness that Amaziah Cohen allowed his children. Yet over time Nubin's definition of holiness also changed. She seems to have been a consistent source of support for Tharpe throughout her career. The unmistakable presence of Nubin in Tharpe's life did not escape the notice of the editors of one magazine. In a 1941 feature article on Moe Gale, the magazine included a photograph of Tharpe and her mother in a recording studio. The editors commented on the close relationship between mother and daughter. "Where Sister goes," the caption read, "there goes her mother."[65] Marie Knight suggested that Nubin may have in fact encouraged Tharpe to move to the nightclub circuit. Like Arizona Dranes, Nubin probably welcomed the possibility of some relief from the hardships of a missionary life. Knight explained that Nubin recognized that the extraordinary talent her daughter possessed had economic potential and worked to exploit that potential. "Rosetta," Knight stated, "was her meal ticket."[66]

The willingness of Nubin to alter her conception of holiness is particularly clear in her interaction with jazz pianist Sammy Price, a house musician at Decca Records. In 1944 managers at the record company approached Price about accompanying Tharpe on a series of songs. Price felt reluctant to apply his jazz techniques to religious music. He later explained, "I came from a long line of religious singers, and you could be banished from the clan if you sang gospel songs or if you sang songs with too much rhythm and that sort of thing." Nubin, however, convinced Price to do the recording by reiterating the ideas Amaziah and Mamie Cohen had expressed to members of their congregation, namely that holiness stemmed not just from outward appearances but also from what individuals felt in their hearts. Price recalled that Nubin explained, "If when a song was played, the thinking behind it was right, then there was nothing wrong with it."[67]

The new faith Tharpe embraced marked a departure from the faith that had taken shape in her religious community. Yet on another level, this new faith was an extension of religious teachings she received growing up. Faced with a new set of circumstances, Tharpe applied her religious beliefs to make sense of the world in which she found herself. In highlighting her musical talent rather than her religious convictions, Tharpe called attention to the skills that she comprehended as a divine gift. This perspective appears to have been lost on many of her listeners. Reviews of her appearances do not mention the strength of her faith. Many reviewers commented on the tremendous power of her sound, but none seemed to regard that power as having any sacred significance. Yet according to Knight, the creative process for Tharpe was primarily a spiritual experience. As Knight recalled, Tharpe fully recognized that the sounds she wove together onstage and in the studio came directly from God. When songs came to her in the middle of the night, she would always rush downstairs to play them out on the piano.

Working to make gospel meaningful and relevant on the nightclub and theater circuit, Tharpe relied on principles she inherited growing up in the sanctified church. That these principles led her to take actions that many in her community would come to disavow provides a compelling testimony about the transformation of religion among some sanctified believers. Insisting that her popularity was the result of the deep and abiding faith she possessed, Tharpe relinquished the corporeal religion that was such a vital part of daily spiritual practice in the sanctified church. Others, at least in the Church of God in Christ, were also tempering their commitment to corporeal religion. But while these men and women wrestled with their evolving faith within their communities, Tharpe foisted these changes onto the nightclub stage for all the world to see.

——— Tharpe's experiences between 1938 and 1945 provide important lessons about the expansion of secular values in American society. Tharpe rightly understood that she could reach a broader public by conducting her missionary work on the nightclub and theater circuit than she could by confining herself to religious circles. The advantage of an institution such as the Cotton Club rested in more than the men and women who assembled there on any given evening. Media networks converged on the nightclub, broadcasting performances to black and white audiences and transforming the Cotton Club into a symbol of the growing consolidation of the entertainment industry. This consolidation, represented by links between commercial venues, radio networks, newspapers, and recording companies, permeated society in ways religious institutions, perched on the margins of secular society, could no longer command.

Tharpe's success anticipated the popularity of gospel in the postwar years. At the same time, it signaled the expanding role played by commerce in shaping the larger context in which gospel and other musical genres operated. The growth and expansion of a music industry affected the full range of American musical styles, though the issues that emerged differed from community to community. In the case of gospel, critical issues emerged not only around religion but around race. Tharpe was able to give gospel enormous national exposure primarily because the same managers who supported her were instrumental in forging ties that helped consolidate the entertainment industry. Consequently, her rise signaled not only gospel's great appeal but the degree to which corporate interests led by white outsiders were investing in the music. This racially charged context would make Tharpe a target of considerable criticism among some African Americans. Along with a group of jazz musicians accused of "swinging" spirituals, she emerged as a foil that inspired African Americans, once divided by denomination, to come together to preserve gospel. We now turn to that controversy to understand how the music became a racial battleground.

CHAPTER 5

Between Religion and Commerce

Gospel in the Postwar Era

In 1956 the *Cleveland Call and Post*, an African American newspaper, published an editorial by a local minister condemning musicians for commercializing and perverting sacred music. The minister, who linked the practice to the rise of rock 'n' roll, recalled seeing "a famous Negro night-club singer . . . jazz up that beautiful and sacred hymn, 'It's No Secret What God Can Do.'" He went on to explain that the singer "was backed by a swing guitarist who used every technique possible so as to give a modern rock 'n' roll treatment to the hymn."[1]

While she had nothing to do with the incident, the editors of the *Cleveland Call and Post* pointed to Sister Rosetta Tharpe as the source of the problem. Next to the editorial, the newspaper featured a photograph of her that included the following caption: "She started it all—Chief exponent of the swinging of the spirituals was night club entertainer Sister Rosetta Tharpe, who created a sensation many years ago when she first introduced gospel singing in the old Cotton Club. . . . Since that time many records and theater stars have added jazzed up religious numbers to the [their] repertoire."[2]

The caption reflected two significant trends that would help shape the postwar development of gospel music. In singling out Tharpe's Cotton Club appearance, it pointed to the power of the controversy she had sparked when she transgressed well-established boundaries between sacred and secular. In its blurring of distinctions between spirituals and gospel, the caption pointed to the success Thomas Dorsey and his supporters had achieved in their efforts to cast gospel as a key component of African American heritage. Previously a source of divisiveness between middle- and working-class blacks, vernacular music was gradually now becoming a source of race pride across the spectrum of class. Rigid distinctions some middle-class blacks had once made between gospel and spirituals were losing their relevance, and gospel and spirituals had become aligned under the rubric of black sacred music. In the process gospel had gained a degree of legitimacy in black communities it had never enjoyed before. As gospel's popularity exploded in the postwar era, its twin status as a sacred music and an icon of black heritage would both heighten the emotions surrounding it and complicate understandings of what was in fact at stake.[3]

Although many African Americans condemned Tharpe, swinging spirituals, and the commercial music industry, commercial interest in gospel grew unabated. Enterprising individuals, eager to tap into smaller black consumer markets, invested in gospel and intensified the ties between the music and mass commercialized culture. This development changed the ethos that surrounded the music. Increasingly, gospel singers weighed religious and spiritual matters against material considerations: the number of records sold, what percentage of the door one received, and the wardrobe one selected.[4]

In the 1940s, growing commercialism caused particular alarm within the National Convention of Gospel Choirs and Choruses (NCGCC), whose members perceived it as eroding the music's religious significance. Members saw the problem as a loss of autonomy: the music was moving beyond the control of religious communities where gospel had taken shape. With this realization the convention, which had been so instrumental in taking gospel beyond the church, redirected its efforts and its attention toward "preserving" the music. Their work began as an effort to keep gospel separate from jazz and later expanded into an intensive training and education campaign.[5]

Of course the effort to keep gospel separate from jazz contained a certain irony, given that Thomas Dorsey, who served as president of the NCGCC and who saw his reputation as the father of gospel music soar during the postwar era, began his gospel career by applying blues and jazz rhythms to sacred songs. The contradiction holds enormous significance. It signaled the degree to which the landscape in which gospel operated during the postwar era differed from the context in which the music thrived in the early decades of the century. In the earlier period, gospel prevailed mostly in small churches on the margins of the nation's black communities. The controversy over the music was about whether it was at all suited to religious expression. In contrast, during the years between 1945 and 1960 gospel encompassed two divergent and competing outlooks. One was grounded in a mass commercialized culture where showmanship reigned supreme and where disc jockeys, booking agencies, and recording companies competed fiercely for the attention of black consumers. The other revolved around the idea that gospel was a cultural resource. From this perspective, the music had to remain within the auspices of black communities for it to remain sacred. These divergent tracks, which offered a range of opportunities for gospel singers, also prompted a vigorous debate within the gospel community about the meaning of faith.[6]

———— Gospel underwent a significant transformation in the decades following World War II when radio station operators, small independent recording companies, and local promoters took an interest in the music. The efforts of Tharpe, Dorsey, and others linked gospel with commerce as early as the 1920s. Not until the postwar era, however, did gospel emerge as a full-flown agent of commerce and part of a mass commercialized culture. These developments ushered in numerous changes for singers. Many emerged as music professionals able to support themselves with the earnings they received from gospel. An elite corps of these men and women became national celebrities. The mass commercialized culture in which these gospel singers now found themselves nurtured concerns not simply about religion but also about money, image, and fame.

Although recording companies had been investing in gospel since the 1920s, changes in the music industry after World War II placed gospel in a new context. During the war the record business came to a virtual halt due to governmental restrictions placed on shellac, necessary for pressing records, and a recording ban called by the American Federation of Musicians. After the conflict ended, the economy began to recover and a new spirit of entrepreneurship infused the industry. During the 1930s both radio and recordings had been dominated by large companies like Decca Records, which enjoyed a virtual monopoly on recording black singers and musicians. These companies had directed their attention to mainstream, largely white audiences, where they believed profits were more lucrative. As a result, they limited the resources invested in black music to the handful of stars who gained national appeal. After the war, however, large numbers of start-up record companies turned their attention to more local sounds such as rhythm and blues and rock 'n' roll. A few of these small, independent companies, including Apollo, Specialty, Savoy, and Nashboro, devoted considerable attention to gospel.[7]

The changes in radio would prove even more significant. With television looming on the horizon, the Federal Trade Commission began granting radio licenses to small entrepreneurs who did not have the capital to invest in national network programming. These national networks, which monopolized the prewar airwaves, had devoted the lion's share of their programming to white performers. The new entrepreneurs bypassed the expensive network programming and concentrated on developing local shows that appealed to niche, rather than mainstream, audiences. In many communities with large black populations, these shows often concentrated on recordings and live performances by African American singers and musicians. During the 1940s and 1950s many radio stations hosted Sunday morning religious programs that often featured gospel music.[8]

WLAC, based in Nashville, Tennessee, proved especially instrumental in disseminating gospel throughout the South. During the day the 50,000-watt station geared its offerings to white, mainstream audiences. At night the station directed its programming to black audiences, featuring the latest in rhythm and blues as well as plenty of gospel. These nighttime broadcasts reached far beyond the city limits. As other stations signed off the airwaves at night, WLAC's signal blanketed much of the South, reaching legions of eager listeners.[9]

Curtis Lyles described the impact of radio in the black rural Alabama community where he grew up in the 1940s. Every Sunday morning, he recalled, the local radio station sponsored a program that featured black religious music. It was on that show that he first heard Tharpe. Her broadcasts were so popular in his community that they became a weekly ritual in which friends and neighbors who did not own radios assembled to listen to the program. "People would gather around to hear her sing pretty much the way they would gather around the radio to hear Joe Louis fight," Lyles explained.[10]

These broadcasts, Lyles explained, played a meaningful role in fostering racial pride and self-respect within the oppressive context of Jim Crow. Lyles stressed that throughout his childhood, his family protected him from "white domination." He described his community as very poor, pointing out that some people did not have electricity or indoor plumbing. Yet radio connected him to a larger and more cosmopolitan world. Radio became a topic of almost daily conversation. He and his friends frequently shared their radio experiences and swapped information about a new program someone had discovered by turning the dial. "There were no listings of radio programs," he recalled, "so news about a program spread by word of mouth." Lyles moved across a range of stations, looking for programs featuring black music. He vividly recalled the shows that he and his friends patronized. The "Groove Show," which was broadcast at 3:30 P.M., featured African American groups. Local funeral directors hosted the Sunday morning show on which he heard Tharpe. WLAC was particularly popular. It was the station, he stated with absolute assurance, that "everybody listened to."[11]

Programs that targeted black audiences ultimately contributed to the emergence of black radio stations in the late 1940s and 1950s. This development, in turn, sparked a new form of racial change. Even as black programming and, later, black stations helped foster a sense of community among African Americans, these same arenas of mass entertainment offered white audiences access to that community. This access distinguished radio from race records, which were often marketed exclusively to retail outlets in black neighborhoods. In addition, it blurred racial boundaries held in place by legal segregation. With the mere turn of the dial, radio could forge a virtual community of black and white listeners that transcended racially distinct neighborhoods and communities.[12]

This virtual community could pose problems for law enforcement officials when radio stars made local concert appearances. The problem was particularly acute in the case of Tharpe, whose national reputation soared during the mid-1940s. Tharpe left the Lucky Millinder band in 1943 to begin a gospel-focused collaboration with singer and, later, minister Marie Knight. Despite the controversy Tharpe's nightclub forays had generated, the power of the women's singing attracted an enormous following among both blacks and whites. Abner Jay, who worked as Tharpe's agent between 1949 and 1962, described how emotions ran so high at a 1949 concert in Macon, Georgia, that the audiences completely disregarded Jim Crow regulations. "So there was white and blacks all mixed up," Jay recalled. He went on to describe how "the police was running around, 'The white folks all over on the colored side.' The whites usually in the balcony. 'White folks on the colored side.' So there's nothing we can do about it. 'It ain't nothing we can do about it, just leave them alone.'"[13]

Concerts like the one Jay described played a pivotal role in integrating gospel into mass commercialized culture. Before the war, with few exceptions, live gospel performances occupied a distinct domain from that of recordings. The emergence of gospel concerts in the 1940s helped close that gap as singers began using concert tours to promote their recordings. These new concerts differed significantly from the gospel programs that had become popular in black communities across the country during the 1930s. Gospel programs brought together a number of gospel groups for several hours of music and fellowship. Most took place in churches and relied on freewill offerings to pay musicians. Concert organizers issued tickets with stipulated prices and often scheduled the events in theaters.[14]

The move from programs to concerts was a gradual process whose evolution varied in each locality. In New York local booking agents and disc jockeys like Thermon Ruth, Johnny Meyers, and Joe Bostic developed strategies for organizing and promoting the events. Marie Knight described the innovative strategies Meyers deployed:

MK: And he [Johnny Meyers] started this thing with tickets on the door at the Golden Gate Auditorium; that's where he started it. . . . This was between 1944 and 1945. And the people began to wonder why is he going to get away with this. But he did.

JA: So there was a question about whether people were prepared to pay?

MK: There was; it was a question about whether they would want to pay. Because everything, you know, had been free. But by Johnny going around in the city with this loud cow horn promoting this thing . . . That's the way they used to do it, in a truck. . . . And this is the way he started promoting his programs for the Golden Gate Auditorium. And the people were packed. They were packed in there. It was amazing how he did it, but he did.[15]

The transformation of gospel programs into ticketed events pushed the music further into the world of commerce. Knight was amazed that Meyers was able to mount such changes without provoking much opposition. But Meyers was clearly an effective promoter. The cow horn Knight so vividly recalled no doubt lent an element of energy and excitement to the event, generating enthusiasm among African Americans with and without church ties. In addition to advertising on the street, Meyers often arranged for the groups featured in the concerts to sing one or two numbers on the radio or in local churches during Sunday worship services. In this way he built the concerts into exciting, eagerly anticipated events.[16]

The concerts grew bigger and more extravagant in the early 1950s as recording companies expanded into concert promotion, and regionally and nationally based booking agencies turned their attention to gospel. Irving and Israel Feld, based in Washington, D.C., ventured into concert promotion in the late 1940s. Focusing on the area from Baltimore to Norfolk, Virginia, the brothers began bringing in talent for one-night concerts. Whereas booking agents had focused on theaters, the Feld brothers directed their attention to much larger facilities, including sporting arenas and armories.[17] One of their most lavish events was Rosetta Tharpe's wedding concert. Tharpe had parted ways with Thomas Thorpe sometime during the 1940s. After a brief marriage to booking agent Fosh Allen, Tharpe married manager Russell Morrison. With Tharpe's approval, the Feld brothers devised a plan to use her nuptials as the basis for an extravagant concert and promotional tour. In July 1951, 15,000 people descended on Griffith Stadium in Washington, D.C., to witness the ceremony. The gospel concert that followed included appearances by Tharpe, Marie Knight, a backup group called the Rosettes, and two quartets—the Harmonizing Four and the Sunset Travelers. The next day several thousand people turned out for a follow-up commemoration of the wedding ceremony, a homecoming, and a concert held in Richmond.[18]

Many grand and elaborate gospel concerts took place during the 1950s. Art Rupe, owner of Los Angeles–based Specialty Records, expanded into concert promotion at this time. In 1955 Rupe decided to make a live recording of his top-selling gospel groups and organized a concert at the Los Angeles Shrine auditorium for that purpose. The auditorium, which could seat 6,444, was smaller than Griffith Stadium. Yet the capacity crowd assembled was significantly larger than any that had attended earlier concerts organized by local promoters and disc jockeys. Billed as the First Annual Mid-Summer Festival of Gospel Music, the concert included the Pilgrim Travelers, Brother Joe May, the Soul Stirrers, the Caravans, and Dorothy Love Coates and the Original

Gospel Harmonettes. The concert was part of a tour that included major cities as well as small towns. The gospel groups performed together when the tour arrived in major cities and then split into smaller segments when the tour traveled to small towns. Tharpe focused many of her efforts on the South, playing on a developing circuit of ballparks and other arenas.[19]

The promotion so essential to the concerts helped usher gospel into a mass commercialized culture where success hinged on the size of the crowds that turned out, the number of records sold, and the ability to hold, indeed rouse, an audience. In this environment money assumed utmost importance. Perhaps the greatest evidence of the influence money wielded rests in those individuals who left gospel altogether to pursue careers in the more lucrative fields of rhythm and blues and popular music. Over time many of the record companies investing in gospel realized that the most successful gospel singers could make even more money in the secular field. A number of singers reported that record companies had encouraged them to turn to secular styles where revenues exceeded those generated by gospel. Many gospel singers refused to capitulate. Others, however, found the argument persuasive. These men and women, who comprise a veritable who's who of black music, included Sam Cooke, Della Reese, Sarah Vaughan, and Cissy Houston. The pattern became so prevalent that the church gained a reputation as "a school for singing stars."[20]

As gospel gained access to the airwaves, concerts replaced programs and a growing number of recording companies invested in the music. The number of gospel singers who emerged as national celebrities expanded exponentially. Unlike in the field of jazz, which was dominated by men, women emerged as some of gospel's biggest stars. Not since the 1920s and the ascendancy of blues queens like Ma Rainey and Bessie Smith had so many female musicians captured the attention of African Americans. One of gospel's greatest stars, Chicago-based Mahalia Jackson, also expanded the music's visibility among white mainstream audiences. The acclaim and recognition Jackson garnered was so widespread that President John F. Kennedy invited her to sing at one of his inauguration parties in 1960.[21]

As gospel singers emerged as national and local celebrities, flamboyance and showmanship became a staple of performance. These developments found expression in the attire gospel singers selected. Gospel quartets, which once dressed in dark, tailored suits, began wearing colorful slacks and sports coats. Female singers, faced with the ongoing challenge of generating a certain sex appeal without drawing the accusation that they had become too worldly, chose a variety of paths. Mahalia Jackson and many others wore robes, which immediately linked these women to the religious realm, specifically church choirs. Others, like Tharpe, appeared in carefully selected evening gowns whose elegance and taste conveyed a sense of glamour but downplayed sexuality. In the 1950s the Clara Ward Singers wore robes but rendered these traditional garments flashy and perhaps even sexy by choosing bright colors that emphasized style and presence.[22]

The growing emphasis on showmanship and the willingness to ground success in material as well as spiritual concerns were potent indicators that gospel occupied a new landscape. While some gospel fans celebrated the music's success, others voiced concerns, intensifying a decade-old debate over the growing presence of black sacred music in commercial mass culture as well as the meaning of both race and faith.

As the *Cleveland Call and Post* made clear, Rosetta Tharpe had helped propel the issue into public view. The moment Tharpe set foot on the Cotton Club stage, many sanctified believers denounced her and her actions, insisting that in moving to the nightclub and theater circuit, Tharpe had abandoned her faith altogether. "When she went to the Cotton Club," Richard Cohen recalled, "church folk didn't accept the crossover." While she remained popular in many circles, Cohen explained, her reputation suffered permanent damage:

> So when she came back to the church, she was kind of rejected. You know some of the bishops tried to accept her. But she didn't have that wide range where she could just travel anywhere in the United States and go to churches. . . . And you know that was not just true in Pentecostal churches but even Baptist and Methodist churches kind of pulled away from her. See today they do that, they're in and out and nobody says a thing. But back then, you know, it hurt her career in a lot of instances. I think she never, ever felt that she was able to get back to the point where she was [before].[23]

The NCGCC was particularly incensed that a gospel singer would even attempt to bring the music into a nightclub. During the late 1930s an array of students, social workers, and clerical workers employed by the New Deal's

Works Progress Administration visited black communities across Illinois collecting news clippings and conducting interviews for the Illinois Writers' Project. The project's essay on gospel music, tellingly titled "Spirituals of Today," singled out Tharpe for direct criticism:

> Several years ago a choir singer was rendering "Hide Me in Thy Bosom" when Cab Calloway chanced to hear her. He was deeply impressed with her voice and the way she handled the song and engaged her to sing with his band. The singer, Sister Thorpe, won national recognition swinging the song that caused her discovery. Her inflection in saying "Rock Me, rock me in thy love" so swayed [listeners], who could see a double meaning in the words, that her success was assured. However, church groups protested her using the songs in night clubs. Result, she had to stop using it. But with a well established reputation behind her she has gone on to greater heights.[24]

Convention members, unnerved by Tharpe's behavior and deeply troubled by her use of Dorsey's work, could not believe that she was motivated by sincere religious convictions. Many concluded that she was an impostor, a fraud. Members of the Church of God in Christ, similarly incensed, concurred. Some contended that she had left the church. Others questioned whether she had ever harbored heartfelt religious beliefs. Richard Cohen articulated this uncertainty when asked to describe her music. "She was very expressive," he recalled; "I think she sang with a lot of feeling." Yet even as he acknowledged her music skills, he questioned her convictions. "I don't know whether it was part showmanship," he said, "or whether it was just really, you know that she really actually truly deep down felt it."[25]

Members of the Church of God in Christ, to which Tharpe belonged, and the NCGCC, whose music she performed, had particular reason to focus on her behavior. Among other African Americans, however, greater concern was devoted to the fate of the spirituals. At the same time that Tharpe launched her commercial career, a number of prominent jazz musicians, including Louis Armstrong, Cab Calloway, Tommy Dorsey, Benny Goodman, and Jack Teagarden, responded to growing popular interest in the spirituals by integrating the songs into their repertoires. This development created an uproar among a broad spectrum of African Americans, sparking a discussion that would give

Thomas Dorsey and his followers a key opening for their claim that gospel, like the spirituals, formed an important part of African American heritage.[26]

In 1939, the year after Tharpe made her Cotton Club debut, George W. Harvey, associate editor of the *Pittsburgh Courier*, launched a vigorous campaign against swinging spirituals. Harvey, who was also a Baptist minister, declared that "many of our race bands, artists, and orchestras in addition to the records and broadcasting systems are desecrating spirituals." As the *Courier*'s religious editor, he turned the nationally distributed newspaper into a platform for his campaign. The paper appealed directly to readers. "Dr. Harvey," the paper announced, "asks church people to join in a strong militant protest to stamp out the wanton practice of desecrating the songs of our fathers and mothers."[27]

Readers from across the country expressed enthusiastic support for the campaign. Many wrote letters to the paper denouncing swinging spirituals and praising Harvey for his initiative. For two months the paper published letters from a broad cross-section of African Americans, including educated professionals as well as laborers, men and women, students, and the elderly. One older woman recalled being "converted under the influence of some of those old songs."[28] A variety of people active in music, including music teachers and songwriters, amateurs and professionals, also lent their support.[29]

The range of observations these letters voiced served as a snapshot of the many different issues that the modern transformations of black sacred music, as well as black music in general, had raised for African Americans. Some readers focused their comments on spiritual matters. "Well it is true that we as a race have drifted too far from God," wrote one. "We certainly will have to get back to Him."[30] But others touched on a more complex swirl of issues, which included long-standing concerns about individual and racial respectability as well as more recent uneasiness about the fate of African American music within American popular culture.

Many letters emphasized the firm hold that the values of respectability and restraint continued to hold in many corners of African American society. One critic made it clear that he objected not to the secular nature of jazz, but to the values and outlooks he thought the music conveyed. Music, he insisted, "should lift one up" and "inspire the pleasant emotions of man." Another writer prophesied that the emotions swinging spirituals unleashed would have dire consequences: "I join in protesting with all my power. The continuation of such will inevitably upset all sacred rules of home life, destroy the discipline of school life, and in time, if not already, destroy and wreck the fine spirituality of our churches."[31]

Some of these letters moved from denouncing swinging spirituals to criticizing gospel, reiterating long-held distinctions between the refined worship that had been so closely connected to ideas of racial uplift and the emotional rhythms of sanctified services. One writer traced the problem of swinging spirituals directly to emotional worship. "Visit a few of the Negro churches," he counseled, "and you will find the congregations singing the so-called spirituals in 'swing time' stamping their feet and clapping their hands."[32] Harvey himself intimated that emotional religion ceased to be religion with his lament that "beloved hymns and songs of our fore-parents are being played in swing time."[33]

Other letters, however, made it clear that concerns about the spirituals were not always linked to a middle-class agenda. Another reader, for example, directly discounted the weight so many African Americans placed on education, focusing on the way she saw the power of the songs' emotions embodying the defiant spirit of a people and a race:

> It is true that the Negro slaves who gave birth to these spirituals were unlettered and illiterate, whose vocabularies were limited to few words and phrases, but the souls of our slave ancestors were rich in higher things than you can comprehend.
> . . . In spite of sorrow and sadness as daily companions, slaves could feel joy and gladness. In spite of chains, they could still sing such songs as "When the Saints Go Marching In." In spite of bull whips they could steal sway at night and sing, "Swing Low, Sweet Chariot."[34]

Harvey focused his protest on the need he saw for major reform within the entertainment industry, calling for a broad-based religious protest against its various institutions. "The church should rise up in all of its branches and let the amusement world, shows, taverns, musicians, et al. feel the force of united opposition and protest to this growing evil," he wrote. "Music producers, record makers, electric box distributors and all concerned need to know that we vehemently disapprove of this practice, that is widely in vogue today."[35]

Many readers, however, gave the issue a more specifically racial cast, invoking broader issues connected to commercialized black music, especially swing. For many African Americans, the popular enthusiasm surrounding swing was nothing more than an effort by whites to appropriate black music. In a typical complaint, one journalist asserted that jazz "received no consideration among whites until the Original Dixieland Band, aping colored players, blared a hot trail into the Windy City and New York. Then white America started paying attention to the black man's jazz—but only because it was passably rendered by whites."[36] One of the *Courier* letters invoked this concern directly. The writer pointed out that white music critics had criticized musicians for adapting the national anthem to a swing beat but voiced no opposition when spirituals became the target. He cast this silence in conspiratorial terms, suggesting that it laid the groundwork for "desecrating our spirituals or parts of them in order to appear original, creative geniuses."[37]

Some black swing musicians concurred. Count Basie and Lionel Hampton both voiced strong objections to the practice. Basie reportedly declared that he would rather abandon the airwaves altogether than endorse swinging spirituals. Hampton used his weekly column in the *Washington Afro-American* to call attention to the racial implications of the practice. "Nobody would think of swinging 'Ave Maria' or 'Silent Night,'" he wrote, "yet I often hear bands rip into our spirituals and turn them every which way but loose." Hampton pointed to this contradiction as evidence of a blatant disregard among whites for elements deemed sacred in African American communities.[38]

But as many writers pointed out, white bands were not the only ones swinging spirituals. Harvey, who saw the practice as part of a problem with the industry rather than with individual musicians, focused little attention on them. When, for example, he mistakenly criticized Fats Waller for swinging "When the Saints Go Marching In," a spiritual that Louis Armstrong had recorded, he informed readers of the error but gave it little weight.[39] Many readers, however, saw things differently. The letters of protest that poured into the *Courier* focused particular attention on the entertainers, singers, and musicians who were the public face of the industry. Although black and white musicians played swinging spirituals, most of the protest letters focused on black musicians.[40]

One letter offered an especially elaborate chain of reasoning that both revealed a strong conviction about the racial dimensions of music and pointed to the difficulties African Americans encountered when they sought to comprehend the workings of the mammoth, often amorphous music industry. The writer pointed out that both white and black bands swung spirituals. In her mind, however, the real responsibility lay with black musicians. "Most white orchestras are phoney," she stated, asserting that they merely copied black ensembles. Consequently, she insisted, swinging spirituals must have been developed by African American arrangers and orchestras, who "have taken these spirituals and offered them as a sacrifice to the god—Money!"[41]

Florida resident Alto Peeples also focused on black musicians, offering a particularly eloquent appeal to jazz trumpeter Louis Armstrong that touched on both the hopes and the disappointments that black musical stardom embodied. Armstrong's rise to the national stage signaled an important development: as the entertainment industry promoted cultural forms that had taken shape in African American communities, black singers and musicians emerged as national heroes. Many African Americans embraced individuals like Armstrong not only for the music they produced but also for the way their individual achievements could represent the race to the wider public and in the process help eradicate prevailing notions of black inferiority. Peeples alluded to the stature Armstrong enjoyed by explaining that he had regarded the trumpeter as a "credit to our race." He then made a direct plea to Armstrong: "I want Mr. Armstrong to know that we highly protest the judgement of any individual, or group, that will take the only music that America can really feel proud of and rearrange it to satisfy the emotions of a gang of jitter-bugs."[42]

With the words "the only music that America can really feel proud of," Peeples hearkened back to the black intellectuals who had worked to cast the songs as a vital part of African American culture and, indeed, the manifestation of black contributions to American civilization, converting spirituals into racially as well as spiritually sacred songs. The broad-based acceptance of this sentiment allowed Harvey to turn the protest against swinging spirituals into an assertion of race pride, bridging some of the divides that had marked African American culture earlier in the century. As a result, the many dissimilarities among the campaign's supporters did not harden into internal divisions that would have jeopardized the protest. Despite their differences, protesters were united in their belief that swinging spirituals was an affront not only to religious beliefs, but to African American heritage.[43]

This unity offered a significant opportunity for the NCGCC, whose members seized the moment to educate African Americans about the merits of gospel. As the protest escalated, Thomas Dorsey submitted a letter to the *Courier*. Dorsey did not challenge Harvey's views on the aesthetics of musical performance. Instead, he praised the efforts the minister was making and then used the occasion to make a connection between gospel songs and spirituals:

> I am glad some one has seen the value of our songs and has spoken out to preserve them from the dance bands and theaters of this age.
>
> I have written and marketed successfully more than 300 Gospel songs and Spirituals in the past ten years and one of them "Precious Lord Take My Hand" has been sung around the world where the Christian religion is present and I have spent untold sums to keep my songs from being desecrated by the worldly musicians.[44]

Here Dorsey provided a compelling testimony about his struggle to preserve his sacred compositions from the tentacles of an expanding entertainment industry. Rather than bluntly asserting that gospel represented a modern version of spirituals, Dorsey used his story to dramatize the connection between his modern compositions and the nineteenth-century folk songs.

The strategy made the editors of the paper take notice. During the late 1930s the *Pittsburgh Courier*, and the black press in general, devoted little attention to gospel or any of the new secular styles of music taking shape in black communities. The religion section typically featured church activities and focused on preachers. Gospel programs and especially gospel singers received only the most cursory treatment. Less than a month after Dorsey's letter was published, however, the *Courier* editors published a speech Dorsey had delivered on the significance of spirituals. The editors made an even more unprecedented move by assigning a feature article on Dorsey and his gospel publishing operation. In just one month the *Courier* published a letter by Dorsey endorsing the campaign against swinging spirituals, a speech he delivered on the significance of the songs, and an article on his work as a gospel composer. Such coverage supplied Dorsey with the kind of national exposure that allowed him to blur the boundaries between gospel and spirituals. The strategy lent a significant boost to gospel.[45]

In subsequent years, the NCGCC would launch its own campaign to protect the sacred nature of gospel music. The convention could not reform the entertainment industry or compel musicians to change their repertoires. However, members could provide alternative paths for sacred singers, and the organization could use its public standing to set community-based standards for performers. In 1939 the convention developed a mission statement that highlighted the importance of keeping religious music sacred and established a new set of goals:

> To perpetuate the beautiful SPIRITUALS, that were the spontaneous outbursts of the Negroes' hearts in the dark days of slavery and which have proven themselves to be such a priceless contribution to American civilization; to promote and appreciate the Gospel Songs of this day and time which touch the hearts of men; to prepare singers to carry the Gospel in song in an intelligent manner; and to make it clear that there is a vast difference between the songs that are inspired by our Heavenly Father and the common "jazz" music so prevalent today we herewith organize this National Convention.[46]

The statement makes clear that the convention's vision had significantly changed in six short years. Once devoted primarily to organizing choirs and choruses and to spreading gospel music, it was now taking on new projects that included training singers and protecting both gospel and spirituals from jazz. The offensive posture it initially adopted was now balanced by a defensive mission: keeping gospel separate from jazz.

As ties between gospel and mass commercial culture deepened in the aftermath of World War II, the convention devoted more and more of its attention to protecting and preserving spirituals and gospel from commercial exploitation. Sallie Martin, who had been so active in helping Thomas Dorsey popularize gospel, played a particularly prominent role in these endeavors. Martin had struck out on her own in 1940, establishing an independent gospel publishing studio with associate Kenneth Morris and a new group, the Sallie Martin Singers, to promote the company's songs. The Martin and Morris Music Studio became the country's largest publisher of gospel sheet music, and Martin, who died in 1989, remained associated with the business until 1975. She also remained a central figure in the NCGCC. In 1949 she laid out her concerns about mainstream commercial gospel:

> Recently the enormous growth of gospel and Evangelistic singing in our churches has been widespread and self-evident. This is due to the enormous popularity and public reception of this type of music. . . . It is sad to note though that even though Evangelistic and gospel singing is based on the highest type of songs conducive to the greatest spiritual values, the recent advent of "Followers after Fishes and Loaves" has reduced the effectiveness of this type of music and has brought down upon it the finger of scorn and derision. Too many of our contemporary Evangelistic or gospel singers are in it "for what they can get out of it" or for purely commercial reasons.[47]

Several years earlier Thomas Andrew Dorsey had conveyed his support in song. In 1941 the composer filed to copyright "I'm Going to Live the Life I Sing About in My Songs."[48] Specifically addressing gospel singers, Dorsey used the song to remind them that the Christian message, which set gospel apart from blues and jazz, placed a certain onus on practitioners like himself. In the mid-1950s Dorsey reiterated these sentiments in an interview: "We cannot sing this gospel and when the program is over go out to the hotels, taverns, and good time joints and mix with the people in the world."[49]

The organization made a concerted effort to keep gospel tied to a concrete religious community by concentrating on training gospel singers and choruses. Members of the convention did not seek to isolate themselves or gospel from the commercial arena altogether. Rather, they wanted to maintain some measure of control over the music. Through education and training the convention sought to keep singers and groups tied to a concrete community that members hoped would influence the terms on which gospel practitioners interacted with recording companies. They also asserted their religious authority, identifying standards of conduct for gospel singers and then launching an educational campaign to disseminate those standards. In her 1949 essay Martin emphasized standards that all bona fide gospel singers should uphold. She asserted that gospel singers should maintain "regular membership and be in good standing in some recognized church." Such membership, she cautioned, needed to be active and engaging, not merely token.

"The singer should also first display an attitude of cooperation towards his church and its auxiliaries," she wrote, "before attempting to display his talents abroad." This stipulation signaled just how much gospel had changed since the 1930s, when some ministers voiced such strident opposition to the music that even Martin felt compelled to venture beyond the auspices of the church and organize community-based gospel choirs. Gospel had gained such wide acceptance that the church now served as an agent that could protect the music.[50]

A second standard revolved around musical training and knowledge. Martin insisted that all gospel singers discover the range and depth of their own music skills. Such advice sought to undercut the influence of popular recordings that often led singers to try to imitate the latest gospel stars. Martin urged singers to distinguish between emulating individuals who inspired them and merely seeking to "copy . . . every note and mannerism." Martin stressed the importance of singers gaining knowledge about not only the range of sacred songs suitable for worship but also the intended spiritual message of each song. For Martin, understanding a song's message involved more than merely knowing the words. It required personally feeling the intended message. The convention used its annual meeting and its member unions to spread such knowledge, educating its members about the history of the music generally and the appropriate use of different songs.[51]

Lastly, Martin pointed to the display of Christian conduct as a critical qualification that all gospel singers must possess. According to Martin, music skills and talent alone were insufficient to qualify an individual as a gospel singer. "It certainly should be a requisite for the singer of the gospel story of Christ to be Christ-like," she wrote. Martin further explained that "a singer certainly cannot lead others into the experience and reality of Christ and himself know nothing of it." Voicing these sentiments Martin insisted that a gospel singer had "to be a devout Christian with a good reputation."[52]

——— The interest promoters, recording companies, and radio stations took in gospel, together with the efforts of the NCGCC to preserve the music, produced a gospel spectrum. At one end sat popular acclaim and the resulting material success, and at the other sat concerns about preserving the music's sacred qualities under the auspices of black religious communities. Like Sister

Rosetta Tharpe, talented gospel singers were faced with a series of dilemmas about where and how to focus their abilities. Examining how specific individuals moved across this continuum perhaps helps to illuminate the nature of the possibilities they faced. The experiences of Marie Knight and Dorothy Grant, talented singers who chose different paths, highlight the contours of those different worlds.

Born in 1923, Marie Knight grew up in Newark, only a short ride from New York's legendary commercial venues such as the Apollo Theater and the Savoy Ballroom. When Knight was a young woman, however, such venues never figured in her imagination. In a 1993 interview Knight recalled the central place the church occupied in young people's lives. Even for those who had graduated from school and entered the workforce, the church was a critical component of their leisure time: "In those days the churches were loaded with young people. They were loaded with the Youth Department because that's all the, say pleasure, that we really had. Because what's going on now wasn't happening then, so it was secluded. It wasn't as open as it is now, such as nightclubs and clubs and all that stuff. They weren't around. That was our only outlet—the church."[53] The vibrant religious community that nurtured Knight serves as a reminder that even as commercial venues proliferated in urban areas like New York and Newark, drawing the attention of many African Americans, the church remained an important center of African American life.

Religious communities also nurtured those, like Knight, who were musically gifted. Knight recalled in vivid detail how an auspicious meeting with Francis Robinson, an evangelist based in Philadelphia, opened a new world:

I started to travel with Francis Robinson in 1939. . . . She was an evangelist at the church, and she decided to take me on the road with her and all to help her. So I first jumped from home to Chicago and Detroit, and met a minister there by the name of Rev. Whitehurst. And his brother joined us, James Whitehurst. . . . [Then] we went to California. Then we didn't know anything about flying. We always went on the train. And we went out to the west coast and started running revivals. That's when revivals was 30 days, not 3 days—30 days. And the young people came from all over the Bay area because we stopped in Oakland, California. And we didn't live in hotels then. The pastor of the church usually kept the evangelists and her help.[54]

As gospel programs gave way to gospel concerts in the 1940s, Knight ventured into more commercial circles, joining the lineup of soloists and groups that appeared at civic auditoriums. Tharpe heard Knight at one of these concerts, and by the mid-1940s the two had begun a fruitful collaboration. Lacing their duets with inventive phrasing, Tharpe and Knight used their individual voices to create a dynamic vocal interplay. Recordings such as "Didn't It Rain" and "Up Above My Head I Hear Music in the Air" became some of gospel's biggest-selling hits, and as they traveled across the country during the 1940s and 1950s, the two women drew capacity crowds.[55]

Knight recalled in great detail the crowds that came to see them perform and the lucrative contracts they had with booking agencies: "Wherever we had concerts, we'd have sometimes concerts with people in the South where they come, they would come with wagons. . . . And sometimes you'd have an audience of 3,000–4,000 people. . . . We would serve in the tobacco barns where they would store tobacco. And they would hook the wagons together to put the instruments on the wagons so we would perform there. This is through the South."[56] In New York City audiences embraced the music with such enthusiasm that Tharpe and Knight had to travel by ambulance to get from the downtown clubs where they performed to the uptown engagements. As Knight explained, "The way that they transported us, they transported us in the ambulance because we were working from downtown [to] uptown. And to get us from downtown they had to put us in an ambulance and turn it wide open to get us back uptown . . . to the Apollo Theater to do the next show. That's just how big the call was for our act."[57] This degree of success brought rich financial rewards. "Our salaries," Knight recalled, "were running like—oh we'd go out on Sundays and [the next week] when you came back, you got yourself $5,000 to $6,000." These sums were possible "because the contracts were not booked under $1,000."[58]

Even as Knight found this new world exciting, she recognized that a palpable difference separated practicing gospel under the auspices of a church and engaging the music in the commercial arena. "There was a different group of people, a different set of people altogether," she recalled. "With Francis

Robinson the group was more serene," Knight pointed out. "It was always ministers or an evangelist or what not." But she explained that "with Rosetta, a lot of times we were with show people, in show business; a lot of times we were in the hotels, a lot of show acts and what not was in the hotels where we were. We would go to different things, have different things—go to parties all kind of stuff like that. It was a different group, different set-up altogether. Different strokes for different folks you know. Like I said, it was just that difference there, but [there] was a certain part of it that you'll never forget."[59]

Success and excitement, however, represented only one facet of this fast-paced life. Callousness and tragedy marked the other, as Knight discovered in 1948. "I was in California, Rosetta and I were in California—Oakland, California—on a concert, and I got the call that my mother and both my children were destroyed in a fire." Knight's decision to go to her family in New Jersey posed difficulties for the tour promoters, who were forced to cancel bookings. Only so many dates could be broken before a tour would suffer financially. Knight recalled that immediately after the funeral, she had to return to the road to resume her appearances. "We had to go right back out to Des Moines, Iowa," she expressed with regret, "just after I buried my people."[60]

This tragedy, a critical turning point in her life, prompted a spiritual pilgrimage that would ultimately lead Knight to abandon commercial gospel for the ministry. In the midst of her profound grief and despair Knight met Dolly Lewis, a prophetess whose spiritual gifts had led her to establish Gates of Prayer, a nondenominational church in Harlem. Lewis immediately detected the pain Knight was experiencing and felt moved to minister her back to health. Subsequently Lewis joined Knight and Tharpe on the road, becoming an integral part of their concerts. "When we got up and sang, that was our part of the program," Knight explained. "And when she got up with prophesy, that was her part of the program." Several months later, when Knight had recovered, Lewis resumed independent travel. But her influence remained. Knight recalled the advice Lewis imparted: "Marie I will always be there for you. But I have to teach you how to stand on your own two feet. . . . There are some things that I can do for you that I'm not going to do. But I'm going to see to it that you do them."[61]

Like the religious journey of Thomas Dorsey, Knight's spiritual pilgrimage took a number of twists. Once her collaboration with Tharpe ended in the mid-1950s, Knight pursued a solo career in gospel and had a brief stint in "show business." Eventually, however, she returned to the embrace of the church, settling in New York and joining Gates of Prayer, where Lewis presided. In 1972 she was ordained a minister by Lewis, and when Lewis died in 1990, Knight became pastor of the church.

The trajectory of Knight from gospel into the ministry embodies important changes that transpired in black religious life during the twentieth century. Looking back on her life, Knight regards the commercial arena and the fast-paced lifestyle it fostered as an aberration from the spiritual work she was destined to do. "At that particular time," she recalled, "I didn't have sense enough to know that it was boring and that it was taking something out of me." Yet in the late 1930s when Knight began her missionary work, women like herself were largely barred from the pulpit. Music, and gospel in particular, emerged as a vehicle through which they could conduct missionary work. Over time, women gained greater access to the pulpit. Knight recalled the difficulties Lewis encountered when she established Gates of Prayer in 1948: "The preachers didn't want to recognize her in their pulpit by her being a woman. They didn't want to recognize her in the pulpit, but I got news for you by 11:00 at night or 9:00 or 10:00 they out there on that doorbell coming in—they want help. Yeah they come to her for help at night."[62] The inroads Lewis made for female preachers, together with her mentorship, led Knight to pursue spiritual work as a minister. Knight would continue to record gospel music during the 1970s, but her career as a professional gospel singer became subsumed under her ministerial work. In the process Knight abandoned the commercial arena.

The life of Dorothy Grant, who spent the bulk of her musical career within the confines of the Baptist church, traced an alternate route, one laid out by the efforts of gospel's church-based supporters. Grant grew up in Pidley, Alabama, a small town on the outskirts of Birmingham. As a child she was a member of First Baptist Church of Pidley, where she sang in the choir. As gospel became more popular during the 1930s and 1940s, she joined some local gospel groups and listened avidly to gospel recordings, using them to shape her style: "I always tried to sing like Mahalia Jackson. I always thought I wanted to be like Mahalia Jackson. And then I heard Roberta Martin, and I always wanted to be like Roberta Martin. And then there was Queen Anderson, who sang one of Mr. Dorsey's songs, and I always wanted to be like her too you know. So as a kid, I just picked up folks I wanted to be like having never seen them, but I bought their records. And their records were those 78s."[63]

Even as recordings had shaped Grant's musical abilities, church institutions offered her role models and opportunities. The efforts of the NCGCC sparked the formation of hundreds of gospel choirs in black communities across the country. Grant remembers always singing and recalled that she "got in the choir before I joined the church." At age eleven she saw a woman directing a community choir and was immediately inspired. "I'd never seen a lady director, I'd always seen men." The experience gave her resolve: "It was a desire of mine to direct."[64]

Grant's interest in church work was momentarily pushed aside by an avalanche of other opportunities. The upsurge of gospel groups in the 1950s swept over Birmingham and engulfed Grant. She sang with the Bradford Specials for a period and then with Golden Dreams, which gave her an opportunity to travel across the country. In 1956 she left Birmingham for Chicago to tour with the Gospel Caravans, but she arrived too late. The setback proved a turning point. Rather than return to Alabama, Grant settled in Detroit, where she had come to sing a year earlier. She joined Springhill Baptist Church, which had hosted her in 1955, and her skills immediately won her the position of choir director. Reflecting on her experiences, Grant described the important role that the NCGCC played in giving her the direction and guidance she needed at a vulnerable point in her life. When she was asked to direct the Springhill choir, Grant sought assistance for the daunting task from Goodwill Musical Union, a Detroit-based choral union that belonged to the NCGCC. "In Goodwill we learned how to direct, how to sing correctly, just everything about singing," she said. The knowledge and training Grant gained through Goodwill eased her passage into her new career.[65]

The union also helped dispel the aura that surrounded many of the gospel singers who made recordings. When Grant was a starstruck youngster trying to imitate the latest recordings of Mahalia Jackson and Roberta Martin, these women seemed larger than life. As she became more active within the convention, she met and interacted with many of them. In the process these luminaries emerged as human beings like herself. Grant vividly recalled when Roberta Martin conducted a workshop for Goodwill members and taught members of the local union how to sing particular songs, encouraging those assembled to join their voices to hers.[66]

The knowledge and training the convention disseminated offered critical support to individuals like Grant who possessed music skills but had little previous experience directing a choir. Grant found the personal guidance and direction critical:

> So in joining Goodwill, they sort of just helped to bring me out. I was a singer in my own right. But they enhanced my gift. And it was because of this Convention that they knew how to do it.
>
> See people—when I came to the city, people were pulling at me. They were after me to sing with them. And I'm talking about the Meditation Singers, the various churches, the different groups. You know, I could have been in any number of groups. But I was destined to be a single, you know, I was not supposed to belong to any national acclaimed [group]. I was not to be mixed and mingled with the world.

At a time when many in the gospel community were lured by the more lucrative earnings they could receive in secular music fields like rhythm and blues and rock 'n' roll, Goodwill provided Grant with a network of support that helped her find her voice amid the opportunities.[67]

Both Knight and Grant were enticed by the money and fame of the commercialized culture that engulfed gospel. Yet amid the excitement came new difficulties, namely the realization that excitement could precipitate emotional and spiritual dissatisfaction. Each woman moved across the continuum of gospel as she searched for ways to make sense of her circumstances. Moving from revivals and gospel programs to concerts, Knight ultimately emerged as a nationally recognized gospel singer. The money and fame she enjoyed during the years she worked with Tharpe were exciting, indeed intoxicating. Yet the lifestyle proved harsh and brutal, and she eventually returned to church-based work. Listening to gospel music as a child, Grant wanted to sing like Mahalia Jackson and other celebrities. Later, when she had the opportunity to record, she found the experience profoundly dissatisfying. Grant found solace and, indeed, her own voice in the NCGCC.

——— Together the singers and audiences of gospel, along with those who invested in it, forged a place for the music at the interstices of church and commerce, lodging it between the secular and the religious. This development generated a degree of consternation inside the music community over just what constituted gospel. How much could the music be modified and still remain gospel? This question raised another: what made gospel sacred? Some insisted that the sacred nature of the music hinged on context, on where it was played. Others saw sacredness as inseparable from style. Still others pointed to the intent of the singer as the primary criterion. While the debate generated little consensus, it did signal the emergence of gospel as a critical space for the articulation of the twentieth century's diverse perspectives on the meaning of faith.

For Dorsey, style did not determine whether a song was sacred. Gospel songs could have blue notes and upbeat rhythms and still remain sacred as long as the context in which the music was played was conducive to worship. Reflecting back on his career, Dorsey conveyed these views in a discussion of how he integrated elements from blues into the gospel songs he composed: "If I could get into the gospel songs the feeling and the pathos and the moans and the blues . . . and that got me over into gospel songs. Got me over. For it was something different. They'd just sing 'Spiri-tual-fel-lowship-of-the-Jordan-land,' one of those kinds of things. Wasn't nothing to it. I got that turned like them blues moans in there, and the folks started to flocking."[68]

In the postwar era Dorsey became more rigid about style. As ties between gospel and mass commercialized culture intensified, he began to express concerns about the way groups, soloists, and choirs interpreted sacred songs: "A number of songs have been made to be disliked, not by the way the music is written, but by the way the song is played or sung. I have heard some of the most beautiful hymns jazzed so badly that I do not know what was being played or sung. I have heard some played and sung in such a bad way until I know what was being played and sung was not on the music sheet."[69] Here Dorsey rejected the very idea of merging elements from another style into gospel. These sentiments suggest that the training and education program the NCGCC spearheaded helped put a stylistic standard in place.

Despite such modifications, however, Dorsey consistently maintained that context comprised a critical component of what made gospel sacred. This perspective helps explain his fierce disapproval of Rosetta Tharpe's venture into nightclubs. Stressing the importance of context in a 1957 interview, Dorsey counseled that practitioners of gospel must not "mix with the world."[70]

Other musicians, however, saw the boundaries between church and world as far more fluid. Thermon Ruth began his career in gospel in the late 1920s as a member of a quartet and later turned to radio and promotion. During the mid-1950s Ruth was instrumental in making inroads for gospel at the Apollo Theater, part of the nightclub circuit where Tharpe sang in the late 1930s. Ruth recalled the large crowds that assembled at the theater to attend his Gospel Caravan, a week of shows devoted exclusively to gospel. The Sunday shows generated considerable enthusiasm. "I had a line up and around the Apollo Theater," he explained, "on the street around one corner to the other—folks trying to get there on Sunday." The theater had become legendary by the mid-1950s as the capital of black entertainment. Yet the audiences and singers who assembled there turned the space of secular amusement into a church. Ruth conveyed the delicate nature of this balance as he reflected on some of the challenges he encountered in the course of organizing the shows:

> I always believed that you could take gospel anyplace. So they [gospel singers and groups] came in, and I had a little trouble at the beginning with them because they wanted to stay onstage too long. And I had to pay overtime if they stayed on too [long]. Once I told them, "You got to cut the spirit down. Don't let the spirit run away with you." So they got wise and stopped.
>
> And I had the ushers in the Apollo Theater with me. When the women started shouting and getting happy, I had two ushers [to] take care of them.[71]

With profits in mind, Ruth sought to manage the dynamics of religious emotion. Still, the initiative singers took to extend their allotted time onstage and the shouting that took place during the shows suggest the degree to which performers and audiences felt themselves on sacred ground.

In his autobiography Ruth, the consummate promoter, included recollections of audiences to emphasize the important contributions he made to gospel. Many of these reflections called attention to the parallels between the gospel shows at the Apollo and church services: "The gospel shows were great, you'd go there and it would be like a church, there would be such a spirit in the building. The songs they sang would reach you and touch somebody in the audience, or a group of many people, and it just felt like the ceiling was gonna burst open. People would faint. You'd be overexcited or we'd get happy and shout." Ruth received strong criticism from some who objected to holding a gospel program in a theater. Initially his shows sparked a vigorous debate. Tellingly, one source of religious support came from the leading authority of the Church of God in Christ, Bishop Washington, who pointed to ongoing flexibility in the sanctified church over musical evangelism. Ruth recalled that "when I went into the Apollo Theater for gospel, the pastors of the churches got against me. Said I was taking sin into gospel [by appearing] at the Apollo. But a preacher told me. Bishop Washington told me. He said, 'Now Brother Ruth, when you get ready to catch fish, you don't go to the fish market. You go to the river and catch whatever comes out. So you go right on in the Apollo.' I went on in the Apollo with gospel and my first show was a bang. But I mean they criticized you."[72]

As he described his endeavors, Ruth touched on a critical question about the purpose of religious music. Should music focus on praising God and nurturing the faithful? Or should it be directed toward the unregenerate? Those who ventured outside church walls often stressed evangelism. Rosetta Tharpe had proclaimed that "there are more souls in the nighteries that needed saving than there are in the church." Ruth justified his endeavors by pointing to the advice he received from Bishop Washington. Clara Ward echoed those words in the early 1960s, when she turned to Las Vegas nightclubs to sing gospel. Dorsey, on the other hand, placed greater stress on the importance of context and directed most of his efforts at church members.[73]

For many in the church, justifying a move into secular realms in evangelical terms seemed an example of either cynical rationalization or outright deception. The story of Rosetta Tharpe, however, suggests a different view. Tharpe's attitude derived from her unique perspective on what constituted gospel. She insisted that the sacred value of gospel rested with the singer.

Since she firmly believed that her music skills came from God, Tharpe maintained that neither style nor context determined the sacred value of music. Instead she maintained that an individual's personal relationship with God governed the sacred value of gospel. Her perspective would gain considerable currency within gospel circles. Sam Cooke, who generated enormous popular appeal during the 1950s as lead singer of the Soul Stirrers, left the group in 1957 to pursue a career in popular music. His father, Charles Cooke, a Baptist minister, encouraged his son to make the move: "It isn't what you sing that is so important," Charles maintained, "but rather the fact that God gave you a good voice to use. He must want you to make people happy by singing, so go ahead and do so." With this advice the Baptist minister invoked an argument that closely paralleled the sentiments Tharpe embraced. Because his son's music skills came from God, he argued, any opportunity for expanding those skills was divinely sanctioned.[74]

As members of the gospel community disagreed about what made gospel sacred, they engaged in a discussion about the meaning of religion and the more critical question of what constituted faith. This question assumed enormous importance in a world where fame, fortune, and status gained widespread recognition as hallmarks of success. In such a society money wielded a level of power and authority that served as a formidable challenge to individuals and institutions. No objective standard determined whether the omniscience of the divine outweighed the authority money commanded or whether the exact opposite were true. Instead these matters hinged on individual interpretation. In such a world, just where did one invest his or her faith? The answer varied depending on how a person balanced material against spiritual concerns. Lodged between the secular and the religious, gospel supplied a middle ground where singers and audiences engaged this issue. Not surprisingly, singers used the music to offer a range of perspectives on the meaning of faith.

Tharpe, who emphasized the personal relationship an individual had with God, worked to privatize faith. Since she considered herself and, indeed, her music as instruments of God, Tharpe could explore a range of music styles. Her perspective explains the ease with which she mixed gospel with jazz or country and western, as well as blues. This context no doubt explains the charges that the *Cleveland Call and Post* leveled against Tharpe in 1956. The paper, which pointed out that commercializing gospel helped proliferate rock 'n' roll, understood the full implications of her activities. As she mixed gospel with a range of music styles, she also rendered the boundaries between sacred and secular decidedly amorphous. In a society where commerce wielded ever-increasing influence, her efforts raised an important question about whether religious communities should isolate themselves from the world or work to redraw the boundaries between secular and sacred. Tharpe seems to have preferred the latter option.

Sallie Martin, in contrast to Tharpe, insisted that faith must assume public expression and equated singing gospel with preaching gospel. The assertion had enormous implications for women who for generations had ventured into singing precisely because the pulpit had been closed to them. Martin insisted that the public arena in which singers performed supplied them with a pulpit that extended beyond church doors. The perspectives of Tharpe and Martin serve as examples of the emergence of gospel as a critical space for the articulation of diverse perspectives on the meaning of faith.

——— The controversy that surrounded gospel during the postwar years underscores that in the twentieth century music comprised an arena where critical social and cultural transformations unfolded. The divergent outlooks that encompassed gospel signal two important developments: the intrusion of commerce in daily life and the ways that intrusion influenced race and religion. The radio stations and recording companies that invested in gospel were instrumental in industrializing culture—mass producing it and disseminating it across the nation and around the world. Once the music began to lose its moorings in black religious communities, these developments sparked a wide-ranging discussion. As gospel gained greater exposure to the mass public, radio broadcasts and recordings made it available to audiences far removed from the black religious communities where the music had taken shape. Yet the exposure gospel gained also removed it from local control. For many who had come to regard gospel as a vital source of race pride and identity, this way of removing racial boundaries undermined black cultural autonomy and felt more intrusive than liberating.

As the ties between gospel and mass commercial culture became stronger during the postwar era, a debate emerged in gospel music circles over what made gospel sacred. This debate certainly felt new and different. Yet in many ways it was part of an ongoing debate that had always pervaded gospel: just what comprised faith in a modern world where material and secular values held increasing significance? Those who believed that the sacred quality of the music hinged on either context or style insisted that faith had to have a public dimension. Others advocated privatizing faith. The debates that surrounded the music during the postwar years ensured that gospel remained relevant, indeed modern enough to survive in the world of commerce, and most of all sacred enough to lend meaning to daily life.

Epilogue

In 1977 a concert that featured the choir of Tougaloo College, a historically black school in Mississippi, offered a dramatic illustration of the popularity gospel had gained during the twentieth century. Music scholar Romeo Phillips later recalled that near the end of the program, at the point when spirituals were traditionally performed, the conductor announced that two gospel numbers would be sung instead. Aware that he was breaking with tradition, the conductor explained that the students were so adamant about including gospel songs that unless he capitulated, "he would have a riot on his hands." The incident provides a telling example of the expanding acclaim gospel had acquired in African American communities. At the turn of the twentieth century, the music lingered in obscurity relative to the enormous popularity of arranged spirituals. More than seventy years later, college students were embracing gospel, and members of an older generation, Phillips among them, were lamenting the passing of the revised spirituals.[1]

In the 1990s a new generation made gospel its own. Singers such as Yolanda Adams and Kirk Franklin infused gospel conventions with elements from jazz, hip-hop, and rhythm and blues. Their recordings reached the top of the charts, and their live performances packed huge auditoriums, bringing a resurgence to gospel as young people found their sound a refreshing alternative to the decidedly secular tone of hip-hop. Adams and Franklin became so popular that radio stations that typically featured secular music began to include gospel on their playlists. Today, recording companies have taken note of the appeal the sound has generated and have begun to turn their attention to gospel.[2]

Gospel scholar and practitioner Horace Boyer points to one source of the music's continuing power in a description of its appeal among black college students:

Gospel music is the unifying element of Black students all over the campuses of the United States. Gospel choirs began on college campuses to provide some continuity between the black church and the academic life, but students found that they liked it and wanted to perpetuate its existence. On many predominately white campuses—and I happen to work at one of these—the gospel choir is the one visible evidence of the presence of Black students. They're not in the theater group; they're not in the symphony orchestra; they're not in the ballet troupe. They are in the gospel choir because they find, through it, some means of expression.[3]

The stress Boyer placed on gospel's unifying qualities, and on black students' desire for self-expression, makes clear the degree to which the music had become not simply a form of religious expression but a key source of African American identity.

Placing their passions in song, twentieth-century African Americans rendered music a receptacle of identity and of hope. What compelled African Americans to invest their hopes in a resource so amorphous as sound? The transformation of gospel and the controversies the music provoked offer some answers to this question. As a style of vernacular music, gospel took shape initially among laboring black men and women who found that freedom gave them only minimal control over many aspects of their lives. Since industrial jobs eluded African Americans until the advent of World War II, the vast majority of black laboring men and women found work in service industries that in the early decades of the century were considered the most degraded jobs and offered the lowest pay. For these men and women, the body and the soul it harbored offered refuge from a world marked by discrimination as well as physical violence and intimidation. Song, which was not subject to such outside controls, emerged as a vehicle for giving voice to individual and community aspirations as well as the pain that lingered within. Over time, growing numbers of African Americans would come to embrace the power and solace of such intense emotional expression.

Music, an aural medium, is the elusive manipulation of time through space. As sound, then, gospel was intractable, fluid, and impervious, properties that allowed it to cross normally impassable racial barriers. Writing in 1951, novelist James Baldwin described the broad appeal styles of black music enjoyed over the course of the twentieth century, in part because their full messages remained hidden. "It is only in his music, which Americans are able to admire because a protective sentimentality limits their understanding of it, that the Negro in America had been able to tell his story," Baldwin wrote. While music could not wholly transcend the racial divide, it afforded black Americans an opportunity to speak across those boundaries.[4]

As gospel became a commercial success, it also allowed a small number of singers and musicians to slip across racial barriers. No one illustrates this upward mobility more dramatically than Sister Rosetta Tharpe. Marie Knight described how the notoriety Tharpe enjoyed enabled her to enter places traditionally off-limits to African Americans. During the mid-1940s the two women did a concert tour across the South, traveling by bus. Jim Crow made such travel difficult for most African Americans, who were often denied access to public restaurants and restrooms. Knight recalled how Tharpe used her personality and image to venture beyond those restrictions:

> Everybody knew Rosetta Tharpe. Cops and everybody else. But they figured she had money on her. Cause she was always showing off you know. Talking a whole lot of stuff and what not. She was just—that was her life. That's the way she was. Her personality . . . And we went in a lot of places where blacks weren't even allowed—in the bathrooms and what not. But the minute there [the bus pulled into a gas station], she'd go to work and call my name and tell them who she was.
>
> And [the attendant would respond with enthusiasm,] "What now come on around here."
>
> Plenty of that went on.[5]

With such promises, however, came disappointments. As Baldwin noted, few whites understood the full significance of black music. Even as large numbers of whites embraced gospel, they did not necessarily relinquish long-standing attitudes about black inferiority. As a result, even as black music styles enjoyed greater popularity, African Americans' musical skills came to be regarded as the result of a biological predisposition of blacks to rhythm and emotion. Similarly, it became clear that while black stars formed the bedrock of the gospel music industry, control of the industry remained firmly in the hands of corporate entities that employed few black executives. Given this context, many African Americans began to see commercial gospel's prominence as evidence of whites attempting to appropriate black music—a stance that often cast black musicians as collaborators. Such concerns only heightened long-standing tensions over whether music spread mainly through commercial channels could remain sacred.

The experiences of Sister Rosetta Tharpe show how those eager to use technologies of mass communication to disseminate religion encountered an entertainment industry armed with managers equally eager to convert music into a commodity. In this context gospel singers became workers exercising variable degrees of control over music they regarded as a divine gift. In the public arena these same singers emerged as national celebrities, complete with the material trappings of fame and fortune that had become part of popular stardom. These experiences placed many gospel singers on a tightrope commanding considerable visibility but offering little room to maneuver. Amid the pulls exerted by both sacred and secular concerns, as well as the increasingly charged racial politics that swirled around the music, it was easy to lose one's balance.

Tharpe's experience suggests that while gospel has served as a reservoir of hope, it has also been a locus of enormous pain. I encountered this pain in my own fieldwork as I ventured to Chicago in search of people who knew Sister Rosetta Tharpe when she lived there in the late 1920s and mid-1930s. I discovered that mentioning Tharpe by name could bring a steadfast resistance and sometimes even animosity. On one occasion when a minister assisting me inquired whether she knew Rosetta, a woman spoke proudly of her relationship with Tharpe. Yet that same woman refused to speak with me when I approached her for an interview. On another occasion I telephoned a gospel disc jockey who was undoubtedly familiar with Tharpe. The disc jockey refused to talk, insisting that she did not know anything about Tharpe. No doubt the disc jockey had ample knowledge of Tharpe but did not wish to share that knowledge with me. Experiences such as these helped me recognize that profound pain resided in the silence.

———— The last years of Tharpe's life dramatically illustrate the vicissitudes of the commercial realm. The popularity she enjoyed in the 1940s and 1950s abruptly declined when the Internal Revenue Service charged her with tax evasion in 1957. The bureau seized her house in Richmond for failure to pay back taxes. "Took everything she had," Abner Jay recalled, "and she still owed $7,000." With only thirty days to pay the remaining funds, Tharpe approached Joe Glaser, a leading booking agent on Broadway, for assistance. The two worked out an arrangement that would have dire consequences for Tharpe's standing among gospel audiences. Glaser agreed to loan Tharpe the funds she needed, and in return Tharpe gave him exclusive responsibility to book her live performances for thirty days. Glaser booked Tharpe in Europe for twenty-one days and in West Coast nightclubs and theaters for the remaining period. As part of the arrangement Tharpe also seems to have taken out a lien on her portion of the ticket sales to pay back the loan she now owed Glaser.[6]

It had been some time since Tharpe had sung in nightclubs and theaters. In the years after World War II, when gospel's popularity soared, Tharpe had begun doing more gospel concerts in auditoriums and ballparks across the South. After the loan was paid, Tharpe planned to return to that southern circuit. However, she met cold resistance from the African American audiences who had once flocked to her concerts. Manager Abner Jay described the steadfast resistance he received as he tried to book concerts for Tharpe at the same locations where she had previously performed. "And here's what I ran into," he recalled: "'Oh we wouldn't be interested in her. She been playing in nightclubs.' I tried to explain to them that she was playing gospel in nightclubs. Still didn't make no difference; they wasn't interested."[7]

Such repudiation significantly differed from the reaction Tharpe had encountered in the late 1930s. While many African Americans—churchgoers and nonchurchgoers alike—expressed outrage at musicians who engaged in "swinging spirituals," Tharpe was still able to build a large following among black audiences. But in the 1950s, as more and more black singers turned from gospel to the more lucrative sounds of secular music, the animosity they inspired hardened sacred and secular divisions. In contrast to the discussions she generated in the late 1930s, in the late 1950s Tharpe encountered abject dismissal. Her fame seemed to vanish overnight. No longer a box office attraction, Tharpe could not command the attention of the most prestigious recording companies. While she had enjoyed a long career at Decca Records, Tharpe recorded with five different companies between 1956 and 1968. Jay described the dramatic reversal of fortune, recalling that attendance at her concerts dropped 99 percent. In the late 1940s when Jay had begun working with Tharpe, he had found it difficult to locate places big enough to hold the throngs of people who came to see her perform. Since churches were often too small to hold the large crowds she attracted, Jay worked to secure tobacco warehouses, auditoriums, and baseball parks for her performances. Jay recalled how these circumstances had completely changed by the late 1950s: "Wasn't no point in looking for no big place now. That little old church would be fine—the little old CME Methodist church, the little old Holiness church. The AME church was too big. Don't need no school gym, no ball park."[8]

The circumstances Tharpe encountered must have been extremely difficult. Once able to give money away almost indiscriminately, she now had to struggle to make ends meet. Her earnings barely covered expenses. The array of personnel that once managed her bookings and concerts all but disappeared. Tharpe traded in a luxurious bus in which she traveled across the South for a worn-out limousine. The trappings of fame and success seemed to evaporate almost overnight. Yet Tharpe continued to sing and travel with her music.

While audiences no longer came in droves, she seems to have retained a small corps of supportive admirers. Curtis Lyles remembers a performance Tharpe gave in 1965. She was touring with gospel singer Brother Joe May, and the two appeared together at a church in Greensboro, Alabama:

> And the church was packed. And that was in the late sixties. Now her popularity had declined enormously in this country. . . . But there was still a lot of people who remember her—her name still held magic, a certain amount of magic. I remember that performance at St. Matthews. She had been suffering from a cold. And it didn't matter. She was such a great artist. It was interesting because a lot of people joked about it—my sister and other people in the community—because Brother Joe May wanted the people to shout. It's very interesting she played a counterpoint to him. . . . And so she knew that the state of her voice at that time would not allow her to compete with him but she played a counterpoint. And it worked. She ended up stealing the show.[9]

Tharpe had recognized the fame she enjoyed as a blessing. How did she comprehend the suffering that descended on her life? Tharpe never offered a public explanation for the turn of events. If she had come to believe that she was as invincible as her admirers imagined, the loss of her fame certainly disabused her of that notion. The situation did not leave Tharpe bitter but filled her with resolve. She gritted her teeth and continued to travel with her music. Growing up in the sanctified church, Tharpe knew that getting through difficulties and disappointments hinged on faith. And for Tharpe music had always been an arena where she had articulated that faith. She never let go of her music, the divine gift she had been given.

Gospel scholar Anthony Heilbut points out that the criticism and rejection filled her with a determination to reclaim her fame. He recalls the strategies she perpetually envisioned for mounting her comeback: "While her husband plays the Pilgrim Jubilee's swinging, 'Won't It Be Wonderful There,' she prances about, kicking her leg up to chin level. 'I'm fifty. I know I don't look it,' she says. The age varies, the formula never. She's perpetually announcing a change of fortune: 'It's my big comeback, I'm hot like I used to be—but I don't like to brag.'" In another interview she envisioned producing an autobiography that detailed her experiences. Tharpe told Heilbut, "Someday I'm gonna write the story of my life, the people will cry and cry. I've been robbed, cheated, married three times, but God is so good."[10]

In 1903 W. E. B. Du Bois could not have been expected to imagine a life such as Rosetta Tharpe's, one in which the color line he so vividly described would become entangled in social and economic transformations that would obscure its significance and blur its boundaries. Tharpe would deal with race throughout her life. She grew up in the Church of God in Christ, a black Pentecostal community that flourished within the color line. When she crossed the color line and moved to the Cotton Club to expand her missionary work, she was faced with the conventions of minstrelsy. When she launched her southern tour, she confronted race at every turn. Given the paucity of sources that offer insights into Tharpe's thinking, what she made of these experiences remains an open question.

It seems clear, however, that Tharpe's main focus was religion, particularly in her early years. Her approach to gospel, which was so deeply rooted in her Pentecostal upbringing, provides the clearest evidence of the significance of religion to her worldview. In the Church of God in Christ, identity revolved around religion, not race. The notion that music skill was a divine gift offers additional evidence that one's relationship to God was the primary source of sanctified identity. In the sanctified church gospel was regarded as a mode of worship and had little relevance as a specific style of music, racial or otherwise.

As Tharpe's career developed, she became increasingly preoccupied with commercial success, pointing to the popularity she garnered as a key measure of her faith. In the twentieth century, however, fame hinged not on an individual's talent, God-given or otherwise, but on one's ability to navigate an expanding entertainment industry that used technologies of mass communication to reach across a wide range of social boundaries in search of the broadest possible audience. Tharpe's life cannot be understood outside this context.

The popularity she achieved and the controversy she provoked stemmed from the multiple boundaries she crossed at once. When she stepped onto the Cotton Club stage, she crossed a conventional boundary between sacred and secular. Tharpe also breached the color line by introducing gospel to white audiences, and she helped transport gospel from local black neighborhoods and communities, where the music had taken shape, to the corporate realm.

Tharpe's experiences make clear the degree to which the color line would blur and bend in the face of a corporate enterprise that eclipsed the local and generated material values celebrating consumption and fame. To understand African Americans in the twentieth century, we need to give more thought to this process. The scanty evidence on Tharpe makes it difficult to use her life and music to explore all these issues with the depth they deserve. Nevertheless, her life makes clear the need for work that can sort through them in more detail.

Deteriorating health cost Tharpe her life in 1973. The onset of diabetes in the early 1970s required that doctors amputate her leg, making travel more difficult. Despite the physical constraints, however, Tharpe continued to travel and perform. One of her last concerts was held at Washington Temple, one of the largest sanctified churches in Brooklyn, with a seating capacity of 3,000. Thermon Ruth, who organized the concert, recalled approaching her with the idea. "I knew she had played the Apollo theater; everybody liked her. . . . She came to my [radio] show one night with Mahalia Jackson and Ernestine Washington. So I knew she would want to play."[11]

In the early 1970s gospel audiences witnessed the death of not only Tharpe but also Mahalia Jackson. The treatment each received from the press provides clear evidence that Tharpe never managed to reclaim the fame she had enjoyed in the commercial arena. In contrast to the laudatory tributes newspapers across the country paid to Jackson—who died in 1972—eulogies for Tharpe were more tepid, focusing on the controversy she generated rather than the power of her music or the popularity she garnered during the 1940s. For example, the *New York Amsterdam News* noted that "she was highly criticized for singing in nightclubs and then singing in church, mixing gospel with blues."[12]

Over the course of her career Tharpe would sing gospel in many different settings, and in the process she would serve as a potent symbol of how much religion had changed. She offered little public commentary on how the controversy she generated affected her. As any human being, Tharpe would make a host of mistakes. But throughout her life her music remained a place where she put her joy as well as her pain. Her interpretations of Dorsey's "Take My Hand, Precious Lord" offer compelling testimonies of how she continuously forged her feelings into music. Tharpe recorded the song in 1941, as she was climbing to the height of her popular appeal, and again in 1968, when her fame had slipped away. In 1941 she delivered the song with a distinctively upbeat tempo. While the song has a somber quality, the quick pace gives it almost a light feeling. The unmistakable rhythmic presence that Tharpe infused into the song helped generate a sense of possibility that lingered in the air. In this version Tharpe delivered a compelling guitar solo that she used to let the complex sentiments of the song settle into consciousness.[13]

When Tharpe recorded the song a second time, her life had changed significantly. The intervening years had taken their toll. No longer the rising star, she was now struggling to reclaim her fame. She infused that pain and heartache into "Take My Hand, Precious Lord." Tharpe slowed the tempo, signaling that she was no longer the young, ambitious star appearing on the stage of the Cotton Club. Over the years she had not only grown older but had also fallen ill. As she witnessed in song, "This old body of mine is worn, oh yes." Yet as she explained, illness, disappointment, and even pain were an integral part of the struggles of life. "But you got to go anyhow in the rain or the storm," she testified. The rhythms that were so much a part of her early recording output remained but now took a backseat to the sentiments she wished to convey. Tharpe sang the song as though she were delivering a sermon. With virtually every line, she uttered a spoken testimony so that the chorus of the song became a compelling prayer:

> Through the storm, through the night,
> *Go on in front of me Jesus.*
> Lead me on to the light,
> *I can't make it unless you go with me.*
> Take my hand, *o-h-h-h-h-h* precious Lord,
> Lead me on.[14]

Notes

INTRODUCTION

1 Du Bois, *Souls of Black Folk*, 13, 204. For examples of historians using Du Bois to understand the twentieth century, see Holt, "Marking," 1–3; Levine, *Black Culture and Black Consciousness*, 136, 151–55.

2 Levine, *Black Culture and Black Consciousness*, 36–55.

3 Hunter, *To 'Joy My Freedom*; Earl Lewis, *In Their Own Interests*; Ruth, "Thermon Ruth and the Selah Jubilee Singers."

4 As historians point out, legal segregation in the South and racial discrimination in the North and Midwest placed African Americans on the margins of an industrial economy, and they found work mostly in service and domestic jobs. For example, see Earl Lewis, *In Their Own Interests*; Spear, *Black Chicago*, 29–49. As the walls of segregation began to crumble during World War II, increasing numbers of African Americans acquired employment in factories and thereby gained a more secure foothold in the industrial economy. Historians have traditionally focused on migration to explore how industrialization transformed daily life for many African Americans; see Grossman, *Land of Hope*; Trotter, *Black Milwaukee*. In fact many music scholars stress how migration influenced the development of blues and jazz as well as gospel; see Carby, "It Jus Be's Dat Way Sometimes"; LeRoi Jones, *Blues People*, 95–121; Levine, *Black Culture and Black Consciousness*. For an insightful discussion of the impact of gospel on the music industry, see Maultsby, "Impact of Gospel Music on the Secular Music Industry." In contrast to Maultsby, who sees the relationship between gospel and the music business as one-directional, I treat the relationship between gospel and the music business as interactive and multidirectional.

5 Carby, "It Jus Be's Dat Way Sometimes"; Harrison, *Black Pearls*; Keil, *Urban Blues*; Murray, *Stomping the Blues*.

6 Higginbotham, *Righteous Discontent*; Lornell, *"Happy in the Service of the Lord."*

CHAPTER I

1 *Negro Spirituals* (reissue recording).
2 Nelson, McIntorsh, and Johnson, *Memphis Gospel* (CD reissue).
3 On the impact of machine production, see Chandler, *Visible Hand*. For a discussion of the impact of industrialization on workers, see Gutman, *Power and Culture*.
4 Bederman, *Manliness and Civilization*.
5 Logan provides an overview of the pervasive prejudice, particularly the racial stereotypes that took shape; see Logan, *Betrayal of the Negro*. For an insightful discussion of how economic competition fueled racial discrimination in employment, see Hunter, *To 'Joy My Freedom*, 111–20.
6 Much of the literature on African American life during the late nineteenth century has focused on competing racial ideologies, conceptions of respectability, and methods of resistance. Yet within these competing frameworks, historians have documented the array of institutions black men and women built during this period. For a discussion of educational institutions, see James D. Anderson, *Education of Blacks in the South*. For a discussion of business enterprises that African Americans developed, see Weare, *Black Business in the New South*. For a discussion of religious institutions, see Frazier, *Negro Church in America*; Harvey, *Redeeming the South*; Washington, *Frustrated Fellowship*, 133–208. For a discussion of mutual benefit societies, see Hunter, *To 'Joy My Freedom*.
7 Rouse, *Lugenia Burns Hope*, 57–90; Stephanie J. Shaw, *What a Woman Ought to Be and to Do*, 41–103.
8 Higginbotham, *Righteous Discontent*, 19–46.
9 Ibid.; Stephanie J. Shaw, *What a Woman Ought to Be and to Do*, 90–103.
10 On the convention movement and the emphasis on education it stressed, see Harvey, *Redeeming the South*, 61–68; Higginbotham, *Righteous Discontent*, 19–20.
11 *United Negro*, 69. On slave worship, see Levine, *Black Culture and Black Consciousness*.
12 Harvey, *Redeeming the South*, 107–35, 227–55; Higginbotham, *Righteous Discontent*, 150–84. Focusing on Richmond, Virginia, Elsa Barkley Brown examines these developments as well as restrictions on women that unfolded during the 1890s; see Brown, "Negotiating and Transforming the Public Sphere."
13 Lornell, *"Happy in the Service of the Lord,"* 1–41; Lovell, *Black Song*, 402–22.
14 Levine, *Black Culture and Black Consciousness*, 166–68; Reagon, "Pioneering African American Gospel Music Composers."

15 Quoted in Brooks, "'Might Take One Disc of This Trash as a Novelty,'" 278.

16 Boatner, *Spirituals Triumphant Old and New*, unpaginated.

17 Johnson and Johnson, *Books of American Negro Spirituals*, 11.

18 *Gospel Pearls* marked the first time the word "gospel" emerged in black religious circles to designate sacred songs. Thomas Andrew Dorsey would later revise the meaning of the term as a music category. Yet when editors used the term as the title for the hymnal, they were not referring to a distinctive style of singing that developed in black communities. Instead they adopted the more generic meaning that prevailed in white evangelical circles. Ira Sankey initially coined the term "gospel hymn" to designate the songs he and others composed for the mass revivals held in cities across the United States during the late nineteenth century; see Sankey, *My Life and the Story of the Gospel Hymns*. The editors invoked the term "gospel" to convey to members of the National Baptist Convention that the songbook included modern, up-to-date songs. The editors made special mention of emerging evangelists, "gospel singers," as they were called, the men and women who traveled from place to place conducting revivals. *Gospel Pearls*, the editors explained, "is a boon to Gospel singers, for it contains the songs that have been sung most effectively by Prof. Britt, Mrs. J. J. Bushell, Prof. Smiley, Prof. Nix, Mrs. Williams, and other prominent singers, telling of His wondrous love, through song" (Townsend, *Gospel Pearls*, i).

19 Townsend, *Gospel Pearls*, iii; see also Dett, "Religious Folk-Songs of the Negro"; Harris, *Rise of Gospel Blues*, 112–18.

20 Boatner, *Spirituals Triumphant Old and New*.

21 Davis, *"Weh Down Souf,"* 54–56.

22 Many of the histories of the Church of God in Christ point to connections between the ecstatic worship and early Christianity; see Cornelius, *Pioneer*; Pleas, *Fifty Years of Achievement*. Many scholars emphasize how denominations like the Church of God in Christ embraced the vernacular music that persisted during slavery. Lawrence Levine, for example, points out that these denominations were part of a "revitalization" movement; see Levine, *Black Culture and Black Consciousness*, 179–81. During the 1930s folklorist Zora Neale Hurston emphatically called attention to these connections; see Hurston, *Sanctified Church*, 79–84. For a broad discussion of the African influences on worship practices in the Church of God in Christ and black Holiness and Pentecostalism generally, see Tinney, "Competing Strains of Hidden and Manifest Theologies of Black Pentecostalism."

23 Pleas, *Fifty Years of Achievement*, 1.

24 Ibid., 2; Cornelius, *Pioneer*.

25 Mathews, "Sanctified South."

26 Synan, *Holiness-Pentecostal Movement in the United States*.

27 Nelson, "For Such a Time as This," 192–96.

28 Quoted in ibid., 198.

29 For an overview of the racial politics animating the Holiness and Pentecostal movements, see Butler, "Peculiar Synergy," 35–38; Taylor, *Black Churches of Brooklyn*, 38–47.

 In their search for authentic religion in the 1890s, Mason and Jones helped give new meaning to the ecstatic worship that had prevailed among slaves. As they studied the Bible closely, these men placed slave worship practices within the context of early Christianity and found support in the discipline and heartfelt religion of the Holiness movement. A decade later when Holiness spawned Pentecostalism, Mason and Jones forged separate denominations. The rudiments of solo gospel took shape in the black Pentecostal denomination Mason helped launch. The Church of God in Christ made inroads for the music by emphasizing the importance of spiritual gifts and making individual testimonies a critical part of worship practice. See Horace Boyer, *How Sweet the Sound*, 18–26.

30 For discussion of black working-class domination of Holiness and Pentecostal churches, see Frazier, *Negro Church in America*, 54–71; Spear, *Black Chicago*, 174–79. On specific churches, see Osofsky, *Harlem*, 144–46; Sernett, *Bound for the Promised Land*, 95; Spitzer, *Saint's Paradise*; Sutherland, "Analysis of Negro Churches in Chicago," 8, 88–91; Synan, *Holiness-Pentecostal Movement in the United States*, 136–37. On the growth of the Church of God in Christ, see "Fastest-Growing Church." While the vast majority of the black working class affiliated themselves with Baptist churches, a number of contemporary scholars and social commentators took note of the proliferation of Holiness and Pentecostal churches taking shape, particularly in cities. See Frazier, *Negro Church in America*, 60–71; Mays and Nicholson, *Negro's Church*, 198–229; Sernett, *Bound for the Promised Land*, 191; Sutherland, "Analysis of Negro Churches in Chicago," 56.

 Precisely when and how the term "sanctified church" emerged to refer to black Holiness and Pentecostal churches remains an unanswered question. The term originally had a pejorative meaning. For example, many contemporary sociologists and religious scholars dismissed the "sanctified" as members of "cults" rather than respectable churches. For an insightful discussion of this pattern, see Sernett, *Bound for the Promised Land*, 180–98. When sociologist Cheryl Townsend

Gilkes engaged the term in a 1985 article, she helped remove "sanctified church" from its pejorative context by carefully explaining that the term referred to a "significant but misunderstood segment of a very pluralistic black church"; see Gilkes, "'Together and in Harness,'" 678–79.

31 For a discussion of how these restrictive and innovative aspects of worship unfolded in Brooklyn, see Taylor, *Black Churches of Brooklyn*, 53–65.

32 As quoted in Patricia Wells, "Historical Overview of the Establishment of the Church of God in Christ," 89.

33 Richard Cohen described the culture around dress permeating the Church of God in Christ community in which he grew up; see Cohen interview, 22 January 1992.

34 Quoted in Pleas, *Fifty Years of Achievement*, 2.

35 Bartleman, *Azusa Street*, 72.

36 Horace Boyer interview.

37 Oliver interview.

38 Mason, *History and Life Work of Bishop C. H. Mason*, 49.

39 Powdermaker, *After Freedom*, 254.

40 For an insightful discussion about testifying as part of a holy encounter, see Hinson, *Fire in My Bones*, 14–20.

41 Levine, *Black Culture and Black Consciousness*, 180.

42 Cornelius, *Pioneer*, 69.

43 Nelson, McIntorsh, and Johnson, *Memphis Gospel* (CD reissue).

44 On observation of T-Bone Walker, see Hentoff, *Hear Me Talkin' to You*, 249–51. On blues as an existential experience, see Murray, *Stomping the Blues*, 3–76; Neal, "Ethos of the Blues." On gospel as transcendence, see Hinson, *Fire in My Bones*, 1–8.

45 Handy, *Father of the Blues*, 9, 12, 11, 10.

46 The following histories of the denomination contain anecdotes about music as religious experience: Cornelius, *Pioneer*; Pleas, *Fifty Years of Achievement*.

47 The tremendous growth of the Church of God in Christ suggests that these religious practices appealed to more and more people as the twentieth century wore on. See "Fastest-Growing Church."

CHAPTER 2

1 Richard Cohen recalled the story Tharpe frequently told to friends; see Cohen interview, 22 January 1992. Most gospel scholars regard Tharpe as an aberration

from other gospel singers, rather than as a pioneer; for these discussions, see Horace Boyer, "Contemporary Gospel Music," 7; Heilbut, *Gospel Sound*, 187–89, 203.

For a broad discussion of the growth of urban spaces of amusement in American society, see Erenberg, *Steppin' Out*; Kasson, *Amusing the Million*; May, *Screening Out the Past*; Peiss, *Cheap Amusements*.

2 For a broad overview of women in the sanctified church, see Butler, "Peculiar Synergy," 35–64, 98–151; Gilkes, "Role of Women in the Sanctified Church"; Gilkes, "'Together and in Harness.'"

3 On the role women played in the Baptist churches, see Higginbotham, *Righteous Discontent*. On the role women played in the Church of God in Christ, see Cornelius, *Pioneer*.

4 Tharpe, *Eighteen Original Negro Spirituals*.

5 According to Social Security records, Rosetta Tharpe was born in 1915 in Cotton Plant, Arkansas. In 1995 I traveled to Cotton Plant and met Sam Scott, who recalled that Tharpe and her mother resided on the Cooperwood plantation. The tristate region that included Mississippi, Arkansas, and Tennessee was a stronghold for the development of a number of Holiness and Pentecostal denominations and congregations, including Assemblies of God as well as the Church of God in Christ. See Synan, *Holiness-Pentecostal Movement in the United States*, 135–39.

James Boyer, who grew up in the Church of God in Christ and whose parents joined the denomination during the early 1920s, recalled that Katie Bell Nubin, or Mother Nubin as she was known in sanctified circles, enjoyed a reputation as "one of the most dynamic evangelist missionaries that the Church of God in Christ has ever had" (James Boyer interview).

6 James Boyer, who pursued gospel during his teenage years, generously supplied materials on Sister Rosetta Tharpe that he had in his collection. These materials included playbills announcing her appearances; the playbill cited comes from a 1950 service.

7 A number of friends and acquaintances of Rosetta Tharpe recalled that Katie Bell Nubin was protective of her daughter; see Cohen interview, 22 January 1992; Hamilton interview.

8 Several blues scholars point out that musicians who were active during the 1910s played mandolin; see Bastin, *Red River Blues*, 16–19; Evans, *Big Road Blues*, 184, 187, 194–95.

9 Cohen interview, 22 January 1992.

10 Hubbard interview.

11 Campbell interview.

12 Tharpe, *Gospel Truth* (live recording).

13 Mays and Nicholson, *Negro's Church*, 101. For a broad discussion of the new outlooks and sensibilities African Americans embraced in the urban districts and neighborhoods where they resided, see Cohen, *Making a New Deal*, 147–58; Hunter, *To 'Joy My Freedom*, 145–86; Earl Lewis, *In Their Own Interests*, 89–109; Locke, *New Negro*, 3–16; Murray; *Stomping the Blues*, 23–42.

14 Blakeny interview.

15 Horace Boyer interview.

16 Quoted in Sutherland, "Analysis of Negro Churches in Chicago," 117.

17 Fenton Johnson, "Negro Churches (Denominational)," Works Progress Administration, Illinois Writers' Project, box 016, Harsh Collection.

18 Cohen interview, 29 January 1992.

19 For an insightful discussion of religious plurality among African Americans, see Gilkes, "'Some Folks Get Happy and Some Folks Don't.'"

20 Higginbotham, *Righteous Discontent*, 211–20, 150–84.

21 Cornelius, *Pioneer*, 22.

22 Cohen interview, 29 January 1992.

23 Butler, "Peculiar Synergy," 35–64; Cornelius, *Pioneer*, 22; Gilkes, "'Together and in Harness.'"

24 Cornelius, *Pioneer*, 22.

25 Cohen interview, 29 January 1992.

26 Knight interview, 14 November 1996.

27 Cohen interview, 29 January 1992.

28 Cornelius, *Pioneer*, 68.

29 Quoted in Patricia Wells, "Historical Overview of the Establishment of the Church of God in Christ," 93.

30 *Souvenir Program*, Thompson collection.

31 Campbell interview.

32 For an overview of the new urban institutions African Americans built, see Hazzard-Gordon, *Jookin*, 76–119; Hunter, *To 'Joy My Freedom*; Reid, "Mrs. Bailey Pays the Rent." For a discussion of how churches responded to these developments, see Higginbotham, *Righteous Discontent*. Another incisive discussion of these issues can be found in the forthcoming UNC dissertation by Angela Hornsby, "'Cast Down but Not Out': Black Manhood and Uplift in North Carolina, 1900–1930"; see chap. 2.

33 Blakeny interview.

34 Roberts and Spearmon interview; James Boyer interview.

35 Oliver interview.

36 *Souvenir Program*, Thompson collection.

37 The documentary *Say Amen Somebody!* includes a fruitful discussion of the challenges travel posed for married women; see Nierenberg, *Say Amen Somebody!*

38 Harley, "'When Your Work Is Not Who You Are,'" 29–30. In her study of black female domestics Tera W. Hunter points out that dancing and dance halls offered a vital antidote to the backbreaking labor these women performed; see Hunter, *To 'Joy My Freedom*, 168–86.

39 *Souvenir Program*, Thompson collection.

40 A discussion of urban commercial strips can be found in Hunter, *To 'Joy My Freedom*; Powdermaker, *After Freedom*.

41 DuPree, *Biographical Dictionary*, 8.

42 Campbell interview.

43 Ibid.; Williams interview.

44 Jay interview.

45 Campbell interview.

46 Knight interview, 20 March 1997.

47 Oliver interview.

48 Cornelius, *Pioneer*, 22.

49 *Souvenir Program*, Thompson collection; Malcolm Shaw, "Arizona Dranes and Okeh."

50 DuPree, *Biographical Dictionary*, 8.

51 Quoted in Garon and Garon, *Woman with Guitar*, 15.

52 Hubbard interview.

53 Campbell interview.

54 Barlow, *"Looking up at Down*," 29–32; Evans, *Big Road Blues*, 25–27. Like Tharpe, independent evangelists such as Rev. Gary Davis and Blind Willie Johnson, who moved to city streets to rescue the unregenerate, adopted a picking style that helped extend the vocal line and bring a more dynamic quality to performance. The overlap between sacred music and blues demonstrates the shared cultural terrain in which evangelists, missionaries, and blues musicians operated. See Oliver, *Songsters and Saints*, 206–17.

55 A discussion of the impact of recording technology on the production of music can be found in Attali, *Noise*; Frith, *Music for Pleasure*.

56 Malone, *Country Music, U.S.A.*, 34.

57 Quoted in Foreman, "Jazz and Race Records," 58.

58 Ibid., 56–58.

59 Quoted in ibid., 138.

60 Quoted in Lieb, *Mother of the Blues*, 23.

61 A discussion of the physical appearance and sexual assertion of blueswomen can be found in Carby, "It Jus Be's Dat Way Sometimes"; Carby, "In Body and Spirit"; Harrison, *Black Pearls*.

62 As quoted in Lieb, *Mother of the Blues*, 8.

63 For an overview of race recordings, see Dixon and Goodrich, *Recording the Blues*.

64 Speir, "Interview with H. C. Speir"; Melrose, "My Life in Recording."

65 Walker, "Who Chose These Records?," 11.

66 For a discussion of the recordings made by ministers, see Higginbotham, "Rethinking Vernacular Culture"; Oliver, *Songsters and Saints*, 141–228. The following sources offer a rich discussion of recordings made by gospel quartets: Lornell, *"Happy in the Service of the Lord,"* 1–4; Seroff, "On the Battlefield"; Tallmadge, *Jubilee to Gospel* (liner notes).

67 DuPree, *Biographical Dictionary*, 232.

68 Nelson, McIntorsh, and Johnson, *Memphis Gospel* (CD reissue).

69 Dranes, *Arizona Dranes* (CD reissue).

70 Ibid.

71 As quoted in Harris, *Rise of Gospel Blues*, 60.

72 Roberts and Spearmon interview.

73 For a discussion of the influence of Dranes on Tharpe, see Heilbut, *Gospel Sound*, 191.

74 Malcolm Shaw, "Arizona Dranes and Okeh."

75 I am especially indebted to Malcolm Shaw for the generosity he extended by sharing with me copies of the correspondence between Dranes and recording company personnel, Consolidated Talking Machine Co., to Arizona J. Dranes, 20 July 1926, Shaw collection.

76 Malcolm Shaw, "Arizona Dranes & Okeh," 85–86.

77 Malcolm Shaw, "Arizona Dranes & Okeh."

78 Ibid.

CHAPTER 3

1 The following sources provide an overview of Martin's life, music, and career: Horace Boyer, *How Sweet the Sound*, 62–64; Heilbut, *Gospel Sound*, 21–35. On her music, see Sallie Martin Singers/Cora Martin, *Throw Out the Lifeline* (CD reissue).

2 Horace Boyer, *How Sweet the Sound*, 62–64.

3 Bontemps, "Rock, Church, Rock!"

4 A number of gospel scholars have given attention to Thomas Andrew Dorsey; see Horace Boyer, "Thomas A. Dorsey, 'Father of Gospel Music'"; Harris, *Rise of Gospel Blues*; Heilbut, *Gospel Sound*, 21–35.

The most extensive treatment of Dorsey to date comes from Harris, *Rise of Gospel Blues*. This insightful study examines some of the intellectual forces that spawned gospel music. Focusing on Dorsey, Harris maintains that the popularity the composer generated for gospel transformed the music into a new mode of religious expression that resolved long-standing tensions among African Americans over appropriate worship. I argue that even as it enjoyed increasing popularity, gospel continued to provoke conflicts over the meaning of religion. While Harris focuses on the inroads Dorsey made for the music in mainline churches, I emphasize the commercial inroads the composer made for gospel in local black communities.

5 To appreciate the similarity between Dorsey's songs and music that reigned in sanctified circles, see Dorsey, *Georgia Tom (Thomas A. Dorsey)*, vol. 2 (CD reissue); Dranes, *Arizona Dranes* (CD reissue).

6 Horace Boyer, *How Sweet the Sound*, 63. See also Harris, *Rise of Gospel Blues*, 256–57.

7 For a broad discussion of entrepreneurial black capitalism, see Cohen, *Making a New Deal*, 148–49; Spear, *Black Chicago*, 192–200.

8 Dorsey seems to have acquired the title "Father of Gospel Music" at some point after 1945, since throughout the 1930s and early 1940s he promoted himself as "America's Foremost Gospel Songwriter." In a 1975 interview Dorsey intimated that the title may have been inspired by the 1941 publication of blues composer W. C. Handy's autobiography, appropriately titled *Father of the Blues*. See Dorsey, "Living Blues Interview," 30. See also Handy, *Father of the Blues*.

The NCGCC warrants a full-scale investigation; however, much of the existing literature on the organization often gets subsumed under Dorsey. For information on the NCGCC, see Horace Boyer, "Thomas A. Dorsey," 24; Harris, *Rise of Gospel Blues*, 211–15, 267–71; Heilbut, *Gospel Sound*, 29–30; Smith, *Life and Works of Thomas Andrew Dorsey*, 7, 19, 38–45, Blues Archive, University of Mississippi; Ricks, *Some Aspects of the Religious Music of the United States Negro*, 137–38. For a noteworthy exception to this pattern, see Nierenberg's film *Say Amen Somebody!*

Gospel scholars typically designate the NCGCC as part of a gospel choral tradition. For insightful background on the gospel choral movement, see "Classic Gospel Song," 12–19, National Museum of American History, Smithsonian Institution, Washington, D.C.

9 Dorsey, *Songs with a Message*, 13, Work Collection, Fisk University.

10 Dorsey, "On His 75th Anniversary," 10.

11 As quoted in Harris, *Rise of Gospel Blues*, 31.

12 Dorsey, "Living Blues Interview," 20.

13 Dorsey, *Songs with a Message*, 20, Work Collection, Fisk University. In his autobiography and subsequent interviews, Thomas Dorsey mentioned his tenure at the Chicago College of Composition and Arranging. See Dorsey, "Living Blues Interview," 18; Dorsey, *Songs with a Message*, 16, Work Collection, Fisk University.

   For a discussion of the commercial possibilities that opened up in blues and the musicians who practiced the music, see Abbott and Seroff, "'They Cert'ly Sound Good to Me'"; Foreman, "Jazz and Race Records."

14 Quoted in Harris, *Rise of Gospel Blues*, 94.

15 Dorsey, *Songs with a Message*, 24, Work Collection, Fisk University. For an extensive discussion of this spiritual crisis, see Harris, *Rise of Gospel Blues*, 93–96.

16 Harris, *Rise of Gospel Blues*, xvii–xxiii, 68–78.

17 For a discussion of men in gospel who preceded Dorsey, see Horace Boyer, "Charles Albert Tindley."

18 On the evolution of Pilgrim Baptist Church, see A. Williams and E. Jennings, "Black Churches in Chicago, Pilgrim Baptist Church," Works Progress Administration, Illinois Writers' Project, box 016, Harsh Collection. The architecture of the 1921 structure is vividly described in Historic American Buildings Survey, 1964, File: HABS No. ILL-1054, "Kehilath Anshe Ma'Ariv Synagogue (Now Pilgrim Baptist Church)," Prints and Photographs Division, Library of Congress, Washington, D.C.

19 Harris provides an insightful discussion of the changes Junius Austin put in place at Pilgrim. Harris points out that Austin's behavior stemmed from his perception of the church as a social service agency. See Harris, *Rise of Gospel Blues*, 180–208. For additional information on Austin, see Burkett, *Black Redemption*, 113–20.

20 Isbelle interview.

21 Quoted in Harris, *Rise of Gospel Blues*, 199.

22 Isbelle interview.

23 As quoted in Harris, *Rise of Gospel Blues*, 197.

24 Dorsey, "On His 75th Anniversary," 6.

25 Harris, *Rise of Gospel Blues*, 182–83.

26 Dorsey summarizes these activities in Dorsey, *Songs with a Message*, 27–28, Work Collection, Fisk University. Harris discusses these issues at great length; see Harris, *Rise of Gospel Blues*, 241–71.

27 Isbelle interview.
28 Smith, *Life and Works of Thomas Andrew Dorsey*, 38, Blues Archive, University of Mississippi; Williams-Jones, *Classic Gospel Song*. In the program notes for a 1985 conference on gospel music, gospel scholar Pearl Williams-Jones pointed out that the gospel choirs and choruses that began to flourish in the 1930s sparked a "widespread Dorsey diaspora of gospel music."
29 Williams-Jones, *Classic Gospel Song*. Dr. Mary Wilks, who joined the convention during the 1940s and remains active, described the NCGCC as "a community organization which provided an opportunity for us to develop our talents and skills." See Wilks interview.
30 As quoted in Heilbut, *Gospel Sound*, 8.
31 "Sallie Martin," *Ebony*, March 1986, 76, 78, 81.
32 National Convention of Gospel Choirs and Choruses, *Welcome to NCGCC*, 9, Grant collection.
33 Dorsey, "Living Blues Interview," 33. For an insightful discussion linking denominational control over sacred music among black Baptist churches to religious activism during the 1890s, see Harvey, *Redeeming the South*, 243–50. The activities of composer Lucie Campbell offer a rich source for examining the role hymnals played in the dissemination of sacred music during the 1910s and 1920s; see Horace Boyer, "Lucie E. Campbell." Describing how Dorsey transformed the dissemination of gospel, Anthony Heilbut observed that Dorsey built the infrastructure that fostered the development of a gospel music industry. Heilbut referred to that infrastructure as the "gospel highway"; see Heilbut, *Gospel Sound*, 21–35. Horace Boyer offers a more detailed analysis of how that process unfolded, in "Thomas A. Dorsey, 'Father of Gospel Music.'"

For a discussion of women who became active in gospel music publishing, see Reagon, "I'll Be a Servant for the Lord"; Williams-Jones, "Roberta Martin."
34 Despite his religious outlook, Dorsey was deeply influenced by the music industry. The groups he organized serve as an example of that influence. Organizing the groups to demonstrate his songs, Dorsey adopted a strategy, known as song plugging, that sheet music publishers had utilized for disseminating their materials. For a summary of the song plugging system as it evolved in the arena of popular music, see David Sanjek, "They Work Hard for Their Money." Looking at the influence of the music industry on Dorsey offers a rich vehicle for ascertaining how his religious outlook influenced his approach to gospel. Even as Dorsey adopted the song plugging system, his willingness to embark on an outmoded enterprise illustrates the innovative techniques he deployed. This perspective significantly differs from that of most scholars of gospel music, who emphasize the

inroads Dorsey made for gospel in the commercial arena without placing his initiatives in the context of the music industry. For a discussion of the cost of the economics of record production, see Sanjek and Sanjek, *American Popular Music Business in the 20th Century*, 20.

35 For a discussion of Dorsey's dominance in the gospel sheet music business during the early years, see Horace Boyer, "Thomas A. Dorsey, 'Father of Gospel Music.'"

36 See Wilks interview. The limited economic potential of sheet music would become more evident a decade later when growing numbers of small-scale entrepreneurs gained a foothold in the recording industry. Alluding to this development, gospel composer and publisher Kenneth Morris recalled that record companies, as well as xerox machines, posed increasing competition to his studio; see Reagon, "I'll Be a Servant for the Lord." For a discussion of the moneymaking pursuits of music publishers in popular music, see Sanjek, "They Work Hard for Their Money."

37 As quoted in de Lerma, *Reflections on African-American Music*, 192. Dorsey discussed the money he made from the song in Thomas A. Dorsey, Scrapbooks, December 1950, File: Guideposts, "From Bawdy Songs to Hymns," Schomburg Center for Research in Black Culture; Dorsey, *Songs with a Message*, 30, Work Collection, Fisk University.

38 Peeples interview.

39 Ricks, *Some Aspects of the Religious Music of the United States Negro*, 142–44; Williams-Jones, "Toward the Inclusion of Black American Gospel Music."

40 Smith, *Life and Works of Thomas Andrew Dorsey*, 54–55, Blues Archive, University of Mississippi.

41 Ibid., 10–11.

42 George D. Lewis, "Spirituals of Today," Works Progress Administration, Illinois Writers' Project, box 051, Harsh Collection.

43 Dorsey, "Living Blues Interview," 30. The willingness to accord religious significance to syncopated rhythms seems to have also stemmed from ministerial opposition Dorsey and his colleagues encountered. In a 1974 interview Dorsey recalled how that opposition revolved around the form that religious articulations ought to take. "You can't sing no gospel," Dorsey recalled the ministers saying, "You can only preach it." See Dorsey, "On His 75th Anniversary," 5.

44 W. R. F. Browning, ed., *A Dictionary of the Bible* (New York: Oxford University Press, 1996).

45 Dorsey, *Professor Thomas Andrew Dorsey* (LP).

46 Isbelle interview.

47 For an insightful discussion of how African American cultural leaders engage ethnic ties, specifically, their African past, to refute notions of black inferiority, see Jackson, "Melville Herskovits and the Search for Afro-American Culture."

48 Dorsey, *Songs with a Message*, Work Collection, Fisk University. For an alternative interpretation of the movement for expressive worship, see Harvey, *Redeeming the South*, 127–32. In his provocative study of religious culture among southern Baptists, black and white, Harvey sees Dorsey's songs as the articulation of a "new sensibility about African American sacred music" that began in the 1920s with the emergence of denominational hymnals and songbooks such as *Gospel Pearls*. This interpretation, while insightful, sidesteps the fierce controversies sacred music provoked among African Americans.

49 George D. Lewis, "Spirituals of Today," Works Progress Administration, Illinois Writers' Project, box 051, Harsh Collection.

50 Dorsey, *Songs with a Message*, 70, Work Collection, Fisk University. Harris astutely points out that the absence of biblical scriptures in Dorsey's autobiography as well as his music signals the emergence of a new religious sensibility; see *Rise of Gospel Blues*, 209–71.

51 Thomas A. Dorsey sheet music, Music Division, Library of Congress.

52 Thomas A. Dorsey, Scrapbooks, December 1950, File: Guideposts, "From Bawdy Songs to Hymns," Schomburg Center for Research in Black Culture; Dorsey, *Songs with a Message*, Work Collection, Fisk University.

53 Dranes, *Arizona Dranes* (CD reissue); Oliver, *Songsters and Saints*, 189–90.

54 Paris et al., *Guitar Evangelists* (CD reissue); Oliver, *Songsters and Saints*, 193.

CHAPTER 4

1 For a reflection on Tharpe's appearance at the Cotton Club and the enthusiasm she generated, see George D. Lewis, "Spirituals of Today," Works Progress Administration, Illinois Writers' Project, box 051, Harsh Collection; Leighla W. Lewis, "Sister Tharpe Swings Hymns at Cotton Club."

2 "Singer Swings Same Songs in Church and Night Club."

3 Allgood, "Black Gospel in New York City," 105–7; Broughton, *Black Gospel*, 61–90. Sister Rosetta Tharpe has puzzled scholars who attribute her nightclub appearances to her move from gospel into jazz. See Horace Boyer, "Contemporary Gospel Music," 7; Horace Boyer, *How Sweet the Sound*, 154–57; Zolten, *Great God A'mighty!*, 69, 142–43. This analysis, which hinges on her reputation rather than her activities, overlooks how her appearances helped carve out a place for gospel in commercial culture.

4 Historians have placed the esteemed reputation that the Cotton Club enjoyed among white elites during the 1920s as part of an emerging fascination with Harlem and African Americans more generally. For example, see Osofsky, *Harlem*, 29–41; Van Vechten, "Negro 'Blues' Singers."

5 Monroe, "Top Notchers at Broadway's Spot"; Leighla W. Lewis, "Sister Tharpe Swings Hymns at Cotton Club."

6 Leighla W. Lewis, "Sister Tharpe Swings Hymns at Cotton Club." Jazz singer Ethel Waters provides an insightful discussion of her trajectory from commercial venues where blacks congregated to nightspots patronized by whites. See Waters, *His Eye Is on the Sparrow*, 121–82.

7 Leighla W. Lewis, "Sister Tharpe Swings Hymns at Cotton Club."

8 The following articles detail the array of nightclub appearances Tharpe made subsequent to her debut at the Cotton Club: Clipping File, Sister Rosetta Tharpe, "Paramount, N.Y.," *Variety*, 7 December 1938, and "Circle, Indpls.," *Variety*, 8 November 1939, Billy Rose Theater Collection. For an overview of Tharpe's career and the recordings she made, see Reitz, *Sincerely Sister Rosetta Tharpe* (liner notes).

9 "Singer Swings Same Songs in Church and Night Club."

10 For a discussion of the "From Spirituals to Swing" concerts, see Barnett Collection, 296, File: 11–28 December 1938, "Meade Lux Lewis Steals Spirituals to Swing Concert at Carnegie Hall," Chicago Historical Society; Hammond, *John Hammond on Record*, 199–210; *From Spirituals to Swing* (CD reissue); Scrapbooks, Music and Musicians, vol. 6, File: "From Spirituals to Swing," *Daily Worker*, 14 December 1939, Schomburg Center for Research in Black Culture; Howard Taubman, "Negro Music Given at Carnegie Hall," *New York Times*, 24 December 1938. On Tharpe's tenure at the Café Society, see "Study in Smiles," *Afro-American* 5 October 1940; Scrapbooks, Music and Musicians, vol. 6, File: "Sister Tharpe Outstanding in Cotton Club Revue," *New York Sun*, 11 May 1940, Schomburg Center for Research in Black Culture.

11 For a broad overview of the emergence of music as commerce, see Attali, *Noise*. Commercialization was not a uniform process but differed from music style to music style. For a discussion of the commercialization of music in jazz, see Hennessey, *From Jazz to Swing*, 122–39; Stowe, *Swing Changes*, 94–140.

12 For a discussion of how this process unfolded in jazz and the growing authority managers assumed, see Hennessey, *From Jazz to Swing*, 9–12, 127–30.

13 Lears, introduction to *Culture of Consumption*, ix–xiii.

14 Sanjek and Sanjek, *American Popular Music Business in the 20th Century*, 7–9; Snyder, *Voice of the City*, 26–41.

15 For a discussion of consolidation in jazz, see Hennessey, *From Jazz to Swing*, 122–39; Stowe, *Swing Changes*, 94–100.

16 Scott DeVeaux links consolidation of the music industry to the popularity of swing and points out that these developments ultimately had a detrimental impact on black musicians, pushing many to the margins of the band business. See DeVeaux, *Birth of Bebop*, 116–57.

17 For a discussion of Irving Mills, see Hennessey, *From Jazz to Swing*, 123–27. See also Calloway and Rollins, *Of Minnie the Moocher and Me*, 110–11; Collier, *Duke Ellington*, 64–74; DeVeaux, *Birth of Bebop*, 122; Feather, "Mills."

18 The Jim Crow policy maintained at the Cotton Club tarnished the reputation the club enjoyed among African Americans. Nevertheless, the nightclub gradually emerged as the artery of black entertainment. According to Jim Haskins, the critical turning point came in 1927 when Duke Ellington's band became the club's house band. Their arrival led the Columbia radio network to begin broadcasting nightly sessions from the Cotton Club across the country. With the arrival of the Ellington band, the Cotton Club began to gain a degree of respect among jazz musicians, black as well as white. For a discussion of these developments, see Haskins, *Cotton Club*, 44–59. See also Ellington, *Music Is My Mistress*; 75–80. The arrival of Ellington combined with the radio broadcasts also accounts for the extensive press coverage the nightclub received. Entertainment pages of black newspapers and the trade press covered the opening of the club's seasonal revues. For the role Irving Mills played in transforming the Cotton Club into an artery of black entertainment, see Feather, "Mills."

19 Leighla A. Lewis, "Sister Tharpe Swings Hymns at Cotton Club."

20 Knight interview, 14 November 1996. On Tharpe's sheet music collection, see Tharpe, *Eighteen Original Negro Spirituals*. As an example of the luminaries who worked with Tharpe, see Zolotow, "Harlem's Great White Father," 68.

21 Tharpe, *Eighteen Original Negro Spirituals*.

22 Precisely how or even when the slogan "spirituals in swing" emerged remains unknown. Decca Records invoked the slogan at least by 1941 when it released an album of Tharpe's 78 rpm recordings. Yet the slogan may have been in circulation at least one year earlier when the trade press coined a similar term, "swinging spirituals," to describe Tharpe's music. See *Lonesome Road* (liner notes); Clipping File, Sister Rosetta Tharpe, "Cotton Club, N.Y.," *Variety*, 8 May 1940, Billy Rose Theater Collection. The slogan may have initially been invented by managers and promoters working with swing bands, since several bands began integrating spirituals into their repertoires during this period. For a discussion of these efforts and the controversy they unleashed, see Chapter 5.

23 Knight interview, 20 March 1997.

24 Ibid., 14 November 1996.

25 For an overview of the corporate culture in which Tharpe worked, see Kenney, *Recorded Music in American Life*, 158–81. In his insightful analysis of the recording business, William Kenney points out that a "hit record culture" began to permeate the industry in the wake of the Great Depression, giving rise to multimedia consolidations and an increasing interest in profit. According to Kenney, this new culture prevailed at Decca, where Tharpe recorded.

26 Clipping File, Sister Rosetta Tharpe, "Paramount, N.Y.," *Variety*, 7 December 1938, Billy Rose Theater Collection. For a discussion of racial conventions, see Huggins, *Harlem Renaissance*, 286–301. For a discussion of gender conventions, see Dahl, *Stormy Weather*, 124–35; Erenberg, *Steppin' Out*, 206–30; Stowe, *Swing Changes*, 167–79.

27 Lionel Hampton, "Swing," *Washington Afro-American*, 21 October 1940.

28 Ibid.

29 Leighla W. Lewis, "Sister Tharpe Swings Hymns at Cotton Club."

30 Quoted in Harris, *Rise of Gospel*, 87.

31 Dorsey, "Living Blues Interview," 27.

32 Knight interview, 14 November 1996.

33 Clipping File, Sister Rosetta Tharpe, "Apollo, N.Y.," *Variety*, 19 July 1939, Billy Rose Theater Collection.

34 Gabler conversation; Price, *What Do They Want?*, 50–52.

35 These guitar evangelists and gospel soloists included Elder Beck, Rev. Johnny Blakey, Elder Bryant, Elder Curry, Arizona Dranes, Elder Edwards, Sister Cally Fancy, Jessie Mae Hill, Bessie Johnson, Blind Willie Johnson, Mother McCollum, Rev. F. W. McGee, Lonnie McIntorsh, and Washington Phillips. See Curry and Beck, *Elder Curry and Elder Beck* (CD reissue); Blind Willie Johnson, *Complete Blind Willie Johnson* (CD reissue); Washington Phillips, *I Am Born to Preach the Gospel* (CD reissue).

36 For a broad discussion of open vocals and the willingness to make calculated use of textured vocals, see Horace Boyer, "Contemporary Gospel Music."

37 Dranes, *Arizona Dranes* (CD reissue).

38 Washington Phillips, *I Am Born to Preach the Gospel* (CD reissue).

39 Tharpe, *Sister Rosetta Tharpe*, vol. 1 (CD reissue).

40 Ibid.

41 Ibid.

42 Heilbut, *Gospel Sound*, 189–96.

43 Reitz, *Sincerely Sister Rosetta Tharpe* (liner notes); Clipping File, Sister Rosetta

Tharpe, "Paramount, N.Y.," *Variety*, 7 December 1938, and "Apollo, N.Y.," *Variety*, 19 July 1939, Billy Rose Theater Collection.

44 Tharpe, *Sister Rosetta Tharpe*, vol. 2 (CD reissue).

45 Lyles interview.

46 Dorsey, "Golden Years of Music," Dorsey Collection, Fisk University.

47 Thomas A. Dorsey sheet music, Music Division, Library of Congress.

48 Tharpe, *Sister Rosetta Tharpe*, vol. 1 (CD reissue).

49 Tharpe, *Sister Rosetta Tharpe*, vol. 2 (CD reissue).

50 While scholars readily acknowledge that gospel music flourished in urban neighborhoods, fewer use the music to explore the changing meaning of religion. See Frazier, *Negro Church in America*, 52–85; Harris, *Rise of Gospel Blues*, 180–208; Levine, *Black Culture and Black Consciousness*, 161–81. For an alternative analysis that engages gospel to explore continuities, rather than changes, in religion, see Hinson, *Fire in My Bones*, 14–20.

51 The intense rhythms she infused into her singing would have permitted Tharpe to transition into jazz with its emphasis on syncopation. In a 1996 interview Marie Knight described Tharpe as a "rhythm singer" and recalled the influence of rhythm on her approach to music. Speaking of Tharpe, Knight explained that "the rhythm was just all over her. Rosetta could sit down without playing music and that rhythm would go to work and get started. Now she wasn't that long, sad, drawn-out singer." See Knight interview, 14 November 1996. In the 1950s a British journalist, on interviewing Tharpe, insisted that she was a jazz singer. Pointing to her gospel roots, Tharpe used the interview to inform the journalist that rhythm assumed a critical place in early gospel music. See "Rosetta Tharpe Says I've Never Been a Jazz Singer."

52 "Night Club Soulsaver," *Afro-American*, 11 January 1941.

53 Leighla W. Lewis, "Sister Tharpe Swings Hymns at Cotton Club."

54 Jay interview.

55 On the pervasiveness of material values and consumerism in American society, see Benson, *Counter Cultures*, 17–48; Lears, introduction to *Culture of Consumption*, ix–xvii; Strasser, *Satisfaction Guaranteed* 15–28; Susman, *Culture as History*, xix–xxx, 271–85. The emergence of celebrity culture with its emphasis on personality also marks the rise of material values; see Lowenthal, *Literature, Popular Culture, and Society*, 106–40; May, *Screening out the Past*, 190–99; Ponce de Leon, "Idols and Icons," 1–72. A discussion of the role of consumerism among the working class and especially African Americans can be found in Cohen, *Making a New Deal*, 147–58. While much of the scholarship on blues emphasizes the

popularity the music enjoyed and how it inspired a distinctive aesthetic and outlook, this literature implicitly demonstrates the place consumer values assumed
in blues culture. For an example of how blues singers endorsed consumerism as
an ideal, see Harrison, *Black Pearls*, 3–15.

56 Leighla W. Lewis, "Sister Tharpe Swings Hymns at Cotton Club."

57 National Convention of Gospel Choirs and Choruses, *Welcome to NCGCC*, Grant
collection; Mason, *History and Life Work of Bishop C. H. Mason*; Pleas, *Fifty Years
of Achievement*.

58 Cohen interview, 22 January 1992.

59 Scrapbooks, Music and Musicians, vol. 6, File: "Sister Tharpe Gets Reprimand
from Her Husband for Not Wearing Hat," *New York Sun*, 5 September 1939,
Schomburg Center for Research in Black Culture. Richard Cohen identified the
minister appearing in the *Life* magazine photograph as Bishop O. M. Kelley; see
Cohen interview, 29 January 1992.

60 Cohen interview, 22 January 1992.

61 Ibid.

62 Ibid.

63 Calhoun, "Woman on the Go for God"; Cornelius, *Pioneer*, 23–27.

64 Cohen interview, 22 January 1992.

65 Zolotow, "Harlem's Great White Father," 40.

66 Knight interview, 20 March 1997.

67 Price, *What Do They Want?*, 52.

CHAPTER 5

1 "Is It Sinful to Swing the Hymns?," *Cleveland Call and Post*, 3 November 1956.

2 Ibid.

3 Focusing on educational institutions, several scholars offer an insightful perspective on the struggle of gospel to gain legitimacy: Horace Boyer, "Defining, Researching, and Teaching Gospel Music"; Williams-Jones, "Toward the Inclusion
of Black American Gospel Music." While scholars of gospel typically agree that
the music gained considerable appeal after 1945, Michael Harris insists that widespread acceptance of gospel began in the 1930s, almost a decade earlier. To demonstrate how the music gained acceptance, Harris examines the controversy that
plagued gospel during the 1920s. Yet since his study ends in 1937, Harris does not
explore the new controversies surrounding gospel in the postwar era. See *Rise of
Gospel Blues*, esp. 241–71.

4 For insightful discussions of the impact of commercial investment on gospel, see Kelley, "Notes on the Political Economy of Black Music"; Maultsby "Impact of Gospel Music on the Secular Music Industry."

5 Most scholars have overlooked the transformation of the NCGCC because they often focus on Thomas Dorsey, who served as president, rather than the organization itself. As a result, some scholars attribute emphasis on preservation and training especially to the influence of Dorsey. For an example of this pattern, see "Classic Gospel Song," 12–19, National Museum of American History, Smithsonian Institution, Washington, D.C. While the composer certainly recognized the importance of training, Dorsey was initially more focused on expanding, not preserving, gospel music.

6 Horace Boyer, "Contemporary Gospel Music," 5–11.

7 Nelson George, *Death of Rhythm and Blues*, 15–58; Lornell, *"Happy in the Service of the Lord,"* 166–77. For a broad discussion of the transformation of the music industry during the postwar era, see Sanjek, "They Work Hard for Their Money," 9–15.

8 Horace Boyer, *How Sweet the Sound*, 51–54; Lornell, *"Happy in the Service of the Lord,"* 177–85. For a broad and insightful discussion of radio, see Savage, *Broadcasting Freedom*, esp. 1–12. Savage points out that during the 1930s, the heyday of national radio, networks featured mostly stereotypical images of African Americans. Focusing on public affairs programs, she shows how African Americans during the 1930s and 1940s used radio to mount a national debate on racial equality.

9 Horace Boyer, *How Sweet the Sound*, 51–54.

10 Lyles interview.

11 Ibid.

12 My thoughts on the place of radio in African American life have been enriched by scholars of rock 'n' roll who discuss the influence of radio on white teenagers. For example, see Cantor, *Wheelin' on Beale*, 154–72; Pielke, *You Say You Want a Revolution*, 63–80.

13 Jay interview.

14 Allgood, "Black Gospel in New York City," 105–6; Horace Boyer, *How Sweet the Sound*, 51–54; Ruth interview, 30 September 1996; Ruth, *Gospel*.

15 Knight interview, 20 March 1997. The abbreviation "JA" refers to M. Jacqui Alexander, who helped conduct the oral histories with Minister Knight.

16 Allgood, "Black Gospel in New York City," 105–6.

17 "Feld Brothers Made Good, Get Amphitheater 3 Years," *Evening Star*, 30 December 1954; "The Feld Brothers: What They Like, You Buy—And That's Show-

biz," *Washington Post*, 4 February 1968; "Irvin Feld—the Greatest Showman on Earth?," *Washington Star*, 18 September 1980; "Tips on Tables," *Washington Daily News*, 12 September 1951, all in Washingtonian Collection.

18 "15,000 Attend Sister Tharpe's Wedding," *Richmond Afro-American*, 14 July 1951; "20,000 Watch Wedding of Sister Rosetta Tharpe"; "Colorful Ceremony Performed Outdoors," *Washington Afro-American*, 7 July 1951; "Public to Pay to See Super-Duper Wedding of Sister R. Tharpe," *New York Amsterdam News*, 30 June 1951.

19 Hildebrand and Nations, *Great 1955 Shrine Concert* (liner notes).

20 Black, "How Black Churches Became a School for Singing Stars," 70; Guralnick, *Sam Cooke's SAR Records Story* (liner notes); Hepburn, "Big Bonanza in Gospel Music."

21 Horace Boyer, *How Sweet the Sound*, 83–91; Heilbut, *Gospel Sound*, 67–71.

22 Horace Boyer, *How Sweet the Sound*, 105–11; "Glamour Girl of Gospel Singers"; Ruth, "Thermon Ruth and the Selah Jubilee Singers."

23 Cohen interview, 22 January 1992.

24 George D. Lewis, "Spirituals of Today," Works Progress Administration, Illinois Writers' Project, box 051, Harsh Collection.

25 Cohen interview, 22 January 1992.

26 *Rigler and Deutsch 78 RPM Index*, Motion Picture, Broadcasting, and Recorded Sound Division, Library of Congress. For illustrative examples of these musicians at work, see Armstrong, *Gospel According to Louis* (CD reissue); Teagarden, *Swing Low, Sweet Spiritual* (LP).

27 "Says Swinging Spiritual Is Disgrace to Race."

28 "Teachers, Song Writers and Choir Singers Join in Protest against Swinging Spirituals."

29 "Must Stop Desecration of Spirituals"; "Teachers, Song Writers and Choir Singers Join in Protest against Swinging Spirituals."

30 "Fight against Defilement of Negro Spirituals Continues."

31 Ibid.

32 "Dr. Harvey's Article on Insidious Evil of Swinging Spirituals Brings Many Letters."

33 "Says Swinging Spiritual Is Disgrace to Race."

34 "Teachers, Song Writers and Choir Singers Join in Protest against Swinging Spirituals."

35 "Says Swinging Spiritual Is Disgrace to Race."

36 Barnett Collection, 26, File: 9–11 September 1938, "Hot White Bands Hurting Colored Orchestras," Chicago Historical Society.

37 "Must Stop Desecration of Spirituals."
38 Lionel Hampton, "Swing," *Washington Afro-American*, 28 December 1940.
39 "Baptist Preacher Asks Pardon," *Pittsburgh Courier*, 25 March 1939.
40 "Fight against Defilement of Negro Spirituals Continues"; "Dr. Harvey's Article on Insidious Evil of Swinging Spirituals Brings Many Letters."
41 "Teachers, Song Writers and Choir Singers Join in Protest against Swinging Spirituals."
42 "Must Stop Desecration of Spirituals."
43 For a parallel development among white Americans, see Levine, *Highbrow/Lowbrow*, 104–41.
44 "Teachers, Song Writers and Choir Singers Join in Protest against Swinging Spirituals."
45 "Close-Ups of Chicago's Great Gospel Song Writer, Assistants, Studios," *Pittsburgh Courier*, 20 May 1939.
46 The mission statement is often featured in printed programs of the NCGCC annual meetings and is included in the organization's official by-laws. For an example of the printed programs, see National Convention of Gospel Choirs and Choruses, *Welcome to NCGCC*, Grant collection. Also see National Convention of Gospel Choirs and Choruses, *By-Laws and Constitution*, Berryman collection. The statement seems to have been drafted when the organization was incorporated in 1939.
47 Morris, *Improving the Music in the Church*. For discussion of the Sallie Martin Singers, see DjeDje, *Throw Out the Lifeline* (liner notes). For background information on the publishing studio Martin established with business partner Kenneth Morris, see Reagon, "I'll Be a Servant for the Lord," 332–33.
48 Thomas A. Dorsey sheet music, Music Division, Library of Congress.
49 As quoted in Ricks, *Some Aspects of the Religious Music of the United States Negro*, 149.
50 Quoted in Morris, *Improving the Music in the Church*, 51.
51 Ibid., 48–49.
52 Quoted in ibid., 48.
53 Knight interview, 20 March 1997.
54 Ibid.
55 *Sister Rosetta Tharpe*, vol. 3 (CD reissue). The popularity Knight and Tharpe enjoyed during the 1940s can be discerned from the pages of the *Amsterdam News*, a New York City–based African American newspaper. The paper's entertainment pages frequently featured news and celebrity gossip about these women.
56 Knight interview, 14 November 1996.

57 Ibid., 31 October 1984.

58 Ibid., 14 November 1996.

59 Ibid.

60 Ibid., 20 March 1997.

61 Ibid.

62 Ibid., 2 July 1997.

63 Grant interview.

64 Ibid.

65 Ibid.

66 Ibid.

67 Ibid.

68 Dorsey, "Living Blues Interview," 17.

69 Morris, *Improving the Music in the Church*, 43.

70 As quoted in Ricks, *Some Aspects of the Religious Music of the United States Negro*, 149.

71 Ruth interview, 30 September 1996.

72 Ruth, *Gospel*.

73 Broughton, *Black Gospel*, 91–107; Heilbut, *Gospel Sound*, 103–13; Hepburn, "Big Bonanza in Gospel Music"; Nierenberg, *Say Amen Somebody!*

74 Guralnick, *Sam Cooke's SAR Records Story* (liner notes), 3.

EPILOGUE

1 Romeo Eldridge Phillips, "Some Perceptions of Gospel Music," 167; Williams-Jones, "Toward the Inclusion of Black American Gospel Music," 30.

2 Guthrie P. Ramsey Jr., "Gospel with Its Eye on the Hip-Hop Generation," *New York Times*, 11 July 1999; Richard Harrington, "Yolanda Adams: Gospel Truths," *Washington Post*, 17 November 1999; Lynn Norment, "The Gospel Soul of Yolanda Adams," *Ebony*, August 2000, 42–44, 46.

3 Horace Boyer, "Defining, Researching, and Teaching Gospel Music," 36.

4 Baldwin, *Price of the Ticket*, 65.

5 Knight interview, 20 March 1997.

6 Jay interview; Bob Dawbarn, "Sister Rosetta Makes a Flying Start," *Melody Maker*, 30 November 1957, 6; "Rosetta Tharpe's British Tour," *Melody Maker*, 23 November 1957, 6; "Auction Sales," *Richmond Times-Dispatch*, 25 April 1957.

7 Jay interview; Boatfield, "Sister Rosetta Tharpe and the Gospel Singers," 3. For an alternative account of this turn of events, see Heilbut, *Gospel Sound*, 192–95.

8 Jay interview.

9 Lyles interview.

10 Heilbut, *Gospel Sound*, 190.

11 Ruth interview, 30 September 1996.

12 "Sister Tharpe Is Dead," *New York Amsterdam News*, 13 October 1973; "Sister Rosetta Tharpe Rites Set for Tuesday," *Philadelphia Tribune*, 13 October 1973; "Sister Rosetta Tharpe Is Dead; Top Gospel Singer since 1930's," *New York Times*, 10 October 1973; Max Jones, "Sister Rosetta Tharpe"; Goreau, *Just Mahalia Baby*, 609–10.

13 Tharpe, *Sister Rosetta Tharpe*, vol. 1 (CD reissue).

14 See Tharpe, *Precious Memories* (reissue recording), for a rendition of the performance. The music and lyrics for the song, however, originated with Thomas A. Dorsey.

Bibliography

Primary Sources

ARCHIVES AND COLLECTIONS

Berryman, Gladys. Private collection, Boston, Mass.
  National Convention of Gospel Choirs and Choruses. *By-Laws and Constitution*.
    1947.
  Records and programs of the National Convention of Gospel Choirs and
    Choruses
Boyer, James. Private collection, Manhattan, Kans.
  Information on songs sung in the Church of God in Christ
  Sister Rosetta Tharpe playbills from the 1950s
Carnegie Hall Archives, New York, N.Y.
  Concert programs
Chicago Historical Society, Chicago, Ill.
  Claude A. Barnett Collection
  Chicago city directories and music scrapbooks
  Jack Cooper Papers
City of Richmond, Court of Chancery, Richmond, Va.
DuPree, Sherry Sherrod. Private collection, Gainesville, Fla.
  Information on the Pentecostal movement and the Church of God in Christ
Fisk University, Nashville, Tenn.
  Thomas Andrew Dorsey Collection
    Thomas A. Dorsey. "Golden Years of Music." [1970]. Box 6.
  John W. Work Collection
    Thomas A. Dorsey. *Songs with a Message with My Ups and Downs: A Book
      of Songs-Poems-Readings and Life Story*. Chicago: Thomas A. Dorsey, 1941.
Grant, Dorothy. Private collection, Detroit, Mich.
  Programs produced by the National Convention of Gospel Choirs and Choruses
  National Convention of Gospel Choirs and Choruses. *Welcome to NCGCC:
    We're Fulfilling the Dorsey Dream*. [1988].
Vivian G. Harsh Collection. Carter G. Woodson Branch of the Chicago Public
  Library, Chicago, Ill.

Works Progress Administration, Illinois Writers' Project
    Native Sons: Music and Art. Box 051.
    Promised Land: Churches. Box 016.
Library of Congress, Washington, D.C.
    Music Division
        Copies of sheet music produced by Thomas Andrew Dorsey
    Motion Picture, Broadcasting, and Recorded Sound Division
        Rigler and Deutsch 78 RPM Index
Billy Rose Theater Collection. New York Public Library for the Performing Arts, New York, N.Y.
    Clipping file, Sister Rosetta Tharpe
Schomburg Center for Research in Black Culture, New York Public Library, New York, N.Y.
    Scrapbooks, Clippings from Vertical Files of Schomburg Collection, 1920–1966, Music and Musicians, vol. 6
Shaw, Malcolm. Private collection, Denver, Colo.
    Correspondence between Arizona Dranes and Consolidated Talking Machine Company
Smithsonian Institution, Washington, D.C.
    Program in African American Culture, National Museum of American History
        Transcripts of proceedings for the conference "Classic Gospel Song: A Tribute to Thomas A. Dorsey," October 1985
State of Illinois, Cook County Department of Health
State of Missouri, Secretary of State, Department of Corporations
Thompson, Mamie. Private collection, Chicago, Ill.
    Pamphlets and programs from Roberts Temple Church of God in Christ
    Souvenir Program: Eighteenth Annual Convocation, Churches of God in Christ, Illinois. Edited by Elder A. A. Childs. Chicago: Unity Press, 1937.
University of Mississippi, Oxford
    Blues Archive
        Ruth A. Smith, *The Life and Works of Thomas Andrew Dorsey: The Celebrated Pianist and Songwriter Poetical and Pictorial*. Chicago: Thomas A. Dorsey, [1935].
Wilks, Dr. Mary. Private collection, Detroit, Mich.
    Information about programs produced by the National Convention of Gospel Choirs and Choruses

Washingtonian Collection. Public Library, Washington, D.C.
Feld Family, clipping file

INTERVIEWS

Blakeny, Susie. Interview by Jerma Jackson. Tape recording. Chicago, Ill., 13 April 1993.

Boyer, Horace. Interview by Jerma Jackson. Tape recording. Via telephone, 23 January 1992.

Boyer, James. Interview by Jerma Jackson. Tape recording. Via telephone, 17 January 1992.

Campbell, Agnes. Interview by Jerma Jackson. Tape recording. Via telephone, 26 April 1993.

Cohen, Richard. Interview by Jerma Jackson. Tape recordings. Miami, Fla., 22, 29 January 1992.

Dorsey, Thomas Andrew. "Georgia Tom Dorsey." By Bob Rusch. *Cadence: The American Review of Jazz and Blues* 4, no. 11 (December 1978): 9–13.

———. "Living Blues Interview: Georgia Tom Dorsey." By Jim O'Neal and Amy O'Neal. *Living Blues: A Journal of the Black American Blues Tradition* 20 (March–April 1975): 17–34.

———. "On His 75th Anniversary: An Interview with Thomas A. Dorsey." By Alfred Duckett. *Black World* 23 (July 1974): 4–19.

Gabler, Milt. Conversation with Jerma Jackson. Via telephone, 3 January 1992.

Grant, Dorothy. Interview by Jerma Jackson. Tape recording. Detroit, Mich., 5 February 1993.

Hamilton, Gussie. Interview by Jerma Jackson. Tape recording. Miami, Fla., 15 January 1993.

Hubbard, Musette. Interview by Jerma Jackson. Tape recording. Via telephone, 29 April 1993.

Isbelle, Joan. Interview by Jerma Jackson. Tape recording. Chicago, Ill., 12 April 1993.

Jay, Abner. Interview by Jerma Jackson. Tape recording. Via telephone, 25 May 1993.

Knight, Minister Marie. Interview by Jerma Jackson and M. Jacqui Alexander. Tape recordings. New York, N.Y., 14 November 1996, 20 March, 2 July 1997.

———. Interview by Karen Johnson. *Blues Stage*. National Public Radio, 31 October 1984.

Lyles, Curtis. Interview by Jerma Jackson. Tape recording. Brooklyn, N.Y., 14 April 1994.

Melrose, Lester. "My Life in Recording." *American Folk Music Occasional*, 1970, 59–61.

Oliver, Maudelle. Interview by Jerma Jackson. Tape recording. Via telephone, 30 April 1993.

Peeples, Marion. Interview by Jerma Jackson. Tape recording. Chicago, Ill., 14 April 1993.

Roberts, Alva, and Spearmon, Elizabeth. Interview by Jerma Jackson. Tape recording. Chicago, Ill., 15 April 1993.

Ruth, Thermon. Interview by Jerma Jackson. Tape recordings. Brooklyn, N.Y., 15 August, 30 September 1996.

———. "Thermon Ruth and the Selah Jubilee Singers: An Interview." By Christopher Lornell. *Journal of Black Sacred Music* 2 (1988): 29–51.

Scott, Sam. Interview by Jerma Jackson and Karen Glynn. Cotton Plant, Ark., 29 July 1995.

Speir, H. C. "An Interview with H. C. Speir." By David Evans. *John Edwards Memorial Foundation Quarterly* 8 (1972): 117–21.

Walker, Frank. "Who Chose These Records? A Look into the Life, Tastes, and Procedures of Frank Walker." By Mike Seeger. In *Anthology of American Folk Music*, edited by Josh Dunson and Ethel Raim, 8–17. New York: Oak Publications, 1973.

Wilks, Dr. Mary. Interview by Jerma Jackson. Tape recording. Detroit, Mich., 5 February 1993.

Williams, Marion. Interview by Terri Gross. *Fresh Air*. National Public Radio, 6 December 1993.

FILMS AND SOUND RECORDINGS

Armstrong, Louis. *Gospel According to Louis*. Collegedale, Tenn.: Black Label, BLCD 4029, 1994.

Curry, Elder, and Elder Beck. *Elder Curry and Elder Beck: Complete Recorded Works in Chronological Order, 1930–1939*. Vienna: Document Records BDCD-6035, 1992.

Dorsey, Thomas A. *Georgia Tom (Thomas A. Dorsey): Complete Recorded Works in Chronological Order*. Vol. 2, *5 February 1930 to 22 March 1934*. Vienna: RST Records BDCD-6022, 1992.

———. *Professor Thomas Andrew Dorsey, the Maestro Sings: A Music and Photo History*. Sound of Gospel Records, 1980.

Dranes, Arizona. *Arizona Dranes: Complete Recorded Works in Chronological Order, 1926–1929*. Vienna: Document Records DOCD-5186, 1993.

From Spirituals to Swing: Carnegie Hall Concerts, 1938/39. Produced by John Hammond. Santa Monica, Calif.: Vanguard VCD2-47/48, 1987.

Johnson, Blind Willie. *The Complete Blind Willie Johnson, 1929–1930.* New York: Columbia, Legacy C2K52835, 1993.

Sallie Martin Singers/Cora Martin. *Throw Out the Lifeline.* Berkeley: Specialty Records SPCD-7043-2, 1993.

McGee, Rev. F. W. *The Complete Recorded Works of Rev. F. W. McGee in Chronological Order.* Vol. 1, *1927–1929.* Vienna: RST Records, 1992.

Negro Spirituals: La Tradition de Concert/The Concert Tradition. France: Fre'meaux & Associe's FA 168, 1999.

Nelson, Sister Mary, Lonnie McIntorsh, and Bessie Johnson. *Memphis Gospel, 1927–1929.* Vienna: Document Records, 1991.

Nierenberg, George T. *Say Amen Somebody!* New York: GTN Productions, 1983.

Paris, Blind Willie, and Wife et al. *Guitar Evangelists, 1928–1951.* Vienna: Document Records DOCD-5101, 1992.

Phillips, Washington. *I Am Born to Preach the Gospel: The Complete Recorded Works of Washington Phillips.* Yazoo 2003, 1991.

Teagarden, Jack. *Swing Low, Sweet Spiritual.* New York: Capitol Records, T820.

Tharpe, Sister Rosetta. *The Gospel Truth.* Live Recording. Mercury MG 20412, 1956.

———. *Sister Rosetta Tharpe: Complete Recorded Works, 1938–1944, in Chronological Order.* Vol. 1, *1938–1941.* Vienna: Document Records DOCD-5334, 1995.

———. *Sister Rosetta Tharpe: Complete Recorded Works, 1938–1944, in Chronological Order.* Vol. 2, *1942–1944.* Vienna: Document Records DOCD-5335, 1995.

———. *Sister Rosetta Tharpe: Complete Recorded Works in Chronological Order.* Vol. 3, *1946–1947.* With Marie Knight and Sam Price Trio. Vienna: Document Records DOCD-5607, 1998.

———. *Precious Memories.* Jackson, Miss.: Savoy Records SCD 5008, 1997.

NEWSPAPERS

Afro-American (Baltimore, Md.)
Atlanta Constitution
Chicago Defender
Cleveland Call and Post
The Freeman

Pittsburgh Courier
Richmond Afro-American (Richmond, Va.)
New York Amsterdam News
New York Times
Washington Afro-American (Washington, D.C.)

BOOKS, ARTICLES, AND DISSERTATIONS

"20,000 Watch Wedding of Sister Rosetta Tharpe." *Ebony*, October 1951, 27–28, 30.

Bartleman, Frank. *Azusa Street.* South Plainfield, N.J.: Bridge Publishers, 1925. Reprinted with foreword by Vinson Synan, 1980.

Boatfield, Graham. "Sister Rosetta Tharpe and the Gospel Singers." *Jazz Journal*, November 1957, 3–4.

Boatner, Edward, ed. and arranger. *Spirituals Triumphant Old and New*. Nashville: Sunday School Publishing Board, National Baptist Convention U.S.A., 1927.

Bontemps, Arna. "Rock, Church, Rock!" *Common Ground*, Autumn 1942, 75–80.

Broonzy, William. *Big Bill Blues: William Broonzy's Story as Told to Yannick Bruynoghe*. New York: Oak Publications, 1964.

Calhoun, Lillian S. "Woman on the Go for God." *Ebony*, May 1963, 78–81, 84, 86–87.

Church of God in Christ. *The Official Quarterly Guide Senior YPWW [Young People Willing Workers]*. Summer 1991.

Cornelius, Lucille J. *The Pioneer: History of the Church of God in Christ*. Memphis: Church of God in Christ Publishing, 1975.

Davis, Daniel Webster. *"Weh Down Souf," and Other Poems*. Cleveland: Helman-Taylor, 1897.

Dett, R. Nathaniel. "Religious Folk-Songs of the Negro." In *The R. Nathaniel Dett Reader: Essays on Black Sacred Music*, edited by Jon Michael Spencer. Special issue of *Black Sacred Music: A Journal of Theomusicology* 5, no. 2 (Fall 1991): 56–67. Durham, N.C.: Duke University Press, 1991.

Drake, St. Clair, and Horace Cayton. *Black Metropolis: A Study of Negro Life in a Northern City*. Vol. 2. 1945. Reprint, New York: Harcourt, Brace and World, 1962.

"Dr. Harvey's Article on Insidious Evil of Swinging Spirituals Brings Many Letters." *Pittsburgh Courier*, 18 March 1939.

Du Bois, W. E. B. *The Souls of Black Folk*. 1903. Edited by Donald B. Gibson. New York: Penguin, 1989.

Ellington, Edward Kennedy. *Music Is My Mistress*. New York: Duke Ellington, Inc., 1973. Reprint, New York: Da Capo Press, 1976.

"Fight against Defilement of Negro Spirituals Continues." *Pittsburgh Courier*, 22 April 1939.

Garrett, Franklin, ed. *Atlanta and Environs: A Chronicle of Its People and Events*. Vol. 2. Athens: University of Georgia Press, 1969.

"Glamour Girl of Gospel Singers." *Ebony*, October 1957, 24–28.

Hammond, John. *John Hammond on Record: An Autobiography*. With Irving Townsend. New York: Ridge Press, 1977. Reprint, New York: Penguin, 1981.

Handy, W. C. *Father of the Blues: An Autobiography*. Edited by Arna W. Bontemps. New York: Macmillan, 1941. Reprint, 1970.

Hentoff, Nat. *Hear Me Talkin' to You: The Story of Jazz as Told by the Men Who Made It*. New York: Dover Publications, 1955. Reprint, 1966.

Hepburn, Dave. "Big Bonanza in Gospel Music." *Billboard*, 23 October 1965, 13–18.
Hurston, Zora Neale. *Mules and Men.* With an introduction by Robert E.
   Hemenway. 1935. Reprint, Bloomington: Indiana University Press, 1978.
———. *The Sanctified Church: The Folklore Writings of Zora Neale Hurston.*
   Berkeley: Turtle Island, 1981.
Johnson, James Weldon. *Black Manhattan.* 1930. Reprint, New York: Atheneum,
   1977.
Johnson, James Weldon, and J. Rosamond Johnson. *The Books of American Negro
   Spirituals Including "The Book of American Negro Spirituals" and "The Second Book
   of Negro Spirituals."* 1925, 1926. Reprint, New York: Viking Press, 1944.
Jones, Max. "Sister Rosetta Tharpe: Queen of Gospel." *Melody Maker*, 27 October
   1973, 40.
Kolodin, Irving. "The Dance Band Business." *Harper's Magazine*, June 1941, 72–82.
Lewis, Leighla W. "Sister Tharpe Swings Hymns at Cotton Club." *Washington
   Afro-American*, 14 January 1939.
Locke, Alain, ed. *The New Negro.* With a new preface by Robert Hayden. 1925.
   Reprint, New York: Atheneum, Albert and Charles Boni, 1977.
Lomax, John A. " 'Sinful Songs' of the Southern Negro." *Musical Quarterly*, April
   1934, 177–87.
The Lonesome Road: Gospel Songs and Other Favorites. Liner notes. New York: Decca
   Records, album no. 224, 1941.
Mason, Mary, ed. and comp. *The History and Life Work of Bishop C. H. Mason.* 1924.
   Reprint, Memphis: Church of God in Christ, 1987.
Mays, Benjamin Elijah, and Joseph William Nicholson. *The Negro's Church.* New
   York: Institute of Social and Religious Research, 1933. Reprint, New York: Arno
   Press, 1969.
Monroe, Al. "Top Notchers at Broadway's Spot." *Chicago Defender*, 8 October
   1938.
Morris, Kenneth. *Improving the Music in the Church.* Chicago: Martin and Morris
   Music Studio, 1949.
"Must Stop Desecration of Spirituals." *Pittsburgh Courier*, 25 March 1939.
Odum, Howard W., and Guy B. Johnson. *Negro Workaday Songs.* Chapel Hill:
   University of North Carolina Press, 1926. Reprint, New York: Negro
   Universities Press, 1969.
Patterson, Bishop J. O., Rev. German R. Ross, and Mrs. Julia Mason Atkins.
   *History and Formative Years of the Church of God in Christ with Excerpts from the
   Life and Works of Its Founder—Bishop C. H. Mason.* Memphis: Church of God in
   Christ, 1969.

Pleas, Charles. *Fifty Years of Achievement, from 1906–1956: A Period in History of the Church of God in Christ*. Memphis: Church of God in Christ, 1956, 1991.

Powdermaker, Hortense. *After Freedom: A Cultural Study in the Deep South*. Madison: University of Wisconsin Press, 1939. Reprinted with a new introduction by Brackette F. Williams and Drexel G. Woodson, 1993.

Price, Sammy. *What Do They Want? A Jazz Autobiography*. Edited by Caroline Richmond. Urbana: University of Illinois Press, 1990.

Reid, Ira De A. "Mrs. Bailey Pays the Rent." In *The New Negro Renaissance: An Anthology*, edited by Arthur P. Davis and Michael W. Peplow, 164–77. New York: Holt, Rinehart and Winston, 1975.

Rodeheaver, Homer A. *Hymnal Handbook for Standard Hymns and Gospel Songs*. 1931. Reprint, New York: AMS Press, 1975.

———. *Twenty Years with Billy Sunday*. Nashville: Cokesbury Press, 1936.

"Rosetta Tharpe Says I've Never Been a Jazz Singer." *Melody Maker*, 19 April 1958, 7.

Ruth, Thermon T. *Gospel: From the Church to the Apollo Theater*. Brooklyn: T. Ruth Publications, 1995.

Sampson, Henry T. *The Ghost Walks: A Chronological History of Blacks in Show Business, 1865–1910*. Metuchen, N.J.: Scarecrow Press, 1988.

Sankey, Ira D. *My Life and the Story of the Gospel Hymns: And of Sacred Songs and Solos*. 1907. Reprint, New York: AMS Press, 1974.

"Says Swinging Spiritual Is Disgrace to Race." *Pittsburgh Courier*, 11 March 1939.

"Singer Swings Same Songs in Church and Night Club." *Life*, 28 August 1939, 36–37.

Spencer, Jon Michael. Introduction to *The R. Nathaniel Dett Reader: Essays on Black Sacred Music*, edited by Jon Michael Spencer. Special issue of *Black Sacred Music: A Journal of Theomusicology* 5, no. 2 (Fall 1991): 1–22. Durham, N.C.: Duke University Press, 1991.

Sutherland, Robert Lee. "An Analysis of Negro Churches in Chicago." Ph.D. diss., Department of Christian Theology and Ethics, University of Chicago, 1930.

"Teachers, Song Writers and Choir Singers Join in Protest against Swinging Spirituals." *Pittsburgh Courier*, 1 April 1939.

Tharpe, Sister Rosetta. *Eighteen Original Negro Spirituals*. New York: Mills Music, 1938. Sheet music collection.

Townsend, Mrs. Willa A., ed. *Gospel Pearls*. Nashville: Sunday School Publishing Board, National Baptist Convention U.S.A., 1921.

The United Negro: His Problems and His Progress. Edited by I. Garland Penn and J. W. E. Bowen. Atlanta: D. E. Luther Publishing, 1902. Reprint, New York: Negro Universities Press, 1969.

Van Vechten, Carl. "Negro 'Blues' Singers: An Appreciation of Three Coloured Artists Who Excel in an Unusual and Native Medium." *Vanity Fair*, 26 March 1926, 67, 106, 108.

Waters, Ethel. *His Eye Is on the Sparrow.* With Charles Samuels. Garden City, N.Y.: Doubleday, 1950. Reprint, New York: Da Capo Press, 1992.

Wells, Ida B. *Crusade for Justice: The Autobiography of Ida B. Wells.* Edited by Alfreda M. Duster. Chicago: University of Chicago Press, 1970.

Zolotow, Maurice. "Harlem's Great White Father." *Saturday Evening Post,* 27 September 1941, 37, 40, 64, 66, 68.

Secondary Sources

BOOKS AND PAMPHLETS

Agnew, Jean-Christophe. *Worlds Apart: The Market and the Theater in Anglo-American Thought, 1550–1750.* Cambridge: Cambridge University Press, 1986.

Allen, Ray. *Singing in the Spirit: African-American Sacred Quartets in New York City.* Philadelphia: University of Pennsylvania Press, 1991.

Anderson, James D. *The Education of Blacks in the South, 1860–1935.* Chapel Hill: University of North Carolina Press, 1988.

Anderson, Robert Mapes. *Vision of the Disinherited: The Making of American Pentecostalism.* New York: Oxford University Press, 1979.

Attali, Jacques. *Noise: The Political Economy of Music.* Translated by Brian Massumi. Minneapolis: University of Minnesota Press, 1985.

Baldwin, James. *The Price of the Ticket: Collected Nonfiction, 1948–1985.* New York: St. Martin's Press, 1985.

Barlow, William. *"Looking up at Down": The Emergence of Blues Culture.* Philadelphia: Temple University Press, 1989.

Bastin, Bruce. *Red River Blues: The Blues Tradition in the Southeast.* Urbana: University of Illinois Press, 1986.

Bederman, Gail. *Manliness and Civilization: A Cultural History of Gender and Race in the United States, 1880–1917.* Chicago: University of Chicago Press, 1995.

Benson, Susan Porter. *Counter Cultures: Saleswomen, Managers and Customers in American Department Stores, 1890–1940.* Urbana: University of Illinois Press, 1986.

Boyer, Horace Clarence. *How Sweet the Sound: The Golden Age of Gospel Music.* Washington, D.C.: Elliott and Clark, 1995.

Broughton, Viv. *Black Gospel: An Illustrated History of the Gospel Sound.* Poole, England: Blandford Press, 1985.

Burkett, Randall K. *Black Redemption: Churchmen Speak for the Garvey Movement.* Philadelphia: Temple University Press, 1978.

Calloway, Cab, and Bryant Rollins. *Of Minnie the Moocher and Me.* New York: Thomas Y. Crowell, 1976.

Cantor, Louis. *Wheelin' on Beale: The Story of the Nation's First All-Black Radio Station.* New York: Pharos Books, 1992.

Chandler, Alfred D., Jr. *The Visible Hand: The Managerial Revolution in American Business.* Cambridge, Mass.: Belknap Press, 1977.

Cohen, Lizabeth. *Making a New Deal: Industrial Workers in Chicago, 1919–1939.* New York: Cambridge University Press, 1990.

Collier, James Lincoln. *Duke Ellington.* New York: Oxford University Press, 1987.

Cone, James H. *The Spirituals and the Blues: An Interpretation.* New York: Seabury Press, 1972.

Dahl, Linda. *Stormy Weather: The Music and Lives of a Century of Jazzwomen.* New York: Pantheon, 1984.

de Lerma, Dominique-Rene. *Reflections on African-American Music.* Kent, Ohio: Kent State University Press, 1973.

DeVeaux, Scott. *The Birth of Bebop: A Social and Musical History.* Berkeley: University of California Press, 1997.

Dixon, Robert M. W., and John Goodrich. *Blues and Gospel Records, 1902–1943.* 3d ed. London: Storyville Publications, 1982.

———. *Recording the Blues.* New York: Stein and Day, 1970.

DuPree, Sherry Sherrod. *Biographical Dictionary of African-American, Holiness-Pentecostals, 1880–1990.* Washington, D.C.: Middle Atlantic Regional Press, 1989.

Erenberg, Lewis A. *Steppin' Out: New York Nightlife and the Transformation of American Culture, 1890–1930.* Chicago: University of Chicago Press, 1981.

———. *Swingin' the Dream: Big Band Jazz and the Rebirth of American Culture.* Chicago: University of Chicago Press, 1998.

Evans, David. *Big Road Blues: Tradition and Creativity in the Folk Blues.* Berkeley: University of California Press, 1982.

Frazier, E. Franklin. *The Negro Church in America.* Liverpool: University of Liverpool, 1963. Reprint, New York: Schocken Books, 1974.

Frith, Simon. *Music for Pleasure.* New York: Routledge, 1988.

———. *Sound Effects: Youth, Leisure, and the Politics of Rock 'n' Roll.* New York: Pantheon, 1981.

Garon, Paul, and Beth Garon. *Woman with Guitar: Memphis Minnie's Blues.* New York: Da Capo Press, 1992.

George, Nelson. *The Death of Rhythm and Blues*. New York: Penguin, 1988.

George-Graves, Nadine. *The Royalty of Negro Vaudeville: The Whitman Sisters and the Negotiation of Race, Gender and Class in African American Theater, 1900–1940*. New York: St. Martin's Press, 2000.

Goreau, Laurraine. *Just Mahalia Baby: The Mahalia Jackson Story*. Waco, Tex.: Word Books, 1975. Reprint, Gretna, La.: Pelican Publishing, 1984.

Grossman, James R. *Land of Hope: Chicago, Black Southerners, and the Great Migration*. Chicago: University of Chicago Press, 1989.

Guralnick, Peter. *Sweet Soul Music: Rhythm and Blues and the Southern Dream of Freedom*. New York: HarperCollins, 1986. Reprint, HarperPerennial, 1994.

Gutman, Herbert G. *Power and Culture: Essays on the American Working Class*. Edited by Ira Berlin. New York: Pantheon, 1987.

Harris, Michael W. *The Rise of Gospel Blues: The Music of Thomas Andrew Dorsey in the Urban Church*. New York: Oxford University Press, 1992.

Harrison, Daphne Duval. *Black Pearls: Blues Queens of the 1920's*. New Brunswick: Rutgers University Press, 1988.

Harvey, Paul. *Redeeming the South: Religious Cultures and Racial Identities among Southern Baptists, 1865–1925*. Chapel Hill: University of North Carolina Press, 1997.

Haskins, Jim. *The Cotton Club*. New York: Random House, 1977.

Hazzard-Gordon, Katrina. *Jookin': The Rise of Dance Formation in African American Culture*. Philadelphia: Temple University Press, 1990.

Heilbut, Anthony. *The Gospel Sound: Good News and Bad Times*. 3d ed. New York: Proscenium Publishers, 1989.

Hennessey, Thomas. *From Jazz to Swing: African-American Musicians and Their Music, 1890–1935*. Detroit: Wayne State University Press, 1994.

Higginbotham, Evelyn Brooks. *Righteous Discontent: The Women's Movement in the Black Baptist Church, 1880–1920*. Cambridge, Mass.: Harvard University Press, 1993.

Hinson, Glenn. *Fire in My Bones: Transcendence and the Holy Spirit in African American Gospel*. Philadelphia: University of Pennsylvania Press, 2000.

Hirshey, Gerri. *Nowhere to Run: The Story of Soul Music*. New York: Time Books, 1985.

Huggins, Nathan Irvin. *Harlem Renaissance*. New York: Oxford University Press, 1971.

Humez, Jean. Introduction to *Gifts of Power: The Writings of Rebecca Jackson, Black Visionary, Shaker Eldress*. Edited by Jean Humez. Amherst: University of Massachusetts Press, 1981.

Hunter, Tera W. *To 'Joy My Freedom: Southern Black Women's Lives and Labors after the Civil War*. Cambridge, Mass.: Harvard University Press, 1997.

Jones, LeRoi. *Blues People: Negro Music in White America*. New York: William Morrow, 1963.

Kasson, John. *Amusing the Million: Coney Island at the Turn of the Century*. New York: Hill and Wang, 1978.

Keil, Charles. *Urban Blues*. Chicago: University of Chicago Press, 1966, 1991.

Kenney, William Howland. *Recorded Music in American Life: The Phonograph and Popular Memory, 1890–1945*. New York: Oxford University Press, 1999.

Lears, T. J. Jackson. Introduction to *The Culture of Consumption*. Edited by Richard Wightman Fox and T. J. Jackson Lears. New York: Pantheon, 1983.

Levine, Lawrence W. *Black Culture and Black Consciousness: Afro-American Folk Thought from Slavery to Freedom*. New York: Oxford University Press, 1977.

———. *Highbrow/Lowbrow: The Emergence of Cultural Hierarchy in America*. Cambridge, Mass.: Harvard University Press, 1988.

Lewis, Earl. *In Their Own Interests: Race, Class, and Power in Twentieth-Century Norfolk, Virginia*. Berkeley: University of California Press, 1991.

Lieb, Sandra A. *Mother of the Blues: A Study of Ma Rainey*. Amherst: University of Massachusetts Press, 1981.

Logan, Rayford W. *The Betrayal of the Negro from Rutherford B. Hayes to Woodrow Wilson*. New York: Da Capo Press, 1965. Reprinted with a new introduction by Eric Foner, 1997.

Lornell, Kip. *"Happy in the Service of the Lord": African-American Sacred Vocal Harmony Quartets in Memphis*. 2d ed. Knoxville: University of Tennessee Press, 1995.

Lovell, John, Jr. *Black Song: The Forge and the Flame*. New York: Macmillan, 1972. Reprint, New York: Paragon House, 1986.

Lowenthal, Leo. *Literature, Popular Culture, and Society*. Englewood Cliffs, N.J.: Prentice-Hall, 1961.

Malone, Bill C. *Country Music, U.S.A.: A Fifty Year History*. Austin: University of Texas Press for the American Folklore Society, 1968.

May, Lary. *Screening Out the Past: The Birth of Mass Culture and the Motion Picture Industry*. New York: Oxford University Press, 1980.

Mazur, Eric Michael. *God in the Details: American Religion in Popular Culture*. New York: Routledge, 2001.

Meier, August. *Negro Thought in America, 1880–1915: Racial Ideologies in the Age of Booker T. Washington*. Ann Arbor: University of Michigan Press, 1963.

Murray, Albert. *Stomping the Blues*. New York: McGraw Hill, 1976. Reprint, Random House, 1982.

Oliver, Paul. *Songsters and Saints: Vocal Traditions on Race Records*. New York: Cambridge University Press, 1984.

Osofsky, Gilbert. *Harlem: The Making of a Ghetto, Negro New York, 1890–1930*. New York: Harper and Row, 1963, 1968.

Peiss, Kathy. *Cheap Amusements: Working Women and Leisure in Turn-of-the-Century New York*. Philadelphia: Temple University Press, 1986.

Pielke, Robert G. *You Say You Want a Revolution: Rock Music in American Culture*. Chicago: Nelson-Hall, 1986.

Ricks, George Robinson. *Some Aspects of the Religious Music of the United States Negro: An Ethnomusicological Study with Special Emphasis on the Gospel Tradition*. New York: Arno Press, 1977.

Rouse, Jacqueline Anne. *Lugenia Burns Hope, Black Southern Reformer*. Athens: University of Georgia Press, 1989.

Sanjek, Russell, and David Sanjek. *American Popular Music Business in the 20th Century*. New York: Oxford University Press, 1993.

Savage, Barbara Dianne. *Broadcasting Freedom: Radio, War, and the Politics of Race, 1938–1948*. Chapel Hill: University of North Carolina Press, 1999.

Sernett, Milton C. *Bound for the Promised Land: African American Religion and the Great Migration*. Durham, N.C.: Duke University Press, 1997.

Shaw, Stephanie J. *What a Woman Ought to Be and to Do: Black Professional Women Workers during the Jim Crow Era*. Chicago: University of Chicago Press, 1996.

Snyder, Robert W. *The Voice of the City: Vaudeville and Popular Culture in New York*. New York: Oxford University Press, 1989.

Spear, Allan H. *Black Chicago: The Making of a Negro Ghetto, 1890–1920*. Chicago: University of Chicago Press, 1967.

Spencer, Jon Michael. *Blues and Evil*. Knoxville: University of Tennessee Press, 1993.

Stowe, David W. *Swing Changes: Big Band Jazz in New Deal America*. Cambridge, Mass.: Harvard University Press, 1994.

Strasser, Susan. *Satisfaction Guaranteed: The Making of the American Mass Market*. New York: Pantheon, 1989.

Susman, Warren I. *Culture as History: The Transformation of American Society in the Twentieth Century*. New York: Pantheon, 1984.

Synan, Vinson. *The Holiness-Pentecostal Movement in the United States*. Grand Rapids, Mich.: Eerdmans, 1971.

Taylor, Clarence. *The Black Churches of Brooklyn*. New York: Columbia University Press, 1994.

Titon, Jeff Todd. *Early Downhome Blues: A Musical and Cultural Analysis*. Urbana: University of Illinois Press, 1977.

Toll, Robert C. *Blacking Up: The Minstrel Show in Nineteenth Century America*. New York: Oxford University Press, 1974.

Trotter, Joe William, Jr. *Black Milwaukee: The Making of an Industrial Proletariat, 1915–45*. Urbana: University of Illinois Press, 1985.

Washington, James Melvin. *Frustrated Fellowship: The Black Baptist Quest for Social Power*. Macon, Ga.: Mercer University Press, 1986.

Weare, Walter B. *Black Business in the New South: A Social History of the North Carolina Mutual Life Insurance Company*. Urbana: University of Illinois Press, 1973. Reprint, Durham, N.C.: Duke University Press, 1993.

Williams-Jones, Pearl. *Classic Gospel Song: A Tribute to Thomas A. Dorsey*. Washington, D.C.: National Museum of American History, Smithsonian Institution, 1985.

Zolten, Jerry. *Great God A'Mighty! The Dixie Hummingbirds: Celebrating the Rise of Soul Gospel Music*. New York: Oxford University Press, 2003.

ARTICLES

Abbott, Lynn, and Doug Seroff. "'They Cert'ly Sound Good to Me': Sheet Music, Southern Vaudeville, and the Commercial Ascendancy of the Blues." Edited by David Evans. Special issue of *American Music: New Perspectives on the Blues* 14, no. 4 (Winter 1996): 402–54.

Allgood, B. Dexter. "Black Gospel in New York City and Joe William Bostic, Sr." *Black Perspective in Music* 18 (Fall 1990): 101–15.

Bailey, Ben E. "The Cotton Blossom Singers: Mississippi's Black Troubadors." *Black Perspective in Music* 15 (Fall 1987): 133–52.

Black, Doris. "How Black Churches Became a School for Singing Stars." *Sepia*, 22 February 1973, 70–78.

Boyer, Horace. "Charles Albert Tindley: Progenitor of African American Gospel Music." In *We'll Understand It Better By and By: Pioneering African American Gospel Composers*, edited by Bernice Johnson Reagon, 53–78. Washington D.C.: Smithsonian Institution Press, 1992.

———. "Contemporary Gospel Music." *Black Perspective in Music* 7 (Spring 1979): 5–58.

———. "Defining, Researching, and Teaching Gospel Music: A Contemporary Assessment." In *Black American Culture and Scholarship: Contemporary Issues*, edited by Bernice Johnson Reagon, 33–40. Washington, D.C.: Smithsonian Institution Press, 1985.

———. "Lucie E. Campbell: Composer for the National Baptist Convention." In *We'll Understand It Better By and By: Pioneering African American Gospel Composers*, edited by Bernice Johnson Reagon, 81–108. Washington D.C.: Smithsonian Institution Press, 1992.

———. "'Take My Hand, Precious Lord, Lead Me On.'" In *We'll Understand It Better By and By: Pioneering African American Gospel Composers*, edited by Bernice Johnson Reagon, 141–64. Washington, D.C.: Smithsonian Institution Press, 1992.

———. "Thomas A. Dorsey, 'Father of Gospel Music': An Analysis of His Contributions." *Black World* 23 (July 1974): 20–28.

Brooks, Tim. "'Might Take One Disc of This Trash as a Novelty': Early Recordings by the Fisk Jubilee Singers and the Popularization of 'Negro Folk Music.'" *American Music* 18, no. 3 (Fall 2000): 278–316.

Brown, Elsa Barkley. "Negotiating and Transforming the Public Sphere: African American Political Life in the Transition from Slavery to Freedom." *Public Culture* 7 (1994): 107–46.

Carby, Hazel V. "In Body and Spirit: Representing Black Women Musicians." *Black Music Research Journal* 11, no. 2 (Fall 1991): 177–92.

———. "It Jus Be's Dat Way Sometimes: The Sexual Politics of Women's Blues." *Radical America* 20 (1986): 9–22.

Cohen, Lizabeth. "Encountering Mass Culture at the Grassroots: The Experience of Chicago Workers in the 1920's." *American Quarterly* 41 (1989): 6–33.

Cureau, Rebecca T. "Kemper Harreld and Willis James: Music at Atlanta University, Morehouse College, and Spelman College." *Black Music Research* (Columbia College), Spring 1989, 5–7.

DjeDje, Jacqueline Cogdell. "Los Angeles Composers of African-American Gospel Music." *American Music* 11, no. 4 (Winter 1993): 412–57.

Erenberg, Lewis A. "From New York to Middletown: Repeal and the Legitimization of Nightlife in the Great Depression." *American Quarterly* 5 (Winter 1986): 761–78.

"Fastest-Growing Church." *Ebony*, August 1949, 57–60.

Feather, Leonard. "Mills: A Life of Being in Swing." *Los Angeles Times*, 28 April 1985.

Filene, Benjamin. "'Our Singing Country': John and Alan Lomax, Leadbelly and the Construction of an American Past." *American Quarterly* 43 (December 1991): 602–25.

George, Luvenia A. "Lucie E. Campbell: Her Nurturing and Expansion of Gospel Music in the National Baptist Convention, U.S.A., Inc." In *We'll Understand It Better By and By: Pioneering African American Gospel Composers*, edited by Bernice Johnson Reagon, 109–19. Washington, D.C.: Smithsonian Institution Press, 1992.

Gilkes, Cheryl Townsend. "The Role of Women in the Sanctified Church." *Journal of Religious Thought* 43, no. 1 (Spring/Summer 1986): 24–41.

———. "'Some Folks Get Happy and Some Folks Don't': Diversity, Community and African American Christian Spirituality." In *The Courage to Hope: From Black Suffering to Human Redemption*, edited by Quinton Hostord Dixid and Cornel West, 200–213. Boston: Beacon Press, 1999.

———. "'Together and in Harness': Women's Traditions in the Sanctified Church." *Signs: Journal of Women in Culture and Society* 10, no. 4 (Summer 1985): 678–99.

Harley, Sharon. "'When Your Work Is Not Who You Are': The Development of a Working-Class Consciousness among Afro-American Women." In *"We Specialize in the Wholly Impossible": A Reader in Black Women's History*, edited by Darlene Clark Hine, Wilma King, and Linda Reed, 25–37. Brooklyn: Carlson, 1995.

Higginbotham, Evelyn Brooks. "En-Gendering Leadership in the Home Mission Schools." *American Baptist Quarterly* 12, no. 1 (1993): 10–25.

———. "Rethinking Vernacular Culture: Black Religion and Race Records in the 1920's and 1930's." In *The House That Race Built: Black Americans, U.S. Terrain*, edited by Wahneema Lubiano, 157–77. New York: Pantheon, 1997.

Holt, Thomas C. "Marking: Race, Race-Making, and the Writing of History." *American Historical Review*, February 1995, 1–20.

Jackson, Walter. "Melville Herskovits and the Search for Afro-American Culture." In *Malinowski, Rivers, Benedict and Others: Essays on Culture and Personality*, edited by George Stocking, 95–126. Madison: University of Wisconsin Press, 1986.

Kelley, Norman. "Notes on the Political Economy of Black Music." In *Rhythm and Business: The Political Economy of Black Music*, edited by Norman Kelley, 6–23. New York: Akashic Books, 2002.

Mathews, Donald G. "The Sanctified South: John Lakin Brasher and the Holiness Movement." *Southern Cultures* 2, no. 1 (Spring 1996): 115–18.

Maultsby, Portia K. "The Impact of Gospel Music on the Secular Music Industry." In *We'll Understand It Better By and By: Pioneering African American Gospel Composers*, edited by Bernice Johnson Reagon, 19–33. Washington, D.C.: Smithsonian Institution Press, 1992.

Neal, Larry. "Ethos of the Blues." In *Sacred Music of the Secular City*, edited by Jon Michael Spencer. Special issue of *Black Sacred Music: A Journal of Theomusicology* 6, no. 1 (Spring 1992): 36–46. Durham, N.C.: Duke University Press.

Phillips, Romeo Eldridge. "Some Perceptions of Gospel Music." *Black Perspective in Music* 10 (Fall 1982): 167–78.

Reagon, Bernice Johnson. "I'll Be a Servant for the Lord: A 1987 Interview Conducted and Edited by Bernice Johnson Reagon." In *We'll Understand It Better By and By: Pioneering African American Gospel Composers*, edited by Bernice Johnson Reagon, 329–41. Washington, D.C.: Smithsonian Institution Press, 1992.

———. "Pioneering African American Gospel Music Composers: A Smithsonian Institution Research Project." In *We'll Understand It Better By and By: Pioneering African American Gospel Composers*, edited by Bernice Johnson Reagon, 3–18. Washington, D.C.: Smithsonian Institution Press, 1992.

"Sallie Martin." *Ebony*, March 1986, 76, 78, 81.

Sanjek, David. "They Work Hard for Their Money: The Business of Popular Music." In *New Approaches to the Twentieth Century: American Popular Music*, edited by Rachel Rubin and Jeffrey Melnick, 9–28. Amherst: University of Massachusetts Press, 2001.

Seroff, Doug. "On the Battlefield: Gospel Quartets in Jefferson County, Alabama." In *Repercussions: A Celebration of African-American Music*, edited by Geoffrey Haydon and Dennis Marks, 30–53. London: Century, 1985.

Shaw, Malcolm. "Arizona Dranes and Okeh." *Storyville*, February 1970, 85–89.

Williams-Jones, Pearl. "Roberta Martin: Spirit of an Era." In *We'll Understand It Better By and By: Pioneering African American Gospel Composers*, edited by Bernice Johnson Reagon, 255–74. Washington: D.C.: Smithsonian Institution Press, 1992.

———. "Toward the Inclusion of Black American Gospel Music in the Curricula of Academic Institutions." In *Black American Culture and Scholarship: Contemporary Issues*, edited by Bernice Johnson Reagon, 27–31. Washington, D.C.: Smithsonian Institution Press, 1985.

LINER NOTES

DjeDje, Jacqueline Cogdell. *Throw Out the Lifeline*. Berkeley, Calif.: Specialty Records SPCD-7043-2, 1993.

Guralnick, Peter. *Sam Cooke's SAR Records Story, 1959–1965*. New York: ABKCO Music and Records, 2231, 2-CD set, 1994.

Heilbut, Anthony. *The Great Gospel Women*. Vol. 2. Reissue, Shanachie 6017, 1995.

Hildebrand, Lee, and Opal Nations. *The Great 1955 Shrine Concert*. Reissue, Berkeley, Calif.: Specialty Records SPCD-7045-2, 1993.

Reitz, Rosetta. *Sincerely Sister Rosetta Tharpe: Sacred and Secular Gospel-Blues-Jazz.* Reissue, New York: Rosetta Records, 1988.

Romanowski, Ken. *Arizona Dranes: Complete Recorded Works in Chronological Order, 1926–1929.* Vienna: Document Records DOCD-5186, 1993.

———. *Sister Rosetta Tharpe: Complete Recorded Works in Chronological Order.* Vol. 3, *1946–1947.* With Marie Knight and Sam Price Trio. Vienna: Document Records DOCD-5607, 1998.

Spitzer, Nick. *Saint's Paradise: Trombone Shout Bands from the United House of Prayer.* Washington, D.C.: Smithsonian Folkways Recordings SFW CD 40117, 1999.

Tallmadge, William A. *Jubilee to Gospel: A Selection of Commercially Recorded Black Recorded Black Religious Music, 1921–1953.* Los Angeles: John Edwards Memorial Foundation, 1981.

DISSERTATIONS AND UNPUBLISHED PAPERS

Butler, Anthea D. "A Peculiar Synergy: Matriarchy and the Church of God in Christ." Ph.D. diss., Vanderbilt University, 2001, retrieved WorldCat.

Foreman, Ronald Clifford. "Jazz and Race Records, 1920–1932: Their Origins and Their Significance for the Record Industry and Society." Ph.D. diss., University of Illinois, 1968.

Nelson, Douglas J. "For Such a Time as This: The Story of Bishop William J. Seymour and the Azusa Street Revival." Ph.D. diss., Department of Theology, University of Birmingham, England, 1981.

Ponce de Leon, Charles L. "Idols and Icons: Representations of Celebrity in American Culture, 1850–1940." Ph.D. diss., Rutgers, State University of New Jersey, 1992.

Tinney, James S. "Competing Strains of Hidden and Manifest Theologies of Black Pentecostalism." Conference paper presented at the Society for Pentecostal Studies. Oral Roberts University, 14 November 1980.

Wells, Patricia. "Historical Overview of the Establishment of the Church of God in Christ." Ph.D. diss., International Seminary, 1989.

Index

style of, 44–45, 51, 89; recording career of, 44–46, 78, 83

Dress codes, 20, 43, 69, 71, 96, 97, 99, 110–11

Du Bois, W. E. B., 1, 139

Dvořák, Antonín, 13–14

Ebenezer Church, 58

Economic opportunities: gospel music and, 60, 61

Ecstatic worship, 12–13, 65–68, 145 (n. 22), 146 (n. 29)

Eighteen Original Negro Spirituals, 84

Ellington, Duke, 158 (n. 18)

Enslaved Africans, 9–10, 12

Entertainment industry. *See* Industry, entertainment

Evangelism: entertainment industry and, 87, 102; gospel and, 94–97, 145 (n. 18); popular culture and, 101–2; race records and, 46–49; recording industry and, 41, 47–49; street, 40

Famous Ward Singers, 76 (ill.), 111

Feld, Irving and Israel, 109

First Annual Mid-Summer Festival of Gospel Music, 109–10

Fisk Jubilee Singers, 8–9, 13–14, 44–45

Franklin, Kirk, 133

Frye, Theodore, 58

Gabler, Milt, 88

Gale, Moe, 83

Gamble, Nancy, 36, 39–40

Gates of Prayer, 123

Gender: within Church of God in Christ, 25, 28, 30–31, 32–33; mis-sionary work and, 32; popular racial conventions and, 85; preaching and, 28, 31, 47; sexual imagery and, 42, 43, 85, 88

General Recording Company, 41

Glaser, Joe, 137

Goodwill Musical Union, 125–26

Goodwin, William, 37

Gospel (as music): Bible references in, 66; blues and, 23–24; class mobility and, 135; commercialism and, 104; definition of, 64, 145 (n. 18); development of, 2–6, 16–19, 54–59, 84; dissemination of, 60, 62, 84–85; as entertainment, 94; evangelism and, 94–97, 145 (n. 18); importance of lyrics in, 62–63; instrumental accompaniment and, 22–24, 39–40, 45–46, 89–90; jazz and, 118; promotion and preservation of, 34, 54, 58, 59, 61–65, 84, 117–18; publishing of, 60; race and, 6; religious faith and, 115–20; rhythms of, 63–64; role of the composer in, 61, 152 (n. 4); as sacred, 4–5; as sacred vs. secular, 127–32; sheet music and, 60–63; solo, 3–4, 8–9, 22–23; spirituals and, 84, 103–4, 117–18, 134; spread of, 58–63; vocalizations in, 23–24, 46, 52, 88–90, 160 (n. 51); women and, 4, 39–40. *See also* Dorsey, Thomas Andrew; Music, sacred; "Swinging spirituals"

Gospel (as religious practice): definition of, 64; development of, 17–18, 28, 34–38, 64–65, 65–66, 68; ecstatic worship and, 12–13, 65–68,

108–9, 122–23; as minister, 123–24; on race mobility, 135; sanctified singing and, 38–39; solo gospel career of, 124; and tenure with Sister Rosetta Tharpe, 75, 83, 100–101, 107, 109, 122, 135, 160 (n. 51)

80, 85–86; Count Basie, 115; Duke Ellington, 158 (n. 18); Famous Ward Sisters, 76, 111; Kirk Franklin, 133; Lionel Hampton, 85, 115; Louis Armstrong, 116; Lucky Millinder band, 91, 93, 107; Mahalia Jackson, 141; Mamie Smith, 41; Ma Rainey, 42, 54, 61; Memphis Minnie, 39–40; Sam Cooke, 130; Sammy Price, 88, 100; Tampa Red, 54; T-Bone Walker, 23; W. C. Handy, 24; Yolanda Adams, 133. *See also* Dorsey, Thomas Andrew; Dranes, Arizona; Knight, Marie; Martin, Sallie; Tharpe, Sister Rosetta

National Baptist Convention, 12, 14, 32, 43, 56–58, 59, 64
National Convention of Gospel Choirs and Choruses (NCGCC), 59, 64, 104, 111, 118, 125
National Training Institute for Women, 32
Nelson, Douglas J., 18
"Nobody's Fault but Mine," 88
Nubin, Katie Bell, 27, 29–30, 35, 49, 69 (ill.), 100, 148 (n. 5)

Okeh Records (General Recording Company), 41, 46, 47–48, 83
Oliver, Maudelle, 21, 35–36, 39

Paramount Records, 42, 86
Parham, Kitty, 76
Peeples, Alto, 116–17
Peeples, Marion, 62
Pentecostalism, 17, 18–19, 23

Performance, 60, 61–65, 86, 108–10
Phillips, Romeo, 133
Phillips, Washington, 89
Pianos/piano playing, 45–46
Pilgrim Baptist Church (Chicago), 50, 55–57, 58
Pilgrim Travelers, 109
Popular culture, 85, 101–2. *See also* Culture, commercial
Post-Reconstruction, 9–11
Powdermaker, Hortense, 22, 25
Preachers: income of, 47; in minstrel shows, 87; music and, 39; women as, 31–32, 34, 39
Price, Sammy, 88, 100
Promotion, music, 77–80, 108–11, 117–19, 120–24

Quinn Chapel, 31

Race: commercialization of music and, 115–16, 135–36; development of gospel and, 9–11; gender conventions and, 85; promotion of gospel and, 78, 79, 80, 82, 101–2, 106–7, 108–11, 115; sexual conventions and, 78, 88, 106–8, 162 (n. 8)
Race records, 41–49, 53
Radio, 81–82, 106–8, 162 (n. 8)
Record companies: Columbia Records, 42; Decca Records, 84, 88, 105, 158 (n. 22), 159 (n. 25); Okeh Records (General Recording Company), 41, 46, 47–48, 83; Paramount Records, 42, 86; Specialty Records, 109
Reinhart, Fannie, 57
Religious practice: commercial music

Spirituals: arranged, 13–14; enslaved Africans and, 1; gospel vs., 84, 103–4, 117–18, 134; in jazz music, 112–13, 115–16, 118, 133, 158 (n. 22). *See also* "Swinging spirituals"
Spirituals Triumphant, 14
Steadman, Francis, 76
Swing (music), 82, 83–84
"Swinging spirituals," 74, 83–84, 103–4, 112–20

"Take My Hand, Precious Lord," 66–67, 68, 141–42
Tampa Red, 54
Testifying, 20–21, 25
Tharpe, Sister Rosetta, 6, 72–75 (ills.); birth of, 29, 148 (n. 5); and commercial music, 27, 86, 103–4; commercial success and, 94–96, 136–41; in commercial venues, 80, 91–92, 94, 100, 101, 137–38; Cotton Club performances of, 74, 77–80, 97, 103–4, 111; friendship with women and, 30; guitar playing of, 40, 75, 90; and "Hide Me in Thy Bosom," 92; holiness and, 96, 100–101; jazz and, 160 (n. 51); Jim Crow and, 95; Katie Bell Nubin and, 27; Lucky Millinder band and, 91, 93, 107; Marie Knight and, 75, 86–87, 107, 122–24; marriage of, 33, 86, 97; migration and, 30, 94; minstrelsy and, 87–88; missionary work of, 28–29, 33, 37–38, 73, 90, 94–97; musical innovation of, 88–92; public image of, 83–84; religious commitment of, 86–87; Richard Cohen and, 33–34, 127–32;

and "Rock Me," 92; sacred music and, 91, 92–93, 129, 141–42; secular world and, 49, 103–4, 111–13, 136–42; sexual images of, 85, 88; street evangelism of, 37–38, 39–40; vocalization and, 46, 88–90, 91, 141–42, 160 (n. 50); white audiences and, 78, 79
"That's All," 89, 90
Thorpe, Thomas J., 33, 86, 97

Urban communities, 35, 36–38

Vaudeville, 41–42
Vocalizations, 23–24, 46, 52, 88–90, 160 (n. 51)

Walker, Frank, 42–43
Walker, T-Bone, 23
Ward, Clara, 76, 129
Ward, Gertrude, 76
Ward, Willa, 76
Washington Temple, 140
Wesley, John, 17
"What He Done for Me," 91
Williams, Marion, 37, 76
WLAC (radio station), 106–7
Women: in blues, 39, 41; church and, 30–33; in commercial arena, 4; in gospel music publishing industry, 60; as missionaries, 35–36; popular culture and, 85; as preachers, 34; race records and, 41–49; sanctification and, 5, 25–26, 27–28, 40, 43, 47, 49; sexual images of, 42, 43, 85, 88; social reform and, 32; worship and, 25

Women, sanctified: community and, 49; evangelism of, 4; gospel choirs and, 59–60; income generation of, 47; music and, 28, 38–49; in the public sphere, 28, 40, 131; sexuality and, 43; worship and, 25–26. *See also* Dranes, Arizona; Martin, Sallie; Tharpe, Sister Rosetta

Work of the Holy Spirit in Churches, 16

Worship: ecstatic, 12–13, 65–68, 145 (n. 22), 146 (n. 29); educated, 11–13, 15–16; impact of sheet music on, 61–62; interracialism and, 17–19, 145 (n. 18); music as, 22–23, 55–58, 115–20; religious practice and, 19–20, 56–58; sacred music as, 4, 21–26; women and, 25–26. *See also* Religious practice

CPSIA information can be obtained
at www.ICGtesting.com
Printed in the USA
LVHW091740290819
629266LV00002BA/147/P